D

(

ED

)

MULTI-MEDIA COMPUTER ASSISTED LEARNING

Edited by

Philip Barker

Kogan Page, London/Nichols Publishing, New York

First published in Great Britain by Kogan Page Ltd
120 Pentonville Road, London N1 9JN

Typeset by DP Photosetting, Aylesbury, Bucks
Printed and bound in Great Britain by
Billing & Sons Ltd, Worcester

British Library Cataloguing in Publication Data

Barker, Philip G. (Philip George), *1944–*
   Multi-media computer aided learning
   1. Computer-assisted learning
   I. Title
   371.3'9445

   ISBN 1-85091-862-7

First published in the United States of America
In 1989 by Nichols Publishing, an imprint of
GP Publishing Inc., PO Box 96, New York,
NY 10024

Library of Congress Cataloging in Publication Data

Multi-media computer assisted learning.
   Includes index.
   1. Computer-assisted instruction. 2. Audio-
visual education. I. Barker, Philip G.
II. Title: Multimedia computer assisted learning.
LB1028.5M85 1988   371.3'9445   88-19699
ISBN 0-89397-328-9

Contents

Preface

The use of computers as an instructional resource is now quite widespread. Indeed, the phrase 'Computer Assisted Learning' (CAL) has come to be regarded as something of an umbrella term that is used to describe, collectively, the many different teaching, training and learning applications of computers. Multi-media CAL, as its name suggests, involves using a variety of instructional media in conjunction with a computer in order to implement learning and training processes. Using this approach to instruction often means that a significant range of both computing and other instructional resources can be utilized within a given learning context. Thus, for any given learner an optimal learning strategy could, in principle, be derived. Furthermore, provided care is taken in their design, multi-media teaching systems can often produce methods of knowledge/skill transfer that are far more effective than many approaches that are based on the use of more conventional methodologies. This book attempts to describe some approaches to the realization of multi-media CAL.

Multi-media computer assisted learning techniques can be used to create a wide variety of different interactive learning environments. These environments are usually designed in such a way that learning processes are (1) learner controlled, (2) participative, and (3) highly motivating. Central to the multi-media approach is the use of some sort of microcomputer system to which is interfaced a wide range of peripherals and devices.

This combination of peripherals and microcomputer is commonly referred to as a workstation. Where it is appropriate multi-media workstations may be connected both to local area and wide area networks in order to facilitate the dissemination of instructional materials, to provide access to shared resources, and to enable the collection of student statistics for course analysis and administration purposes.

The peripherals that are interfaced to a workstation constitute the 'interaction environment' in which a student learns. Usually, these peripherals are carefully chosen in such a way that particular learning/training processes are initiated and optimized. The peripherals that constitute the student's interaction environment fall into three broad categories:

(a) those used to effect the presentation of learning material (text, graphics, sound, exhibits, animatrons, and so on);

(b) those used to facilitate the collection of student responses and behavioural data; and

(c) those that are specifically chosen to make the learning experience more active, participative and motivating.

This book presents a collection of papers, each one dealing with some aspect of multi-media CAL. The various chapters from which the book is comprised have been prepared by an international group of authors each having significant expertise and experience of the topic about which they write. In the introduction that follows, a synopsis of each chapter is presented; these will enable the reader to see how each author's contribution fits within the overall theme of the book. At the end of the book some concluding remarks are presented in order to bring together the various ideas that have been presented and in order to set the scene for future developments within this very important area of computer-based education.

Introduction

Multi-media CAL offers many interesting possibilities for both the instructional designer and the implementer of interactive computer-based teaching/learning systems. For this reason the chapters in this book cover a wide range of topics. However, despite the many different topics that are covered, within each chapter there is a common theme: the use of advanced information processing technologies for the development of more effective, more efficient and more exciting ways of learning. Because of the diverse range of topics that have been brought together in this book we believe that the material that is presented will be of value to many instructional designers who are interested in using multi-media CAL methods for the provision of a computer-based teaching or learning facility.

Several of the chapters in this book have been previously published in journal form and so can be read quite independently of any of the other chapters. Obviously, to preserve the individuality and cohesiveness of each author's contribution some duplication of ideas and material from one chapter to another is therefore unavoidable. The task of editing the book has thus been one of attempting to minimize duplication (where this is possible without losing effect), ensuring consistency of presentation, and drawing together links and cross-references between individual chapters. In order to provide a smooth transition into the various contributions that follow, this introduction provides a short overview of each chapter and also attempts to bring out the various relationships that exist between the different sections of the book.

The book commences with an overview chapter the aim of which is to summarize the basic tenets of multi-media CAL and the ways in which different types of technology can be brought together to effect learning/training processes. Some of the major pedagogic communication resources are discussed: the use of text, the use of sound, and the use of graphics. Other important factors are also introduced – workstation design, the authoring of courseware, courseware delivery, and the dissemination of learning resources through open learning environments. Each of these topics is later 'picked up' and expanded upon by various authors within subsequent chapters.

In Chapter 2, John Whiting undertakes the extremely important task of making the case for multi-media CAL. He does this by looking at the evidence that exists to support both the use of conventional CAL and the multi-media approach. His conclusions are thus based on evidence taken from his own research findings and also the results that have been produced by a number of other researchers who have studied the impact and utility of this approach to instruction.

Learning can take place in a wide variety of different contexts. Because of their importance for stimulating learning within both young and adult learners the third chapter of the book is devoted to some of the considerations that need to be taken into account when designing multi-media workstations. Major emphasis is given to new types of human-computer interaction technology and the use of optical disc facilities for the creation of electronic books and advanced interactive video workstations. An outline description is then given of some of the new types of learning paradigms and metaphors that new technologies make available. Many of the topics introduced in this chapter are later examined in much greater depth in Chapters 7, 11, 12 and 13.

Mathematics and science are obvious areas for the application of CAL methods. In Chapter 4, Yeow-Chin Yong outlines some of the CAL approaches being used at the Mathematics and Science Centre at Ngee Ann Polytechnic. Over the last few years this Centre has been extremely active in developing both induction and remediation courseware to support a wide variety of mathematical and scientific topics. The rationale underlying these activities is outlined and some indications of possible future directions of development are presented.

There are many different ways of employing multi-media CAL for teaching. In Chapter 5, Geoffrey Reynolds and Ken Meierdiercks outline the approach that they have been using for the computer-assisted teaching of a module on Linear Integrated Circuits within an Electronics course. In their system students learn through the use of video-based teaching, CAL methods, the use of a workbook and conventional one to one tutor/student contact at various intervals during the course; no formal lectures are given. The authors describe the way in which the teaching resources have been prepared and the mechanism for implementing the course using a test group of 40 students. The case for using this approach to learning is then discussed both in terms of its overall effectiveness and in terms of the attainment of greater degrees of student control over the learning process.

Simulation techniques play an extremely important role in the development of multi-media CAL resources. They can be used in a variety of ways to make learning more exciting. The appropriate design of simulation rigs also enables the learning/training processes to achieve extremely high degrees of realism. The extent to which this can be achieved is illustrated in Chapter 6 by the contribution from R.F. Short wherein the use of simulators for the training of deck officers is described. In his system a complete 'mock up' of a ship's bridge is used to give students experience in navigational skills. The approach that is presented here is not unlike that used in many other training environments in which, were it not for simulators, costly equipment would otherwise have to be used.

Pictures play an important part in developing effective and efficient multi-media CAL strategies. In Chapter 7, Barker, Manji and Tsang describe the approaches that they have been using in order to develop pictorial interfaces to computer-based instructional resources. The relative merits of two types of interface are discussed: paper-based and cathode ray tube (CRT)-based. Paper-based interfaces offer a low-cost method of generating graphic communication strategies that do not involve any substantial programming effort. Although they are extremely useful they are less reactive and are often less convenient to use than pictorial interfaces that are based upon the use of a CRT. The final section of this chapter considers the use of low-cost image acquisition and image processing equipment for implementing a number of new types of learning metaphor.

Over the next decade satellite communication techniques are likely to provide an increasingly popular method of disseminating instructional resources. Because of the importance of this technique in the context of multi-media CAL for open learning, in Chapter 8 Gareth Jones discusses some of the problems, possibilities and likely advantages associated with the use of satellite broadcasting. The chapter commences with a general introduction to the use of satellites within education. This is then followed by an in-depth description of Project Olympus – a recent European experiment in the use of satellite transmission for the dissemination of educational material.

Continuing with the theme of communications, Robert DeSio in Chapter 9 discusses the role of instructional television for promoting opportunities in the context of continuing education. In a short historical perspective he outlines some of the approaches that have been used by universities and industries in North America in order to provide life-long continuing education programmes for working professionals in high technology subjects. The steps leading up to the creation of the USA's National Technological University (NTU) in 1984 are then outlined. NTU consists of a consortium of 24 universities that use instructional television based on satellite transmission. Industrial collaboration figures prominently in NTU's planning rationale since the corporate classroom is a major target for many of the resources that are produced. The importance of academic/industrial collaboration in this area is then discussed and debated.

Satellite broadcasting deals with the distribution of CAL resources. Dissemination of resources is an extremely important task. Of equal importance, however, are techniques for efficiently and effectively organizing knowledge upon the media that are used to contain it. This is the theme of chapter 10. Knowledge engineering is concerned with techniques and methods for representing knowledge within computer systems. It is obviously a topic that is of vital importance in the context of developing flexible approaches to the use of CAL methods. In this chapter the origin of knowledge is outlined and techniques for its representation are discussed. In order to produce adaptable learning systems any realistic modelling system must support multiple views of knowledge domains; the difficulties of realizing such a requirement are then outlined. The chapter concludes with a description of a linguistic interface that is capable of providing an instructional designer with a set of tools for creating and manipulating sophisticated knowledge based structures for CAL applications.

Chapters 11 and 12 are devoted specifically to the pedagogic applications of interactive video disc systems. George Teh's chapter discusses in considerable detail the steps involved in designing and producing interactive video disc resources for use in an instructional environment. As well as describing the various phases involved in developing a video disc this chapter also presents the results of some evaluative studies that were designed to investigate the attitudes of student teachers towards the use of interactive video.

In her chapter, Judith Mashiter discusses the rationale and ideas underlying the work of the Interactive Learning Project (ILP) that is currently underway within the School of Education at Newcastle University in the UK. This project is intended to develop interactive video learning materials for the teaching of basic mathematics and science in secondary schools. The chapter commences with a short description of the potential of video in schools; it then gives a brief outline of several interactive video projects and then follows on with an in-depth discussion of the ILP work in which she is involved.

The production of courseware for use in a multi-media CAL environment raises the problem of authoring. This is therefore the theme of the final chapter of the book. Within this chapter some of the problems of creating multi-media courseware are discussed. A variety of courseware development tools now exists to facilitate the production of the instructional software that is needed to support this approach to learning. Some of these tools are reviewed and described and, where appropriate, some of their shortcomings are identified.

In the conclusion to the book the editor is set the very difficult task of bringing together the significant ideas and findings of each of the authors that has contributed to the book. In trying to accomplish this two underlying criteria have been used. First, an attempt is made to identify those ideas and findings that establish the firm foundations upon which multi-media CAL should be based. Second, an attempt is then made to bring out those ideas that lead to the development of architectural and procedural guidelines that can be used to aid the future development of sound instructional systems that embody this approach to CAL.

Before concluding this introduction it is important to express my gratitude to all those who have made contributions to this book. Indeed, were it not for the energy and enthusiasm of each of the contributors this book would not have been possible. As editor of the book I would like to thank them all for the effort that they have each put in and commend them for the very high standard of professionalism that they have each shown in the contributions that they have made.

Philip Barker
Interactive Systems Research Group
School of Information Engineering
Teesside Polytechnic, UK

Chapter 1
Multi-Media CAL

Philip Barker
Teesside Polytechnic

1.1 Background

The use of multi-media computer assisted learning has grown quite
considerably over the last few years. This growth has been primarily due to
three major factors:

(1) the relatively low cost of the terminals and the other types of resource needed to
implement it;
(2) some degree of dissatisfaction with conventional approaches to computer
assisted learning; and, least of all,
(3) the effectiveness of the instructional strategies that can be produced using multi-
media CAL.

We believe, therefore, that this approach to the use of computers for
learning has much to commend it. Evidence to support this claim will be
found in many of the subsequent chapters of this book.

For those readers who are unfamiliar with CAL methods the initial part
of this chapter attempts to provide the background needed to understand
what follows in later chapters. The material presented in this chapter is
therefore broadly subdivided into four basic areas. First, a description is
given of the rationale for and nature of multi-media computer assisted
learning. Those factors that contribute to the effective utilization of this
technique are then outlined. Some indication is then given of workstation
requirements for use in a mixed-mode, multi-media authoring environment. Finally, some discussion is presented of how this technique might
usefully be implemented within the framework of a global open learning
facility.

1.1.1 Introduction

A large proportion of conventional learning and training situations involve
the communication of knowledge, experience and skills either to a single
student or to an organized group of learners. In the context of knowledge
transfer most trainers, teachers and instructional designers are agreed
upon the inadequacy of a single medium of instruction. Thus, while text is
good at communicating some types of information it is very poor at

conveying others. It is for this reason that books, particularly technical ones, are often heavily dependent upon pictures and other graphic forms. They use these 'additional channels' in order to improve both their efficiency of communication and, for their users, the ease of assimilation of the information that they contain. Unfortunately, even well illustrated conventional books have their limitations: they cannot produce sound and they are unable to generate animation and moving pictures. In order to produce these effects instructional designers must resort to the use of other media. They might use audio tape for sound production, video tape for the display of high quality life-like pictures, and a computer as a source of computed imagery. Situations that involve the use of a number of different media in order to implement a learning/training strategy are often referred to as multi-media instructional (MMI) strategies (Barker, 1986a; 1987a). Sometimes the acronym MMI is used as an abbreviation for Man-Machine Interaction; this latter meaning is not implied anywhere in this chapter. MMI embraces a wide range of instructional activities. These can involve: (a) using a computer directly, (b) performing some task on an item of equipment that is connected to a computer and monitored by it, and (3) undertaking one or more exercises that do not directly involve the computer. Consider, for example, some possible approaches to learning to drive a motor car. A student might work through some computer assisted learning (CAL) material dealing with the procedures and skills relating to driving through a busy city. Subsequently, the student might then spend a period of time in a training rig or simulator (a mock-up of a motor car) that is connected to a control computer. This generates the views that the student sees through the windscreen, side windows and mirror; it also creates events for the student to cope with and monitors his/her reactions and performance. After the session in the simulator the student might be directed towards some self-study material located in books or on a video disc system. Undoubtedly, in addition to these activities, the student will also be 'coached' by means of training sessions in a real motor car accompanied by a human instructor.

This chapter is concerned with two particular aspects of multi-media CAL. First, the design and fabrication of workstations that are able to provide a suitable environment for the realization of this approach to instruction. Second, the use of such workstations to facilitate both open and distance learning over a geographically large area – such as the continents of Asia, Europe, Africa or North America. However, before these issues are discussed it is necessary to outline some of the commonly accepted models of CAL and also provide an overview of the nature of multi-media interaction with computers. These topics are discussed in the immediately following sections of this chapter.

1.1.2 Models of CAL and computer based training (CBT)

From the point of view of the work that is to be covered later in this chapter there are three important models of CAL that need to be considered. These are illustrated schematically in Figure 1.1. They are often referred to as 'the

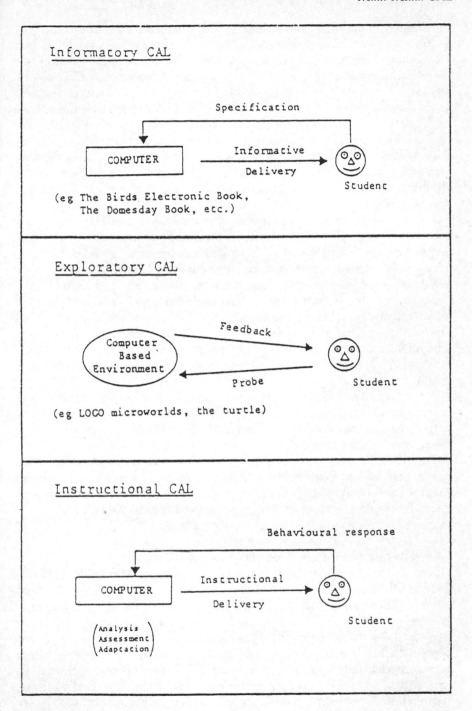

Figure 1.1 *Models of computer assisted learning*

informatory', 'the exploratory', and 'the instructional' realizations of CAL. Each requires a different approach. The first simply presents information to students; perhaps just to satisfy their curiosity, to facilitate some research orientated task, or to aid a decision making process. The second approach involves the provision of both a computer based learning environment and a set of tools that will enable this environment to be explored by the student; essentially, the methodology involved in this realization of CAL is based upon the 'microworld' approach advocated by Papert (1980). The third approach to CAL uses the computer as a delivery vehicle for previously planned, prepared, and tested courseware material; although reminiscent of programmed instruction, it is far more sophisticated.

Instructional CAL is usually much more difficult to implement than any other form. Complexities arise from a number of different sources, of which just three will be cited. First, the courseware involved must be adaptable – both with respect to the student's pre-knowledge and his/her preferred modes of learning. Second, in order to be adaptable the courseware must attempt to assess how well the student is (a) acquiring the skills, and (b) assimilating the knowledge that constitute the domain of instruction. Third, the courseware should be able to function in a generative fashion; that is, it should be capable of producing instructional mechanisms and material that has not been previously pre-programmed into it.

A number of important courseware development tools and techniques are now becoming available. These are capable of providing significant help with respect to the realization of instructional CAL. The use of knowledge bases and student modelling techniques are two examples. These are discussed in more detail elsewhere (Barker, 1986b; Barker and Proud, 1987; Barker, 1988a) and in other chapters of this book. Therefore, this present chapter concentrates on the nature of the interaction environments that might be needed to support the above approaches to CAL. This topic is discussed in more detail in the following section.

1.1.3 The nature of multi-media interaction
Within a conversational CAL system the student's interaction environ-ment is often defined in terms of the local collection of devices, aids, and other facilities that are needed for the propagation of the various learning/ training processes that it is designed to support. Four basic models are frequently used as a basis for designing interaction environments (1) the keyboard/CRT model, (2) the workstation model, (3) the interaction surface model, and (4) group interaction models. This present section deals only with a comparison of the relative merits of the first two of these. Further details on the interaction surface and group interaction models are given elsewhere (Barker, 1986a; 1987a).

The keyboard/CRT model is illustrated schematically in Figure 1.2. Essentially, a single cathode ray tube (CRT) display is used to present instructional material to a student or trainee.

In very early CAL systems (based on low resolution displays) this material was essentially textual in nature. However, with the more advanced technology that is currently available (incorporating high resolution screens) pictorial information may also be employed. Indeed, it is now possible to intermix both text and graphic illustrations within a single segmented/windowed display screen in order to produce a particular instructional effect. Invariably, student feedback responses to the material on the CRT screen are mapped onto some form of keyboard facility. In most cases a full 'QWERTY' keyboard is used. However, in some situations (particularly those involving young children or handicapped/disabled people) subset or special-purpose keyboards/keypads are employed. Certain of the latter types of device are often referred to as 'concept' keyboards.

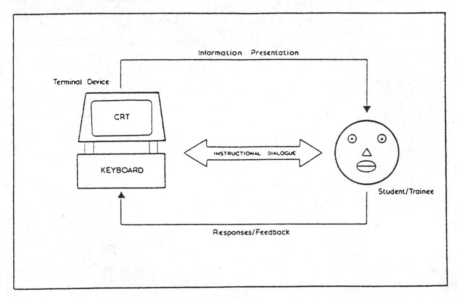

Figure 1.2 *The keyboard/CRT model of interaction*

The workstation model of human/computer interaction (upon which multi-media CAL is based) realizes and acknowledges the central and important role of both the CRT and the keyboard. However, it also realizes the limitations of this basic peripheral combination. Consequently, the workstation model of interaction is one which is based upon the use of a wide range of peripheral devices that are attached to a central controlling element. Each device in the peripheral cluster associated with a workstation is specially selected in order to facilitate some aspect of the human-computer dialogue inherent in normal use of the system. Of course, in the case of CAL workstations each device is purposely chosen to meet the particular requirements of the instructional tasks that are to be fulfilled. Fundamental to this approach, therefore, are the basic ideas associated with multi-channel or multi-media instruction.

Figure 1.3 illustrates the concept of a multi-media interaction environment. It shows how a number of different peripheral devices (of differing information bandwidth and directionality) may be utilized to facilitate student-computer dialogue. This figure depicts only the 'on-line' aspect of the MMI learning process. Of course, this will normally be augmented by many 'off-computer' activities, perhaps involving the use of a special workbook, playing a game, reading a passage from a text book, or using an instrument of some sort.

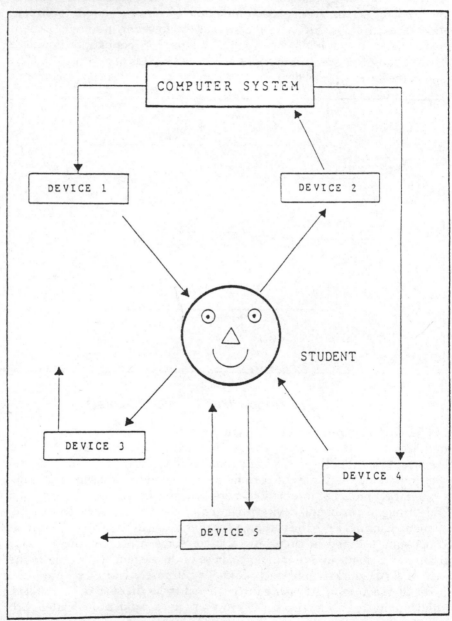

Figure 1.3 *Multi-media interaction environment for CAL*

Fundamental to the successful implementation of any MMI scheme will be:

(i)   an appreciation of the central integrating and co-ordinating role of the computer;
(ii) the realization and acceptance of the fact that many kinds of instructional resource need to be used;
(iii) the optimal integrated deployment of the resources that are available for use; and
(iv) the production of an appropriately designed multi-media resource pack.

The multi-media resource pack is important because it is what the student first 'sees and handles' – usually before any computer contact is made. Considerable thought must therefore be given to both its design and contents. Undoubtedly, one of the essential features of the resource pack will be a workbook. This is likely to contain sheets of instructions describing how to operate the multi-media workstation, pages of notes describing the course units and explaining how to use the resource material, pictures and interface cards for use in conjunction with various workstation devices (such as a digitizer, a concept keyboard or an electronic book), video discs and CDROMs – compact discs with read only memory – (containing text, pictures and sound), and activity lists for the students to work through. Within the resource pack there may also be special items of equipment. Among these might be included specific learning aids such as a micrometer, thermometer or microscope; learning how to use these might be an integral part of the course of instruction. Also included in the pack might be exhibits (such as a set of maps or a butterfly collection) and physical or mechanical models that must be connected to the workstation (for computer monitoring and control). Obviously, the contents of the resource pack will depend critically upon the nature of the training objectives to be realized. This will obviously vary quite considerably from one particular application of the technique to another.

Within a multi-media CAL environment it is important to realize the multiple roles played by the computer itself. Thus, the computer will be responsible for monitoring the student's learning progress and suggesting possible activities that the student(s) might undertake. It may also control some of the other media (such as video, slides, or audio) during the learning/training session. Of course, it may also participate in the teaching process itself, by running a simulation, as a calculator, as a help facility, or by playing a game. The multiple roles played by the computer in MMI are depicted schematically in Figure 1.4. This diagram shows the computer acting in each of its control, record keeping, and instructional roles.

Although there are many positive advantages to CAL based upon MMI methods there are obviously some disadvantages. One major drawback is the problem of developing courseware; this is often difficult and time consuming since there are few useful courseware development tools available. Another disadvantage of the MMI approach is the often difficult nature of the device interfacing that needs to be undertaken; when the peripheral cluster associated with a workstation contains a large number of

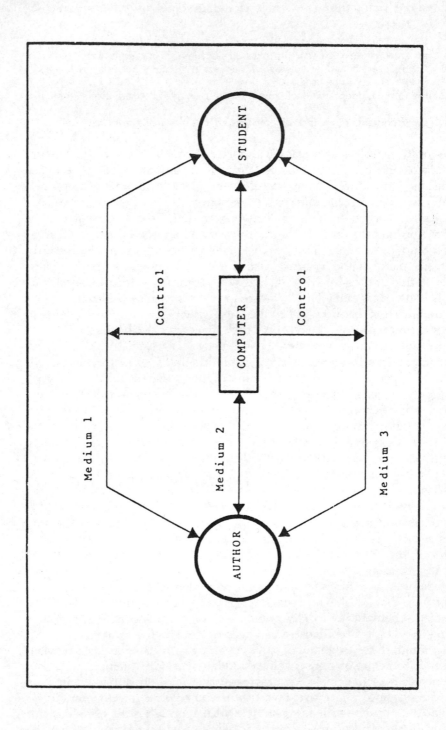

Figure 1.4 *Multiple roles of the computer in multi-media CAL*

devices, connecting and controlling them can be difficult – particularly if they utilize 'non-standard' interfaces. Yet another disadvantage of MMI is its cost; when sophisticated resources are involved (such as a video disc or a complex simulation rig) the cost can be prohibitively high. Of course, there may also be some disadvantages from the point of view of the learner. For example, sometimes before the primary learning goals of an MMI scheme can be realized students may have to acquire some additional ancillary skills. Usually, these are needed in order to operate the workstation or the particular devices that are attached to it. This point can be illustrated by reference to the multi-media Map Reading Resource Packs (Barker, 1987b). Typically, these would each include a set of pictorial interface cards containing sections of a map that have to be used in conjunction with a high resolution digitizer. Before these can be used students have to be taught how to manipulate a pointer (or stylus) in order to (a) 'register' the interface cards on the surface of the digitizer, and then (b) point to objects contained within these interfaces. Although use of this technique involves the acquisition of some new skills the overall benefits gained more than compensate for the extra learning involved.

1.2 Basic resources

Multi-media CAL is concerned with the design and fabrication of teaching systems that optimize learning processes through the most effective use of a variety of different communication channels (as depicted in Figures 1.3 and 1.4). These channels form the basic 'media' via which pedagogic material is presented to students and trainees. This section considers three of the more important of these media (text, sound and pictures) and how they might be optimally integrated within a multi-media workstation in order to provide effective and stimulating learning experiences.

1.2.1 Using text
For a variety of reasons that are discussed in greater depth elsewhere (Barker, 1987c), text has been and will continue to be one of the primary vehicles for both the preservation and the presentation of instructional material. Like any other medium it has both strengths and weaknesses. Furthermore, there are many different ways in which it can be presented to its reader. Within a multi-media CAL situation two of the most important of these are (1) via a CRT screen, and (2) using conventional paper-based methods. These methods differ considerably in a number of ways – impact, effectiveness, acceptability, readability, cost of production and so on. It is important to realize, of course, that both forms of text have a number of vital roles to play. Figure 1.5 illustrates some of the roles that text plays within a workstation environment that is designed to support both implicit and explicit CAL activity (Barker, 1987c).

Text is essentially an organized collection of strings of characters or symbols taken from some alphabet and strung together according to a set

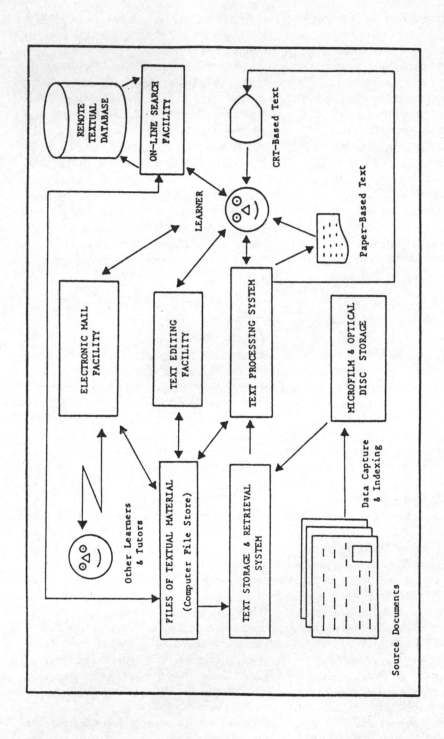

Figure 1.5 *The role of text in a CAL environment*

of reasonably well-defined morphemic, lexical, syntactic, semantic and pragmatic rules. The nature of the alphabet and the rule sets often define the type of text that is produced. This may be mathematical proofs or computations involving strings of numbers; it may comprise collections of symbols representing logical arguments or a sequence of statements that make up a computer program. Alternatively, the symbol combination may represent poetry, prose, scientific reports, or documented records of legal and jurisprudential material. Frequently, the nature of the alphabet employed can be used in order to characterize the 'tongue' in which the textual material is expressed: Russian, French, German, Arabic, Japanese, or English.

Conventional text books are probably one of the most useful means of distributing knowledge. Indeed, books permit self-study and learning in many environments that are distant from the authors who generate the learning material. Unfortunately, conventional books lack many of the useful attributes that computer-based systems can offer – such as interactivity, artificial intelligence, and shared learning partnerships. Computer generated, 'interactive text' can thus offer many new possibilities that conventional text denies.

Some of the possible implications that computer-based reading might have on reading comprehension have been discussed by Waern and Rollenhagen (1983). They emphasize the dynamic nature of visual display unit (VDU) text as compared with text on paper. Indeed, they suggest that:

> On paper the text is just there, in the same way and at the same place, whenever you look at it. On a screen the text may appear and disappear. It may stand still or move. It may present itself page-wise or roll-wise. Depending upon the speed of presentation it may creep slowly over the page, or it may appear so quickly that you notice almost nothing more than a change from blankness to a full-sized page of letters.

These comments are important since they bring out some of the potential advantages of screen based text.

For certain applications there are three important advantages of screen based text over its paper equivalent: spontaneity of update, its potential for reactivity, and the opportunities it offers for incorporating 'special effects'. The first of these advantages simply reflects the fact that the contents of a screen can be instantly updated. This means that the messages it conveys can be made immediately relevant to other things that may be taking place within a workstation environment. Reactivity of text can be achieved through the use of special touch sensitive screens so that when a user touches a word on a CRT display certain 'special' things happen – perhaps automatic dictionary look-up, page turning, jumps to other sections of text, and so on. Special effects can also be built into screen-based text – for example, the use of colour and highlighting, blinking and flashing, sound associations, use of hypertext, and word animation. Screen-based text thus offers many interesting possibilities for use as a resource within a multi-media CAL environment.

1.2.2 Using sound

Ongoing educational processes within members of the human species require for their development and sustenance the acquisition of a number of basic skills. For example, with few exceptions, the ability to read text and comprehend visual images is of paramount importance to virtually all forms of advanced learning and training. Similarly, students who are involved in using computer assisted learning are also required to have some dexterity in tactile communication – usually in the form of keyboard skills.

In many CAL situations the use of sound (through interactive audio) is a necessity. Other situations arise in which this technique can be used to increase the realism of a learning situation, improve its quality or act as a significant source of motivation. Unfortunately, most of the CAL material that has been developed to date has placed greatest emphasis on the learner's visual and tactile communicative abilities. Consequently, until quite recently the human's adeptness at sound processing has been almost totally ignored within CAL environments. This has had two major effects. First, subject domains that are 'sound orientated' – such as music, foreign language instruction, elocution, and so on – have often been neglected as major application areas for CAL. Second, the efficiency of interaction within conventional screen and keyboard CAL systems has not been as high as it might have been if sonic interaction (through audio aiding) had been available. From the point of view of its CAL applications, interactive audio refers to the use of sound processing techniques within the interaction environment of a learner or trainee (Barker, 1984a; 1986c; Barker and Yeates, 1985). It is intended both to enhance learning and provide novel types of interaction (and other effects) which, in the absence of sound, could not be achieved. Our motivation for using this resource therefore stems from the fundamental tenet that synthetic sound (particularly, speech) can significantly enhance the quality of CAL (Gray, 1984; Gull, 1985).

Interactive audio techniques can encompass a wide range of resources: use of telephones, tape recorders, voice synthesizers, speech analysis/ recognition equipment, music synthesizers, audio conferencing systems, and so on. It can involve both the transmission of sound to and its receipt from the learner. This chapter is concerned with only one aspect of the subject: the transmission of sound to the learner via some computer mediated method similar to that depicted schematically in Figure 1.6.

As Figure 1.6 suggests the descriptive material that follows is primarily concerned with sound production equipment that can be connected to (and hence, controlled by) a computer system. The controlling computer may be a stand alone micro or a workstation that is attached to a computer network that forms part of a local or global open learning system. In the latter situation the control information for the sound processing equipment might be held locally within the workstation or stored in a remote host computer. When stored remotely, speech segments (and any other control data) are only transmitted to the workstation as and when they are needed. Of course, the sound material might be stored digitally or in

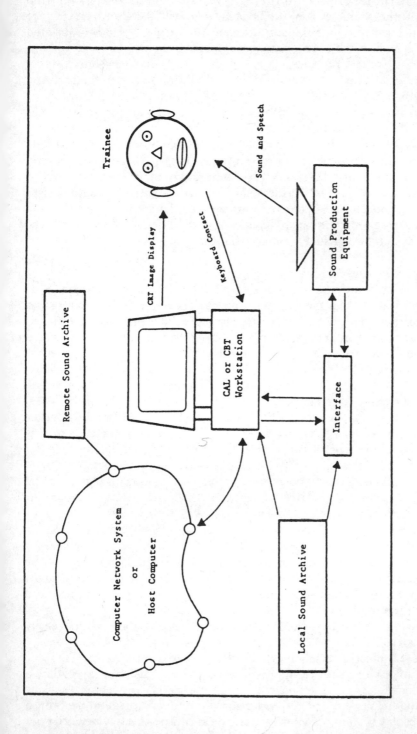

Figure 1.6 *Interactive audio for CAL applications*

analogue form as 'original' recordings. The method of storage and the nature of the transmission media available will dictate the types of transformation to which the sound resources may have to be subjected prior to their dispatch over a network system.

The nature of the interface, shown in Figure 1.6, that is used to connect the sound production equipment to the workstation will depend upon the basic nature of each of these items and upon the communication procedures involved. Locally, within the workstation environment there is likely to be a variety of different resources to produce sound, manipulate it and facilitate its archival and retrieval. Typically, the repertoire of peripherals is likely to include different types of speech synthesizer, sound production units (for special effects generation), tape recorders (both sequential and rapid access), dedicated CDROM systems and random acess audio discs. Substantial volumes of sound material may also be available via a hybrid storage medium such as video disc. Full details of each of these types of system are given elsewhere (Barker, 1986c).

1.2.3 Using pictures

There is a significant volume of evidence to support the use of imagery as an educationally useful medium within a variety of different training and learning situations. Indeed, it is now quite well established that images and pictorial data play an important role in (1) determining the way in which individuals perceive their external environment, (2) facilitating mechanisms of memory and recall, and (3) influencing the efficiency with which people are able to communicate with each other and with computers. Evidence for these statements may be found in the work of Neurath (1939; 1980), Paivio (1980), Barnett (1981), Barker and Najah (1985), and Barker and Skipper (1986). Bearing in mind the importance of pictorial form, it is natural to enquire whether or not this medium could usefully improve the quality, effectiveness, and efficiency of computer-based instruction.

Empirical evidence to support the assertion that 'graphics is useful' can be found in a number of sources. First, the prolific research/development activity currently taking place in this area; second, the amount of instructional software that now incorporates some form of graphic support (Stevens, Roberts and Stead, 1983); and third, the inherent ease with which pictorial information can be assimilated. This latter point can be seen by comparing three ways in which the concept of 'circle' or 'ring' might be communicated to someone. First, as an array of (x,y) pairs, second, as a mathematical equation, and third, as an actual drawing or sketch. Undoubtedly, for most people, the latter method is probably the most easily understood.

Figure 1.7 illustrates schematically the way in which pictorial/graphic support might be used to augment a basic CAL dialogue involving a conventional CRT and keyboard. There are three important ancillary (conceptual) units: an image production system, an image store, and a picture display system. Obviously, this diagram caters for a wide variety of possibilities. For example, the image production system could be based upon conventional manual methods of picture generation involving the use of a drawing board, paints, and/or ink. Alternatively, it might be a highly automated system involving the use of sophisticated computer graphics (perhaps in conjunction with a mouse or light pen device). The unit could equally well employ some form of camera that incorporates conventional film or video.

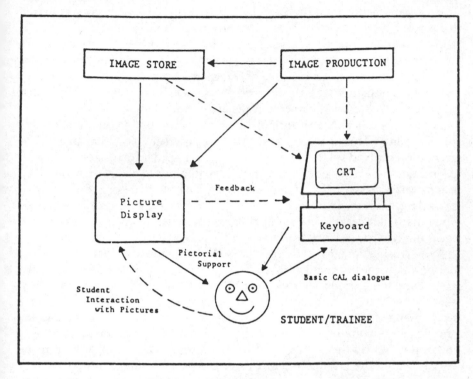

Figure 1.7 *Graphic support for CAL*

The images that are produced by the image production unit can be generated in real-time (that is, created and used as they are needed) or they can be fabricated and then committed to storage for later use. In this latter situation, there is a diverse range of image storage possibilities: conventional paper, photographs, slides, video tape, magnetic storage, video disc, CDROM, and so on. Of course, there is no reason why a combination of storage media cannot be employed.

Of equal importance to image storage and production is the concept of image display. A variety of techniques may be employed. These range from the use of conventional workbooks and other paper-based teaching aids (for example, maps, pictures, circuit diagrams), projection systems (such as slide and film), through to the use of high resolution colour graphics systems. Displayed pictures may be of three basic types: static, dynamic, and animated. Dynamic pictures are 'reactive', that is, things happen when they are touched (or otherwise referenced) by the student. This is easily accomplished in a variety of different ways: on a CRT display (through the use of a touch sensitive screen), on a map (by means of a high resolution digitizer), or on a conventionally designed picture using the 'electronic book' principle. Animated images are, of course, another powerful instructional aid. Animation may be local (to a particular base image) or global (involving the display of a large number of static images in succession (forward or backward at high or low speed). When images are synthesized for display they can of course utilize any combination of static, dynamic, and animated components embedded within each other. Similarly, within an image construction process, it is possible to use part-images from several different storage media (or image fragments computed in real-time) to compose an image having the desired properties. Sometimes this approach to picture production is referred to as 'value added imagery'.

Another important attribute of pictures that needs to be considered is their quality. This usually improves as both the colour capability and resolution of the display medium/device increases. Unfortunately, as these properties increase so does the cost of the equipment needed. It is therefore important to bear this in mind when thinking about alternative ways of providing graphic support. However, the rapidly falling cost of graphics equipment is a very compelling reason for wishing to incorporate this technology into CAL applications.

When using images to support a CAL dialogue the instructor must decide upon the mechanism by which graphic aid will be provided. Like sound and text, graphics provides another 'logical' channel of communication. Some thought must therefore be given to how this logical channel is to be mapped onto one or more physical support channels. For example, should pictorial material be contained in a workbook that the student uses in conjunction with the CRT? Should a second CRT display system be used? Should the graphic support be embedded within the primary CRT/ keyboard device by means of frame swapping, screen segmentation, and/or windowing techniques? Should graphic aiding be built into some other ancillary device such as a graph plotter, a robot arm, or a mechanical turtle having a 'paint brush' attached to its tail? Obviously, a large number of possibilities exist for the realization of the 'picture display system' depicted in Figure 1.7. Because of the diverse range of resources available each learning/training situation must therefore be considered in the context of its own particular pictorial aid requirements and appropriate graphic support facilities designed.

Some mention has already been made of the wide range of graphics resources available for picture production. Before concluding this section brief descriptions of some of these will be presented. Because it is not possible to offer any form of in-depth treatment of specific areas appropriate references are given (where they are needed) to more detailed descriptions of particular topics and techniques.

Conventional images
There exist within the world vast quantities of pictorial material of many

different types. Much of this material is available in the form of paper-based images – as photographs, as illustrations in books, and so on. It is obviously very important that the courseware designer is able to accommodate the use (where appropriate) of some of this material within the computer based teaching strategies that he/she formulates. For example, maps are used in the teaching of both geography and navigation. Computers are also used to help teach these subjects. It would therefore be very useful if paper-based maps and charts could be used to augment computer based tuition. Similarly, in the teaching of electronics, circuit diagrams are extensively used as a graphic aid. Although these are often displayed on a high resolution screen (Barker, 1987a) this does not preclude the need to employ similar circuits drawn on paper.

Paper-based pictorial material for use in a course can often be conveniently incorporated into a workbook (Barker and Yeates, 1985). This can be of either a 'bound' or a 'loose-leaf' form. Sometimes, pages of the workbook may be used in conjunction with a suitably designed input peripheral (such as a digitizer or a microswitch system) in order to make them interactive. This is the principle underlying the 'electronic book' which was referenced in Figure 1.1. A more detailed description of this device is given elsewhere (Barker, Lees and Docherty, 1986).

Computer graphics
Essentially, the term 'computer graphics' encompasses any technique in which a computer system is used to generate a picture – this may be on paper, on a CRT screen, or in the form of a celluloid slide or film. Usually, in order to use this technique the person responsible for generating the picture (the producer) often has to specify suitable algorithms to control the resources available within the image production and/or display system(s) shown in Figure 1.7 (Newman and Sproull, 1979; Giloi, 1978; Foley and van Dam, 1982; Machover and Meyers, 1984). Typically, this may involve controlling the movement of a pen (as in a plotter or turtle – see below) or an electron beam (as in a CRT display). Alternatively, at a less technical level, the producer may simply employ a set of graphical primitives that enable the generation and manipulation of commonly used 'standard forms'. For example, a user might type in the command MAKECIRCLE(A,X,Y,R) in order to generate a circle (notionally labelled A) of radius R centred at the screen location (X,Y). Similarly, a command of the form MOVE(A,X2,Y2) might then be used to move the circle A to a new screen position. Effects of this sort may also be achieved through suitably designed light pen or mouse dialogues based upon selection techniques if these interaction devices are available.

When producing images by means of computer graphics techniques either of two basic modes of usage may be employed – depending upon the nature and extent of the interaction that takes place between the producer and the picture he/she is generating. 'Interactive graphics' is the term commonly used to describe the approach wherein the producer is able to influence the ongoing computational processes responsible for picture production. The producer can thus modify the picture as it is being produced. The other form of graphics is akin to mechanized drafting in which the computer just produces a picture according to a previously specified list of instructions.

In the context of CAL three other important aspects of graphics need to be mentioned: iconics, animation, and sketching. Iconics refers to the design and production of graphic symbols to enable efficient human-computer interaction using pictorial forms (IEEE, 1984; Gittins, 1986). Animation effects (Magnenat-Thalmann and Thalmann, 1983) can be produced and used in a variety of different ways. For example, the computer might be used to generate two closely spaced parallel lines containing a sequence of moving dots to indicate the flow of liquid along a pipe. Alternatively, the computer might be used to generate a series of static images that are subsequently shown in rapid succession in order to produce the illusion of movement. Computer monitored sketching is another useful way of generating pictures. In this approach the producer sketches a picture on a flat surface; the pen movements are monitored, digitized, transformed, stored, and displayed on a CRT screen. Once the sketch data has been captured it can be stored in a data base and recalled for display at any subsequent time.

Because graphics has become so popular an extremely wide range of software packages now exist to support the use of this technique. Many of these are described in the standard graphics text books cited above. These packages can be used to reduce much of the programming effort needed to generate pictures. In addition to graphics packages, many author languages (Barker and Skipper, 1986) also provide in-built facilities for picture generation.

Video disc and tape

Video technology offers the instructor a powerful method of 'capturing reality' for subsequent use in an instructional situation. Through the use of portable video equipment it is possible to capture (at relatively low cost) the details of happenings taking place in a wide variety of locations. In addition to permitting the use of a camera, video equipment also allows the acquisition of material that is broadcast via TV networks. This too can be integrated into an instructional sequence – providing it is appropriately indexed to enable its subsequent retrieval from storage.

The connection of a video tape system to a computer is a relatively simple matter (Laurillard, 1982). The computer can be used to control image retrieval and display. Systems of this type are frequently referred to as 'interactive video' systems. One of the problems associated with the use of video tape as an archival medium for pictorial material is its relatively slow retrieval time. Significant improvements in access speed (and image presentation facilities) can be gained by using video disc instead of tape (Barker, 1985).

In many ways interactive video disc (Duke, 1983) is a far more useful instructional medium than is interactive video tape. A typical system might provide almost instantaneous access to any of 55,000 (or more) static images. Of course, sequences of images can be shown in rapid succession (25 frames/sec) in order to provide normal speed animation; slow or fast motion may also be implemented. Through the use of special effects generators, it is possible to combine pictorial material retrieved from a video disc with material that has been generated using computational graphics. A wide range of stimulating instructional effects can be achieved using equipment capable of providing facilities of this type.

Film, slide and microfiche material

Devices capable of showing closed loop film strip and slides can easily be interfaced to and controlled by a computer system (Barker, 1982; Barker and Yeates, 1985). These media offer useful ways of providing high quality static images (slides) and animation (film). One of the disadvantages of computer controlled slide projection is the relatively small number of images that can be accessed (unless a number of units are operated in parallel). This limitation can sometimes be overcome through the use of a computer controlled microfiche or microfilm system. Alternatively, the slide (and film) material can be committed to video disc storage and used in this form. However, once a slide collection has been stored on disc it may prove difficult to update it.

Television, Teletext, and Telesoftware

Television broadcasts offer an extremely rich source of pictorial information – both static images and animation. Such images can be committed to video tape storage (as discussed above) or digitized (using a 'frame grabber') and stored digitally for subsequent display and/or processing. The advantage of having the pictorial information stored digitally is the ease with which it can then be modified by means of an image processing system. By this means images can be enhanced, mixed with others, replicated, and manipulated in a host of different ways.

Broadcast Teletext is another useful source of medium resolution pictures that can be used for instructional purposes. Many other non-broadcast systems also use the Teletext display standard (Reis, 1976) for the implementation of electronic message board and display systems. For example, the Video-Slide system (Barker and Skipper, 1986) is a microcomputer based instructional facility that incorporates this standard.

Telesoftware is a term used to describe the technique whereby computer programs are transmitted along with TV signals (Hedger, 1978; Coates, 1982). These programs can be captured and stored locally (for example, within a home computer) and then executed. They can be used for a variety of computational purposes – including the generation of graphical effects to support learning activity.

Plotters, Turtles, and Robots

Graph plotters were probably one of the earliest types of computer peripheral capable of supporting the output of pictorial data from a computer. A variety of different types exist – depending upon the way the paper is held (on a drum or a flat bed) and the type of 'marking' technology employed (such as conventional pens or a laser beam). The pictures produced by a plotter may be either monochrome or coloured. During the picture production process a plotter can be operated in either an off-line or an on-line (or interactive) mode; these two modes more or less correspond to the two modes of computer graphics described above. In interactive mode the user is able to directly (and instantaneously) influence the operation of the plotter by means of the commands that are sent to it – just like controlling a turtle.

A turtle is really a special type of 'mobile' graph plotting device. The most sophisticated kinds of turtle are those that are able to roam around a large sheet of paper that is fixed on a flat surface such as a table or a floor. Using one or more of the coloured pens that are attached to it, the turtle is able to draw pictures that trace out a record of its motion. Movement of the turtle is controlled by means of commands that are sent to it directly or which are issued from within a program. The LOGO language (Papert, 1980; Harvey, 1985) is often used in conjunction with turtle graphics. In situations where a mechanical turtle cannot be employed, a CRT based one is used instead. Some types of CRT turtle are able to 'reproduce' themselves under program control; this enables many colourful and stimulating learning effects to be generated.

In addition to the above types of plotting technique a number of other methods exist. Undoubtedly, one of the most impressive is that involving the use of a robot arm which is able, automatically, to select appropriate instruments and use these to produce pictorial forms.

1.2.4 Integrating resources

Teaching, training and learning have always been people orientated activities. Therefore, any discussion of the pedagogical applications of computers should take into account the basic nature of human communication. Humans are naturally multi-channel communicators. That is, they use a number of communication channels (often simultaneously) to get across and receive messages. Consider, for example, a conventional human dialogue between two people. During the conversation process information flow may take place by means of speech, writing, sketching, drawing, doodling, touching, eye movement, facial expression, gesticulation, body movement and pose, and so on. Each of the channels listed conveys important information between those involved in a dialogue process.

The communication channels mentioned above will each have a particular capacity for conveying information. The capacity of a channel (the amount of information transferred per unit time) has previously been referred to as its bandwidth. Some channels, for example, speech and vision, will have greater bandwidth than others (such as touch). When a computer is used as an instructional medium (perhaps as a substitute for a human teacher) many of the natural channels of communication described above are likely to be lost. Thus, unless careful thought is given to the design of an instructional human to computer interaction environment there is likely to be a loss in variety (of communication channel) and possibly a reduction in transmission bandwidth.

Multi-media CAL is concerned with deriving techniques for improving the quality and effectiveness of computer-based instruction by suitably augmenting the basic facilities offered by a computer. This is achieved through the provision of additional communication channels or by enhancing the bandwidth of existing ones. Fundamentally, the requirement for this approach to CAL stems from the realization that computers have significant limitations with respect to skill and knowledge transfer processes. That is, it is not possible to use the computer alone in order to achieve total skill transfer in a CAL environment.

The basic concept underlying the design of a multi-media interaction environment for computer assisted learning has been illustrated in Figure 1.3. Essentially, multi-media CAL deals with the fabrication of instructional workstations that are tailor made to the requirements of particular CAL situations. The instructional environment provided by the workstation may be thought of as consisting of an appropriate collection of interaction devices. The devices depicted in Figure 1.3 fall into three basic classes: (a) those used to present instructional material, (b) those used to exercise motor/cognitive skills, and (c) those used to acquire signals, data and messages from the learner (or the equipment that he/she is using). For the moment the detailed nature of these devices is not important. However, it is important to realize that they provide multiple channels of communication between an electronic teaching machine (or 'simulated' teacher) and its student population. As has already been suggested in section 1.1.3, within such a system the computer has two important roles to play: that of a communication medium (in its own right) and that of a controller. In the latter role the computer can be used to control the activity and use of the other media within the learner's interaction environment. This has already been illustrated in Figure 1.4. In this diagram the concept of an author has been introduced. The CAL author is the person responsible for preparing the instructional material and control specifications for use in the multi-media learning environment. Because of the complexity of these environments special types of programming language are often required in order to specify, fabricate and control the progress of the instructional dialogues that take place. Naturally, it is imperative that these programming tools (called author languages) ease the burden of courseware development, improve author productivity, and reduce the overall software development cost. In order to achieve these goals author languages often contain powerful linguistic primitives for controlling the wide range of instructional resources that need to be used within a CAL workstation. The nature of these author languages and the facilities they provide are briefly discussed in the following section.

From what has been said above it is easy to see that there are many good reasons why the resources described previously in this section should be integrated in such a way as to produce multi-media learning/training experiences. Until recently, however, progress towards the realization of multi-media CAL has been severely inhibited by the lack of appropriate microcomputer architectures to facilitate the development of workstations. For example, so ingrained has been the idea of keyboard dialogue that implementing any other form of user-interaction has been virtually impossible for those without significant technical experience. Similar comments apply to the use of CRTs for information display. Fortunately, with the advent of new types of 'base' microcomputer architectures it is now feasible to fabricate systems that contain a wide range of highly disparate interaction peripherals for both the delivery of instruction and the collection of interaction data. This topic is further discussed in the following section.

1.3 Authoring and delivery

The successful application of computer assisted learning within some target domain depends upon the overall integration of a number of sophisticated design and implementation processes. Each of these is described in considerable detail elsewhere (Barker, 1987a; Barker and Yeates, 1985). Therefore, in this section only two of the more important processes are discussed. They have been selected for inclusion because of their importance in the context of the utilization of multi-media CAL in an open, distributed, distance learning environment. The two fundamental processes that are discussed in this section are courseware authoring and the delivery of instructional material.

1.3.1 Courseware authoring

Earlier in this chapter it was suggested that there are two broad approaches to the realization of CAL: implicit and explicit. These categories differ in a number of ways. Of these, one of the most important is the amount of effort needed to develop courseware and other instructional materials. Implicit CAL requires little, if any, software development on the part of the designer. Examples of this approach include such activities as learning to program in BASIC or PROLOG, using LOGO microworlds, using a word-processing system and so on. In contrast, explicit CAL usually requires a significant amount of authoring activity. In the previous section some mention was made of the wide variety of author languages and authoring systems that are available to facilitate this. A number of authors have given extensive descriptions of the many different types of tool available (Barker, 1987a; Barker and Yeates, 1985; Kearsley, 1982).

Some of our own earlier research in the area of authoring for multi-media CAL (Barker, 1984a; 1984b) was concerned with the development of an authoring facility that might be implemented within a workstation that could be attached to a distributed computer network. The system, called MUMEDALA (an acronym for 'Multi-Media Author Language'), was frame based and could utilize frames from a variety of different sources.

These might be a video disc, a CRT frame store (both low and high resolution), paper-based frames from a 'document cluster' held within a workbook, and 3-D overlay frames (for use with disabled and handicapped students). In addition the system could support the use of sound and 'add on' ancillary equipment such as electronic 'patch boards', simulation panels and robotic aids. Since our early investigations with this system we have moved on to study a number of new approaches to the provision of authoring facilities. In doing this we have moved closer to the instructional design phase of authoring in order to study the problems involved in handling the conceptual aspects of the authoring process. The details of this work are presented in greater depth elsewhere (Barker, 1986b; 1987b; 1988a). This section therefore presents only an overview of our current approaches to the design of authoring facilities for multi-media CAL.

Currently, we are concerned with the provision of a linguistic framework that will allow an author or instructional designer to express ideas in the form of a number of primitive epistemological units. The important units are domains, concepts, topics, relationships and knowledge bases. Once the author has created a conceptual model of the required courseware in terms of these basic building blocks, the knowledge structure that has been produced can then be mapped onto the most appropriate media available within the target application domain.

In defining and creating the prototype of the linguistic framework mentioned above we provided the author with a command driven system that was based primarily upon the use of textual dialogue. Conversations with the system via this type of dialogue were realized by means of a conventional QWERTY keyboard. As commands were input to the system the underlying authoring software could create representations of the allowed epistemological units and the relationships between them. During the authoring process the author could obtain real-time pictorial feedback in the form of a knowledge representation diagram displayed in the screen of a high resolution, colour graphics unit. Our work on this approach to authoring has revealed some of the many severe limitations associated with the use of an authoring dialogue that is based purely upon the use of text. Consequently, in our subsequent work we moved towards the use of a multi-media, mixed-mode dialogue involving the use of pull-down menus, icons and mouse interaction (Cox and Hunt, 1986; Gittins, 1986).

The authoring facility that we have recently been designing places special emphasis on the role of pictorial dialogue, the use of graphic overlays (derived from a data base) and a window management system. Some of these features are illustrated in Figure 1.8. This diagram shows the state of the CRT display during the creation of a relationship within a knowledge domain called D47. Through the type of mechanism illustrated in this figure we intend to produce an author's workbench rather than an author language as such. This workbench will provide all the facilities and tools needed to author knowledge based CAL resources for use in a multi-media environment.

Instructional design, validation and evaluation are each complex and

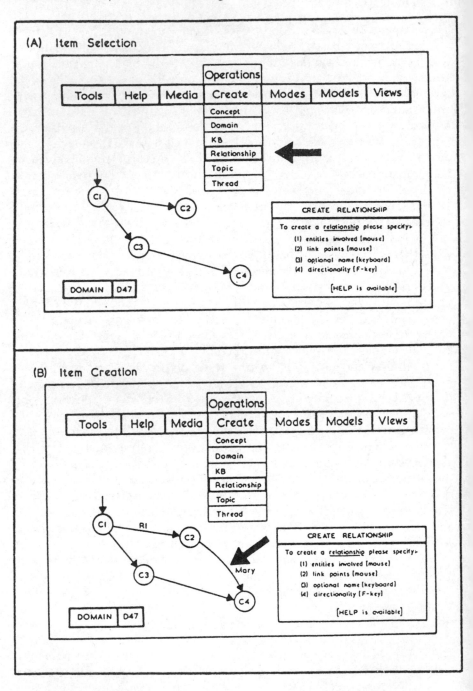

Figure 1.8 *Courseware authoring using pictures*

involved processes. For this reason the workbench described above will need to provide its user with a wide variety of 'intelligent' software tools. These tools must be capable of satisfying all of the authoring requirements encountered in a computer-based teaching and tutoring environment. This environment must therefore provide tools to enable the creation of many different types of user model (of students, of authors, of designers, etc). Similarly, it will need to provide a media specification language that will enable the author to control and manipulate various resources. Because (a) many different media are likely to be involved and (b) resources may be located at may different locations, another obvious requirement will be a set of tools to facilitate instructional resource management. These examples represent just a few of the many different types of facility that will need to be available through the author's workbench. Further details of some of these tools are described elsewhere (Barker, 1988b).

1.3.2 Delivering instruction
In its most general sense the term 'instructional delivery' refers to the many different processes that underlie (and are needed to support) the presentation and control of pedagogic resources during a teaching/tutoring session. In reactive and adaptive tutoring systems student monitoring will obviously play an important role. Its importance stems from the feedback that it provides. Feedback can be used to determine the nature of the instruction that is to be delivered and the strategies involved in its presentation.

When considering the delivery of instructional material to the learner/trainee within a CAL environment, in addition to student monitoring, two other basic issues need to be addressed. First, some consideration must be given to the nature of the workstation itself. Second, some thought must be put into designing an appropriate strategy for providing access to the learning resources via the workstation. Each of these issues is briefly discussed below.

Workstation considerations
It has already been suggested (in part 1 of this chapter) that the implementation of multi-media CAL requires the provision of an environment that contains far more than just a keyboard and a CRT. Effective approaches to multi-media CAL can only be fully realized by the successful 'bringing together' (within the workstation environment) of those interaction peripherals and learning aids that are appropriate to the instructional tasks that are to take place. Guidelines for the fabrication of workstations have been given by a number of authors (Barker, 1987a; Barker and Yeates, 1985; McLean, 1983).

Although the specific composition and structure of individual workstations will depend upon their intended instructional objective, the maxim of 'economy in number' (through large scale production) might usefully be employed in order to reduce their fabrication cost. Therefore, it is likely that a suitably designed 'base' microcomputer could be used as the basic foundation for system building. This will need to contain a number of essential components. For example, it will need to have a powerful 'intelligent' microprocessor (probably 32 bit) having an architecture that is customized with respect to the types of process likely to take place within the workstation. It will need to have significant internal and external memory capacity. It should be able to support a large number of add-on devices such as special effects units, optical storage media, and a range of interaction devices such as a mouse, tracker-ball, joy-stick, digitizers and a variety of different types of keyboard. The ability to support a very large number of 'input-output' channels is therefore a very important pre-requisite. Of course, as is discussed below, the need to be able to attach the workstation to both a local area and a wide area network is also a primary requirement. Some researchers have suggested that two different types of workstation are needed: one to support the authoring of courseware and a second for the delivery of instruction. This is not really necessary since both functions could be subsumed by one common design. However, having said this, the scenario that is presented in the final section of this chapter proceeds to suggest that as many as four different functional types of workstation might be required. It is important to realize, however, that the differences between these is one of role rather than architecture.

The transportation medium

Once a pool of instructional material has been created a major problem facing implementers of distance learning systems is that of 'transporting the resources' to their potential users. A number of strategies are available for providing access to instructional material. For example, the resources could be 'packaged' onto a CDROM or video disc (Barker, 1986d) and then sent to the student/trainee using a postal service. Tuition could then take place using the workstation as a free-standing, autonomous teaching machine; the Advanced Interactive Video (AIV) workstation upon which the British Broadcasting Corporation's Domesday Project is based uses this approach to implement informatory CAL (see Figure 1.1). Alternatively, the workstation could be connected to a high bandwidth communication network (Newman, 1985; Barker, 1986e) that allows resources to be transmitted to the workstation from remote sites or production studios.

When considering the delivery technology that is to be employed in a distance learning environment the instructional designer needs to think very carefully about many of the wider issues associated with the implementation of educational processes. Instructional delivery is not just a matter of simply packaging instructional materials and then 'shipping' them to the student (or the workstation) via a suitable delivery medium. Indeed, of the available possibilities the choice of delivery mechanism needs to be thought about very carefully. In doing this, we contend that particular attention needs to be given to the social and human aspects of the learning process. For example, we believe that it is unrealistic to think of a situation in which learners are isolated from any form of 'live' contact with each other or with their tutors. One way of providing this, of course, is through electronic mail and on-line conferencing facilities (Barker, 1987c). We therefore suggest that an optimal solution to the problems associated with instructional delivery might be sought through the use of an appropriate combination of computer networking based upon the Integrated Services Digital Network (ISDN) (perhaps involving satellite transmission) and the newly emerging optical disc technology. Unfortunately, it is likely to be many years before there is a comprehensive worldwide ISDN coverage. However, in the interim period leading up to this, it may be possible to achieve similar effects through appropriate use of optical disc technology and existing communication network systems.

1.4 The future

Education is likely to be a factor that will significantly influence the future well-being of society. Unfortunately, the creation of educational systems, the bureaucracy to run them and the creation/delivery of instructional resources to ensure their effectiveness are each costly and time-consuming processes. Distributing the tasks of resource production and management over several nations is one way of sharing the costs that are incurred. Such an approach also provides an implicit mechanism for quality control and, to some extent, a facility for standardization. The extent of sharing these tasks, however, depends upon the solution of a number of non-technical problems. These relate to language barriers, cultural differences, and variations in both political and ideological belief systems. Fortunately, in the technical domain these problems are likely to be more easily overcome.

As a 'scenario for the future' let us envisage the existence of a highly distributed, multi-media, open learning facility for some global community of users. What properties should such a system possess and what types of facility should it provide? The remainder of this section attempts to answer these questions and provides one possible indication of how such an open learning facility might appear to its user population.

A co-ordinated distributed learning/training system of the type outlined above is one in which there exists a commonly accessible base of instructional resources along with the means of producing these. It is assumed that instructional materials will be produced and administered by means of suitably designed computer-based workstations. Although capable of operating autonomously, for most applications these will be attached to some form of intelligent computer based communication network (such as the ISDN) that spans the geographical area in which learners, trainers, authors, subject specialists, and tutors coexist. Four basic types of workstation might be available: authoring, enquiry, response and delivery. As its name suggests an authoring station provides access to the mechanisms and resources needed to develop courseware materials. A number of different types of authoring station may be attached to the system depending upon both the locality of the author and his/her authoring requirements. Naturally, it is assumed that distributed authoring is a pre-requisite requirement and that materials may be developed both within some form of production studio(s) and from locations remote to these. A delivery station provides the means by which previously prepared material (held in the form of distributed knowledge-based systems) is presented to the student, his/her reactions monitored and appropriate actions taken towards the realization of particular pedagogic goals. Enquiry stations permit tutors to determine the status of any particular resource, student, author, or tutor. Response stations enable remote and/or mobile tutors to respond dynamically to any demands made of them by the distributed learning/training system. Each of the four types of workstation will need to support different kinds of functionality; guidelines for their fabrication are therefore needed. These are discussed in more detail elsewhere (Barker, 1987a).

The development of instructional material for use within a distributed multi-media CAL environment requires the availability of three basic types of facility:

(1) tools to aid the production of instructional resources (courseware development tools);
(2) a set of resources that are held in a common pool and which may be remote to the learner and/or author (studio resources and remote host resources);
(3) a collection of resources that are held locally at the learner's place of learning (workstation resources).

For any given application the balance of local and remote instructional resources will need to be carefully gauged. Consequently, a variety of instructional design and prototyping tools will need to be available to help designers and tutors create an appropriate learning environment. One class of courseware development tool that is likely to play an increasingly important role in providing access to distributed learning resources is the 'Instructional Designer's Intelligent Assistant' (Barker, 1988b).

The management of studio resources will naturally create many problems with respect to access and sharing – particularly when they involve the use of complex image data or modifications to sophisticated knowledge based structures. Considerable thought must therefore be given (1) to contention problems with respect to views of knowledge, and (2) to the way in which learning resources are distributed between studio(s), remote hosts, and workstation(s). In the previous section it was suggested that workstation operation (be it in the context of authoring or tutoring) often consists of large amounts of highly parallel activity. Thus, during its operation each workstation may spawn a number of parallel (possibly co-operating and/or competing) processes at both a local and global level; these will need to be monitored and controlled by the underlying integrated management support software.

Naturally, in addition to the requirements outlined above, it is assumed that the integrated management and control software for the overall system will possess three basic characteristics:

(1) as hinted above, it will be based upon the use of distributed, multi-media knowledge based systems that can accommodate the facile sharing of stored knowledge;

(2) it is capable of dynamically building models of all the participants involved in the educational processes with which the system deals; and

(3) it will be capable of using these models to produce highly adaptive, reactive, responsive and effective instructional systems.

The technology to construct a powerful multi-media, distributed open learning facility is available today. Therefore, the realization of such a facility depends only upon two major factors: first, the availability of funds to 'bolt' this technology together; and second, a concerted effort on the part of those interested in collaborating in such an extensive and laudable venture.

1.5 References

Barker, P.G., (1982). Computer control of a random access slide projector, *Microprocessing and Microprogramming*, 10, 261-271.

Barker, P.G., (1984a). MUMEDALA – An approach to multi-media authoring, *British Journal of Educational Technology*, 15(1), 4-13.

Barker, P.G., (1984b). MUMEDALA – An approach to multi-media authoring, *Computers and Education*, 8(4), 463-469.

Barker, P.G., (1985). Programming a video disc, *Microprocessing and Microprogramming*, 15, 263-276.

Barker, P.G., (1986a). Multi-media CAL, *Computer Education*, 52, 20-23.

Barker, P.G., (1986b). Knowledge based CAL, 137-143 in *Proceedings of the 5th Canadian Symposium on Instructional Technology*, Ottawa, 5th-7th May 1986.

Barker, P.G., (1986c). A practical introduction to authoring for computer assisted instruction. Part 6: Interactive Audio, *British Journal of Educational Technology*, 17(2), 110-128.

Barker, P.G., (1986d). Video discs in education, *Education and Computing*, 2, 193-206.

Barker, P.G., (1986e). The changing face of computers in education, 29-32 in *National Electronics Review*, Volume 21, National Electronics Council.

Barker, P.G., (1987a) *Author Languages for CAL*, Macmillan Press, Basingstoke.

Barker, P.G., (1987b). A practical introduction to authoring for computer assisted instruction. Part 8: Multi-media CAL, *British Journal of Educational Technology*, 18(1), 20-36.

Barker, P.G., (1987c). Chapter 2 in 'Exploring Multi-media CAL', unpublished manuscript.

Barker, P.G., (1988a). Knowledge engineering for CAL, in *Proceedings of the IFIP European Conference on Computers in Education*, Lausanne, Switzerland, 24th-29th July, 1988.

Barker, P.G., (1988b). Towards an instructional designer's intelligent assistant, 127-134 in *Aspects of Educational Technology, Volume XXI: Designing*

New Systems and Technologies for Learning, edited by Mathias, H., Rushby, N. and Budgett, R., Kogan Page, London.

Barker, P.G., Lees, J. and Docherty, D., (1986). Flexible learning in a multi-media environment, 123-128 in *Aspects of Educational Technology, Volume XX: Flexible Learning Systems*, Kogan Page, London.

Barker, P.G. and Proud, A., (1987). A practical introduction to authoring for computer assisted instruction. Part 10: Knowledge Based CAL, *British Journal of Educational Technology*, 18(2), 140-160.

Barker, P.G. and Najah, M., (1985). Pictorial interfaces to data bases, *International Journal of Man-Machine Studies*, 23, 423-442.

Barker, P.G. and Skipper, T., (1986). A practical introduction to authoring for computer assisted instruction. Part 7: Graphic Support for CAL, *British Journal of Educational Technology*, 17(3), 194-212.

Barker, P.G. and Yeates, H., (1985). *Introducing Computer Assisted Learning*, Prentice-Hall International, Hemel Hempstead, UK.

Barnett, C., (1981). Computer vision can show us what the mind can imagine, *Smithsonian Magazine*, 12(3), 106-113.

Coates, J., (1982). A pilot telesoftware service for education, *International Journal of Man-Machine Studies*, 17(1), 23-32.

Cox, B. and Hunt, B., (1986). Objects, icons and software-ICS, *BYTE: The Small Systems Journal*, 11(8), 161-176.

Duke, J., (1983). *Interactive Video: Implications for Education and Training*, Working Paper 22, Council for Educational Technology, London.

Foley, J.D. and van Dam, A., (1982). *Fundamentals of Interactive Computer Graphics*, Addison-Wesley, Reading, MA.

Giloi, W.K., (1978). *Interactive Computer Graphics: Data Structures, Algorithms, Languages*, Prentice-Hall, Englewood Cliffs, NJ.

Gittins, D., (1986). Icon-based human-computer interaction, *International Journal of Man-Machine Studies*, 24(6), 519-544.

Gray, T., (1984). Talking computers in the classroom, chapter 15, 243-259 in *Electronic Speech Synthesis: Techniques, Technology and Applications*, edited by G. Bristow, Granada, London, UK.

Gull, R.L., (1985). Voice synthesis: an update and perspective, page 525 in *Proceedings of the IFIP WCCE 85 Fourth World Conference on Computers in Education*, edited by K. Duncan and D.

Harris, Norfolk, Virginia, USA, 29th July – 2nd August, 1985.

Harvey, B., (1985). *Computer Science LOGO Style: Intermediate Programming*, MIT Press, Reading, MA.

Hedger, J., (1978). Telesoftware: Home computing via teletext, *Wireless World*, 84(1515), 61-64.

IEEE, (1984). Icon driven systems, Special Edition of *IEEE Computer*, 17(11).

Kearsley, G., (1982). Authoring systems for computer based education, *Communications of the ACM*, 25(7), 429-437.

Laurillard, D.M., (1982). The potential of interactive video, *Journal of Educational Television*, 8(3), 173-180.

Machover, C. and Meyers, W., (1984). Interactive computer graphics, *IEEE Computer*, 17(10), 145-161.

Magnenat-Thalmann, N. and Thalmann, D., (1983). The use of high-level 3-D graphical types on the Mira animation system, *IEEE Computer Graphics and Applications*, 3(9), 9-16.

McLean, R.S., (1983). Ontario Ministry of Education specifies its micro-computer, 436-441 in *Proceedings of the 4th Canadian Symposium on Instructional Technology*, Winnipeg, 19th-21st October, 1983.

Neurath, O., (1939). *Modern Man in the Making*, Knopf, New York.

Neurath, O., (1980). *International Picture Language* (A fascimile reprint of the 1936 edition), Department of Typography and Graphic Communication, University of Reading.

Newman, P., (1985). Information networks: present and future, 67-72 in *National Electronics Review*, Volume 20, National Electronics Council.

Newman, W.M. and Sproull, R.F., (1979). *Principles of Interactive Computer Graphics*, McGraw-Hill, New York, NY.

Papert, S., (1980). *Mindstorms: Children, Computers, and Powerful Ideas*, Harvester Press, Brighton.

Paivio, A., (1980). Imagery as a private audio-visual aid, *Instructional Science*, 9, 295-309.

Reis, C.W.B., (1976). (Editor), Specification of standards for broadcast teletext signals, 76-89 in *IBA Technical Review*, No.2, – Technical Reference Book, ISSN: 03308-423X.

Stevens, A., Roberts, B. and Stead, L., (1983). The use of a sophisticated graphics interface in computer assisted instruction, *IEEE Computer Graphics and Applications*, 3(2), 25-31.

Waern, Y. and Rollenhagen, C., (1983). Reading text from visual display units (VDUs), *International Journal of Man-Machine Studies*, 18, 441-465.

Chapter 2
The Case for Multi-Media CAL

John Whiting
University of Ulster

2.1 Background

Three viewpoints are the minimum when regarding teaching and learning processes: that of the learner, that of the teacher, and lastly, that of the instructional designer. The main dialogue occurs between the learner and the teacher. However, the means by which this dialogue occurs are the province of the instructional designer, whose viewpoint is orthogonal to those of the learner and teacher. The node at which these three viewpoints co-exist may be termed the interface. A variety of interfaces are used. Increasingly, the interface is computer mediated in one form or another. This chapter concerns the nature of the interface, with particular reference to: (a) the scope for multi-media approaches, and (b) the case for using them.

2.2 The multi-media concept

Multi-media is an uneasy concept, like so many in educational technology, and is open to a variety of interpretations. One useful perspective is to regard the term as expressing the number of types of learner-teacher communication channel which are open during tuition. The interface may be a series of sequential, one-way channels such as teacher to learner, learner to teacher using spoken dialogue, accompanied by one or more aids to communication such as a blackboard, slides or overhead projection (OHP) transparencies. Another example of a sequential multi-media interface is a well illustrated textbook which mixes explanatory text, diagrams, photographs, sidebars with self-assessment questions and a running series of illustrative 'real life' case studies and glossaries. More sophisticated examples of sequential multi-media interfaces involve the use of timed learning strategies which contain a variety of learning activities which compliment one another in achieving a set of educational or training objectives. Here, the interface is one which definitely requires the orthogonal influence of the instructional designer, who works to some plan or scheme derived from learning or instructional theory. One of the most powerful of these is the concept of mastery learning (Bloom, 1968; Block, 1971) where learners interact with a variety of defined segments of instruction of varying types at their own pace and in their own way, while under overall control from a tutor (Whiting, 1984; 1985). Figure 2.1 shows, in diagrammatic form, the sequential multi-media perspective that is discussed in this paper.

The time related nature of a multi-media mastery learning stategy is shown in Figure 2.2. This strategy is taken from a course segment that is used to teach a difficult topic in diagnostic microbiology (Whiting, 1985; 1986).

Recent advances in computer technology now offer the possibility of much more diverse and interesting forms of multi-media interface through the use of advanced display facilities, the application of artificial intelligence techniques and the increasing use of telecommunications support for open and distance learners. Exploitation of these technologies is beginning to demonstrate that computer based multi-media perspectives may offer significant advantages over more traditional forms of instruction.

Thus, the concept of the multi-media interface can be seen as a system which has already shown its capabilities, but which will evolve into something much more capable of independent learner support in an environment virtually divorced from traditional educational and training systems. A review of the possibilities inherent in this evolutionary process will be found in Whiting (1988a). For the purposes of this chapter, the main argument is centred around the effectiveness of sequential multi-media methods in which a major element is computer-based.

2.3 Effectiveness of computer based tuition

The majority of the work to which this chapter refers has been reported elsewhere (Whiting, 1984; 1985; 1986). Other evidence for the effectiveness of computer based learning strategies is sparse and scattered in the literature. The work of Johnston (1985a; 1985b; 1985c) in the use of microcomputers in English language teaching, that of Crook and Steele (1987) with infant school pupils and realization of their curriculum through computer generated environments and the results reported by Kenny and Schmulian (1979) are examples of studies which clearly demonstrate the effectiveness of computer-based tuition. Further examples will be found in several of the other chapters of this book.

The multi-media strategy shown in Figure 2.2 (Whiting, 1985; 1986) was devised as part of an investigation into the effectiveness of mastery learning. It employed a mixture of conventional methods (a lecture and some laboratory based practical work) and a computer tutorial. It also incorporated some paper-based analytical exercises using actual experimental data and a series of short questions which were designed to elicit the students' cognitive abilities in terms of Bloom's taxonomy of cognitive objectives (Bloom, 1956). The marking of these questions in terms of the

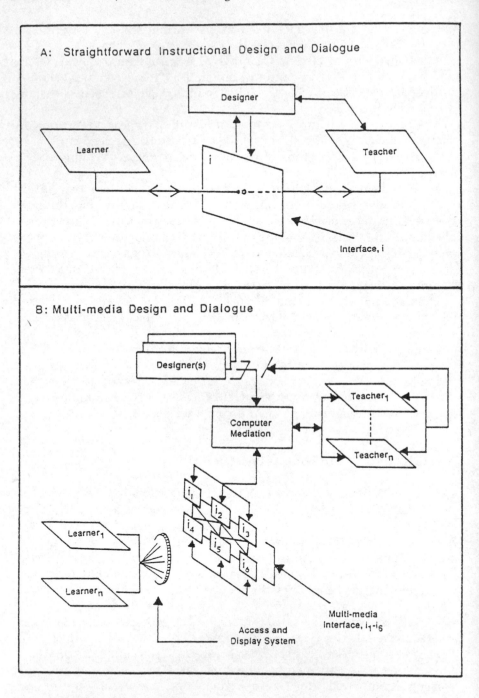

Figure 2.1 *Comparison of traditional and multi-media approaches to instructional design and dialogue*

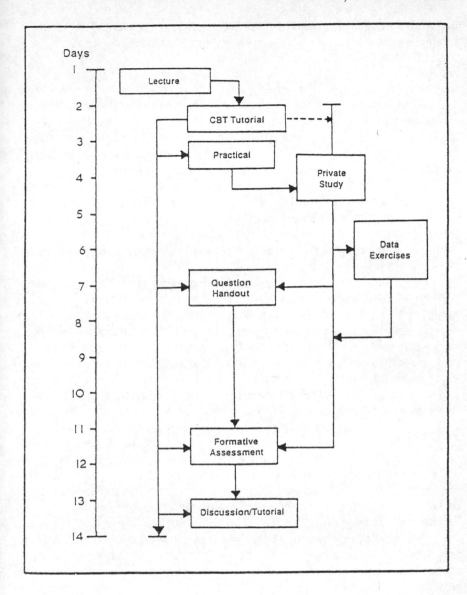

Figure 2.2 *Time schedule and arrangement of mastery learning experience*

taxonomy was allied to rapid formative assessment (essential in mastery strategies) and the seeking of the students' opinions about the effectiveness of the strategy. A similar group of students had been identically taught the previous academic year using the same strategy but with the omission of the computer tutorial. The writing of the computer tutorial was in fact stimulated by the difficulties that were enountered in the human tutoring – mostly in terms of the large amount of time needed by the tutor to guide students through the complexities of the topic. The tutorial was implemented on the University's VAX computer network and was made freely available to the students at any time throughout the three week period. Both groups of students were also exposed to a separate though related learning experience (identical for both groups) which employed a computer simulation of a difficult to control laboratory experiment. The results of this learning strategy were used as a control in order to eliminate any differences between the two student groups, examined through covariance techniques.

The results of the investigations were encouraging in terms of assessed performance. All learning experiences resulted in achievement of mastery levels by a large majority (over 80 per cent) of students. When the differences between human and computer tutorials were examined (after removal of variance due to differences between the characteristics of the two students groups on the basis of the identical control learning experience) some interesting results emerged. The computer taught group demonstrated higher scores for retention of knowledge, its application and its evaluation (Bloom, 1956). While there were no significant differences between the two groups in terms of the three other cognitive categories (comprehension, analysis and synthesis) the mean scores of the computer taught group were higher than those of the human taught group.

Results of the attitudinal assessment (Whiting, 1986) were also interesting. There was a significantly higher preference for the computer tutorial, as long as it was supported by a detailed printed handout (which it was). Females experienced more difficulty in responding to the question posed by the tutorial program than males though they showed a higher opinion of the computer tutorial. There were no significant differences in performance between females and males, which supplies evidence for a greater confidence in the use of computers by males than females, perhaps because use of computers is seen as a 'male' activity by most people. All the users of the program felt less need for human assistance than the human taught group. A further interesting finding was that the use of the tutorial program stimulated the informal assembly of small groups of students (typically two or three) who used a terminal together. Interviews conducted informally with such groups demonstrated that they generally contained one 'holist' and at least one 'serialist' (Pask, 1976). The holist grasped the concepts of the topic quite easily and was able to explain them to the serialists. However, the holists also acquired more detailed information about the topic (which they would otherwise have ignored) as a consequence of their interaction with the serialists. Such spontaneous formation of small peer groups extended to discussion of the questions in the formative assessment questions.

The work reported by Johnston (1985a, 1985b, 1985c) shows many of the same types of result in terms of opinion and gaining of knowledge, though the perceptions of the teachers were more sanguine. Here, the difference was said to relate to the greater acceptance of computer mediated means of tuition by the children and the relative lack of experience in such modes by the teachers. Both the WILT and TRAY programs used in this work were largely aimed at problem solving paradigms. In consequence, the multi-media element came into play in terms of the variety of learning strategies adopted by the pupils, unlike the virtual enforcement and control of cognitive expression in the mastery strategy reported above. The two programs were perceived as open ended problem solving tools rather than explicit parts of the teaching curriculum.

Crook and Steele (1987) chose a different approach toward multi-media computer based learning. The pupils were much younger and the multi-media component resided entirely within a series of choices within a simple 'cat and mouse' chase and catch game related to difficulty, type of activity and speed in pupil response to achieve the game objective (avoidance of 'cat' by 'mouse'). The *laissez faire* choice of difficulty and activity levels on an autonomous basis by the children did not unequivocally demonstrate that choices were made in order to achieve greater mastery of the game. Either the children lacked the mastery-motivation needed to achieve higher levels of ability and performance, or that they showed cognitive limitations in their failure to identify strategies which would encourage mastery or simply ignored (or did not appreciate) the implicit feedback mechanisms the game provided. However, since the game was used autonomously by the children with free choice of approach, the limitations of program design, and more importantly the lack of deliberate guidance toward mastery by the teacher mitigated against the pursuit of mastery strategies. The implication here is to the effect that the program design should be one which more explicitly encourages mastery by its users. This was entirely explicit in the mastery learning strategy adopted for the adult students (Whiting, 1985, 1986) because the computer tutorial contained several assistance routines and its style (deliberatley made similar to that of the tutor) encouraged mastery.

The earlier study of Kenny and Schmulian (1979) restricted itself to direct comparison between a drill and practice CAL program and human teaching. It demonstrated a significant improvement in performance in CAL-taught students, though the groups were small. However, this result is largely in accordance with those of the mastery study.

The conclusions from such work are clear enough. First, that sequential multi-media learning strategies can be very successful in optimizing learning if they are carefully designed. Second, that computer mediated instruction can already be employed to good effect in such strategies by means of fairly straightforward techniques (programming in authoring languages for example). Third, that careful design of such learning experiences can promote the autonomy of learners and simultaneously free the teacher to act in ways which encourage the development of students' cognitive abilities, rather than rote learning and remembrance of facts. In other words, teaching them to think and reason. Finally, since much of the work is based upon private study and an increasing proportion of it is computer mediated, the way towards a distributed, multi-media teaching environment is more open than ever before. This last point is one which requires more discussion in the light of modern advances in computers, telecommunications and information technology.

2.4 Future progress for multi-media approaches

Sequential multi-media approaches restrict themselves to a mixture of conventional technologies, with the recent addition of computer based elements. The interface is limited to keyboard/screen interaction, though increasing use of pointing devices (mouse or light pen) is evident.

Parallel multi-media approaches are now beginning to take two directions. First, the provision of a variety of input and output devices attached to a single server. These include superimposition of video, video disc, CD-ROM, HyperCard, computer generated imagery, pictorial interfaces and window environments and the peripheral I/O devices which are used to interact with them. Second, the application of a variety of instructional approaches embedded in a single interactive computer program. Here, explicit programming in either high level computer languages such as C, Pascal and object oriented languages such as Smalltalk is complimented by or replaced by artificial intelligence (AI) languages such as LISP or Prolog. The use of such methodologies is so far mostly restricted to commercial or business applications packages but their percolation into the fields of education and training is beginning (Whiting, 1988b).

From the educational point of view, such developments are inevitable. However, they are not easy to implement. No authoring systems (more properly termed 'courseware engineering systems') have been constructed as yet and the skills and knowledge to do so are so far unknown. Nevertheless, the aim of transferring more of the instructional and educational process to machine-mediated methods is essential because of the increasing need for education and training (Whiting and Bell, 1987). If a teacher can support more learners than before through the use of computer mediated multi-media tuition (sequential or parallel) then education and training needs can be more properly met in an environment which requires them more and more each year. Here, the role of advanced telecommunications, video conferencing and the formation of dense electronic networks between communities of learners and tutors, supported by AI-driven tutoring and monitoring facilities is paramount. This aspect of multi-media teaching is not often stressed, but the realization that advanced telecommunications have an important role to play in the development of truly distributed open learning environments can only promote the multi-media facilities to support them. In such a universe, the opportunities available to everyone to engage in training and education can only increase. As long as such technological advances are accompanied by both the political and motivational will to implement them in an increasingly fragmented society, the future development of multi-media forms of education and training will be assured.

2.5 Acknowledgements

The author would like to thank Philip Barker both for producing the diagrams that were used in this chapter and for his seemingly endless enthusiasm and encouragement.

2.6 References

Bloom, B.S. *et al*, (1956). *Taxonomy of Education Objective I: Cognitive Domain*, David MacKay, New York.

Bloom, B.S., (1968). Learning for mastery, *Evaluation Comment*, 1, 1-13.

Block, J.H., (1971). *Mastery Learning: Theory and Practice*, Holt, Rinehart and Winston, New York.

Crook, C. and Steele, J., (1987). Self-selection of simple computer activities by infant school pupils, *Educational Psychology*, 7, 23-32.

Johnston, V.M., (1985a) Introducing the microcomputer into English I: Aspects of classroom organization and their consequences for the curriculum, *British Journal of Educational Technology*, 16(3), 118-198.

Johnston, V.M., (1985b). Introducing the microcomputer into English II: an evaluation of WILT as a program using a problem-solving approach to learning spelling, *British Journal of Educational Technology*, 16(3), 199-208.

Johnston, V.M., (1985c). Introducing the microcomputer into English III: An evaluation of TRAY as a program using problem-solving as a strategy for developing reading skills, *British Journal of Educational Technology*, 16(3), 208-218.

Kenny, G.N.C. and Schmulian, C., (1979). Computer-assisted learning in the teaching of anaesthesia, *Anaesthesia*, 34, 159-162.

Pask, G., (1976). Styles and strategies of learning, *British Journal of Educational Psychology*, 46, 128-148.

Whiting, J., (1984). Cognitive and student assessments of a CAL package designed for mastery learning, *Computers and Education*, 8(1), 56-67.

Whiting, J., (1985). The use of a computer tutorial as a replacement for human tuition in a mastery learning strategy, *Computers and Education*, 9(2), 101-109.

Whiting, J., (1986). Student opinion of tutorial CAL, *Computers and Education*, 10(2), 281-282.

Whiting, J., (1988a). New perspectives on open and distance learning, in *World Yearbook of Education, 1988, Education for the New Technologies*, Harris,

N.D.C. (ed.), Kogan-Page, London.

Whiting, J., (1988b). Development of intelligent tutoring systems for open and distance learning, *Engineering Applications of Artificial Intelligence*, 1, 126-137.

Whiting, J. and Bell, D.A., (1987) (eds). *Tutoring and Monitoring Facilities for European Open Learning*, Elsevier-North Holland, Amsterdam.

Chapter 3
Designing Multi-Media Workstations

Philip Barker
Teesside Polytechnic

3.1 Introduction

Over the last decade there have been many new developments in all areas of science, engineering and technology. These developments have had a considerable impact on education and training. Two major consequences of this progress are immediately apparent. First, there is much new material and knowledge to be taught within existing curricula and within existing time scales. Second, many new methods and techniques have become available for teaching and for the dissemination of instructional material. The specific concern of this chapter is therefore to consider how newly emerging technologies can be used to create multi-media workstations that are capable of supporting many new types of learning environment.

New technologies can be used in a variety of interesting ways to generate learning and training opportunities. Currently there is much interest in the ways in which these technologies can be deployed in order to develop different kinds of interactive learning system (Barker, 1987a). An interactive learning system is one which provides rapid feedback (informatory, instructional, remedial or reinforcement) in response to the behavioural activity exhibited by the learner. Learning often involves developing within the student a degree of expertise with respect to some activity or subject domain. This transition from novice to expert is illustrated schematically in Figure 3.1.

The behaviour of an expert is often characterized by the set of concepts, rules, models and procedures that he/she uses in any given problem solving context. In an ideal world the transition from novice to expert can be envisaged in terms of a direct linear traversal between the novice and expert states of knowledge. However, in the real world, learning processes go wrong; for one reason or another students start to develop mal-rules, incorrect concepts, wrong models, bad habits and incorrect procedures. If the development of these unwanted side-effects could be detected early enough they could be corrected and removed through remediation, rehabilitation, practice and rehearsal. Learning can thus be brought back

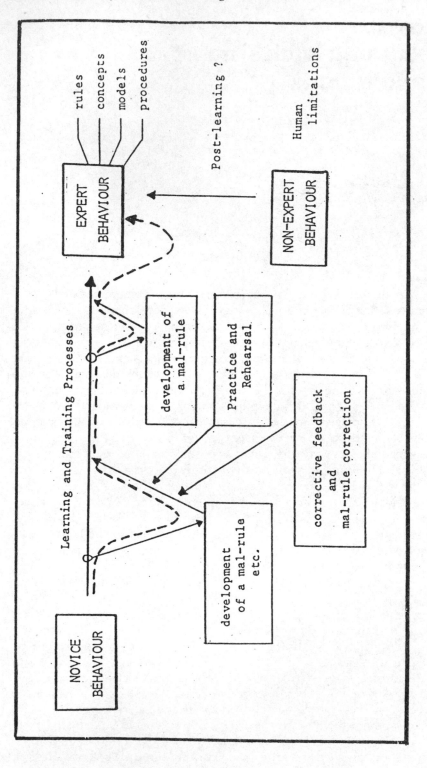

Figure 3.1 *Interactive learning processes*

on-stream. Highly interactive learning systems attempt to meet this objective. Of course, in everyday life it is important to realize that humans are subject to a multitude of innate physical and cognitive limitations. The extent of these limitations varies from one person to another. It is therefore not possible to expect that every person will develop expert behaviour within each and every domain of interest. However, in many pedagogic situations there is considerable evidence to suggest that interactive learning systems can be used to improve and extend human performance quite considerably. Because of their importance as a tool to support interactive learning, the remainder of this chapter is concerned with various aspects of the design of multi-media workstations.

The chapter commences by discussing the supporting hardware and software technologies available for the fabrication of workstations. Two basic design philosophies are outlined: the conventional approach and the multi-media approach. Within the latter particular emphasis is given both to the use of optical disc and to the nature of the peripherals that are needed in order to make interaction effective and meaningful within the context of particular learning/training activities. The potential of multi-media workstations is then illustrated through descriptions of some examples that deal with electronic books and advanced video-based learning environments. The chapter concludes with an outline description of some of the new learning paradigms and metaphors that multi-media workstations are able to support.

3.2 Supporting technologies

When designing workstations to facilitate interactive learning a number of supporting technologies have to be considered. Three important technologies are discussed in this section: computer assisted learning, human-computer interaction, and optical disc. These technologies can be combined and used in a variety of different ways in order to produce many kinds of interactive learning environment. Prior to discussing particular design scenarios involving their use, some introductory background material needs to be presented.

3.2.1 Computer assisted learning

The use of a computer for the realization of a teaching or learning process is often represented diagrammatically in a similar way to that shown in Figure 3.2. Generally, the term computer assisted learning (CAL) is used to describe such activity. CAL may be informally defined as being any application of a computer in which a learning of training process is implemented or initiated (Barker and Yeates, 1985). Within the framework presented by this definition it is possible to identify two basic types of computer-based instructional activity: implicit CAL and explicit CAL.

Implicit CAL is usually the easiest and most cost effective to implement. Some simple examples of situations where this mode of CAL is used include:

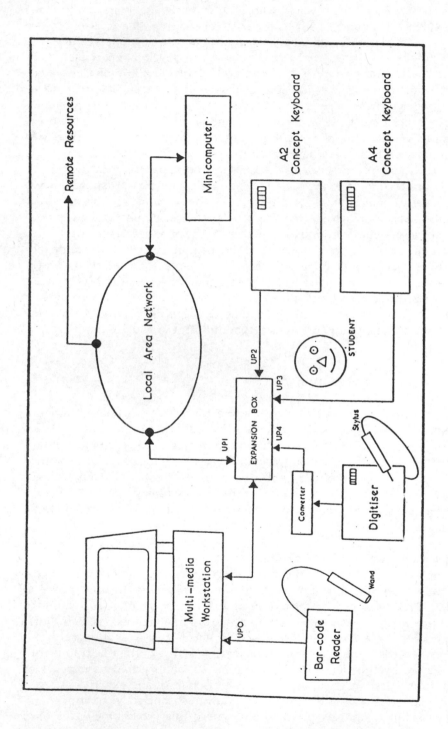

Figure 3.2 *Workstation environment for multi-media CAL*

(a) learning to program a computer in BASIC, Prolog or Pascal;
(b) gaining familiarity and competence in the use of word processing equipment;
(c) making use of a sophisticated graphics package for the design of a manufacturable product; and
(d) consultation with an expert system in order to solve problems within some application domain.

Implicit CAL thus usually involves using 'off the shelf' software products. Because instruction is not their primary intent such software items do not necessarily embed any user monitoring or pedagogic design factors.

More often than not explicit CAL is more difficult to implement than implicit CAL and so is usually more expensive. This mode of CAL actually involves producing instructional software (or courseware) that implements some learning or training process. This software will be designed to meet certain pedagogic objectives and will, optionally, contain facilities to monitor the progress being made by the learner. The information that is collected during the monitoring process may be used to construct a student model and/or guide the subsequent direction that the learning process should take. Currently the most popular applications of explicit CAL fall into three broad categories. These are: informatory CAL, exploratory CAL and instructional CAL.

Informatory CAL is used simply to present information to students, perhaps just to satisfy their curiosity, to facilitate some reseach orientated task, or to aid a decision making process. Our electronic books which are based upon the use of video disc technology are examples of this approach to the realization of CAL (Barker and Manji, 1988b); these are desribed in more detail later. Exploratory CAL involves the provision of both a computer-based learning environment and a set of tools that will enable this environment to be explored by the student; essentially, the methodology involved in this realization of CAL is based upon the 'microworld' approach advocated by Papert (1980) and the 'alternate reality kits' being developed at Xerox PARC (Smith, 1986). The third approach, instructional CAL, uses the computer as a delivery vehicle for previously planned, prepared, and tested courseware material; although reminiscent of programmed instruction, it is far more sophisticated.

Instructional CAL is usually much more difficult to implement than any other form. Complexities arise from a number of different sources, of which, just three will be cited. First, the courseware must be adaptable – both with respect to the students pre-knowledge and his/her preferred modes of learning. Second, in order to be adaptable the courseware must attempt to assess how well the student is (a) acquiring the skills, and (b) assimilating the knowledge that constitutes the domain of instruction. Third, the courseware should be able to function in a generative fashion; that is, it should be capable of producing instructional mechanisms and materials that have not been pre-programmed into it. Each of these problems can be overcome but cause significant increases in the cost of courseware due to the advanced types of software engineering methodologies that are involved.

As a consequence of the rapid progress and major new developments that are taking place in artifical intelligence and human-computer interaction techniques, a number of other important areas of CAL have been emerging over the last few years. Before concluding this section some brief mention should therefore be made of these new developments. The most important of these newly emerging areas are multi-media CAL, ICAL (intelligent CAL), and KBCAL (knowledge-based CAL). As far as this chapter is concerned the most important of these is multi-media CAL. Our rationale for using this approach to instruction is briefly described below.

Conventional approaches to CAL have most often been based upon the use of a CRT screen and a keyboard as the sole interaction peripherals for pedagogic information exchange (see Figure 1.2). In multi-media CAL the view is taken that a wide variety of peripherals should be used. That is, a workstation environment should be developed in which there is a combination of peripherals that are chosen in a way that gives optimum support for the learning/training tasks that are being implemented. Such an arrangement is depicted schematically in Figure 1.3. Two fundamental premises of multi-media CAL are (1) that both on-computer and off-computer learning activities are important and should be appropriately integrated, and (2) instructional delivery should involve the optimum use of sound, text, graphics, animatronics and participative training rigs.

The types of device that might be used within the interaction environments associated with multi-media workstations can vary quite considerably from one situation to another. Broadly, they fall into three categories. First, those needed to allow learners to interact with the computer itself. Second, those needed to support the delivery of instructional material. Third, those that are needed in order to enhance learning by making it more participative. Some of these categories are discussed in more detail in the following sections.

3.2.2 Human-computer interfaces

Human-computer interfaces are important because it is through these that instructional dialogues are fabricated. From the user's point of view these usually involve pecking, touching or pointing operations (for information selection) made during the course of viewing/listening activities.

The most common input interface currently used to facilitate user monitoring is some form of keyboard or keypad. Conventional keyboards have significant ergonomic and usability limitations for many potential applications. Consequently, in some of the case studies outlined below a special purpose 'concept keyboard' is used. This employs special paper-based overlay documents that are easy to design and produce. They can be made easily and economically by teachers and instructors themselves without the need for any substantial programming effort on their part. These devices are robust, easy to use and inexpensive. Another type of input device that is quite commonly used is the 'touch sensitive' screen. Although very robust, these are often less easy to use, more expensive and much more difficult to program. Both the touch sensitive screen and the concept keyboard cater for relatively low resolution touching operations. If greater accuracy is needed then a higher resolution pointing device can be employed – such as a light pen, a digitizer/stylus, a trackerball or a mouse.

In one of the multi-media workstations described in section 3.3 several concept keyboards and a digitizer are used in order to facilitate facile human-computer interaction. The type of workstation environment needed to support such a collecton of peripherals is illustrated schematically in Figure 3.2. This depicts how two concept keyboards, a digitizer and a bar code reader are interfaced to a base microcomputer via an appropriate expansion box (Barker and Manji, 1987a; 1988a). This expansion box also facilitates the connection of the workstation to a remote computing facility via a local area network.

The output of information from the instructional system to the user is most commonly achieved by a single high resolution screen that is capable of supporting both text and graphics. Where greater display bandwidth is required several screens might be used together – either to perform different display functions or to extend the user's physical/logical field of view. Often, the more complex display screens (capable of supporting sophisticated animation and special graphic effects) may be best regarded as being composed from a number of logical screens that each perform a different logical function (Barker and Singh, 1985). The overall display effect can then be deduced by compounding the contributions made by the different logical screens. Where it is necessary (and this is becoming increasingly important in multi-media systems) screen presentations can be augmented by appropriate audio support that is generated by a high quality sound reproduction system (Barker, 1986).

An extremely useful output device, and one which is growing extremely popular for use in workstation fabrication, is the 'bit-mapped' screen. Such screens usually offer a very high resolution output display. Each picture element (or pixel) from which the display is composed is individually addressable; the attributes associated with each pixel (colour, intensity, reactivity, and so on) can also be individually modified. When used in conjunction with appropriate software (for example, a windowing package) and hardware (such as a video frame store) bit-mapped screens can be employed in order to produce many different types of special display effect. They can also be used to facilitate the creation of many novel and exciting ways of interacting with a computer system. This latter facility is illustrated schematically in Figure 3.3 which shows how a bit-mapped screen can be used to display various items of text and pictures. The pictures may be static or animated; they may also be reactive. Because it is not possible to see sound, its availability is denoted by means of a collection of appropriately designed sound icons. Touching any of these reactive icons causes an associated sonic response to be produced. This might be the generation of an English, French or German narrative; alternatively, it might be some special sound effect such as a piece of music or the noise of an aeroplane engine. The arrows shown in Figure 3.3 denote either hypertext or hyper-image references (Conklin, 1987). By touching an appropriate word (within

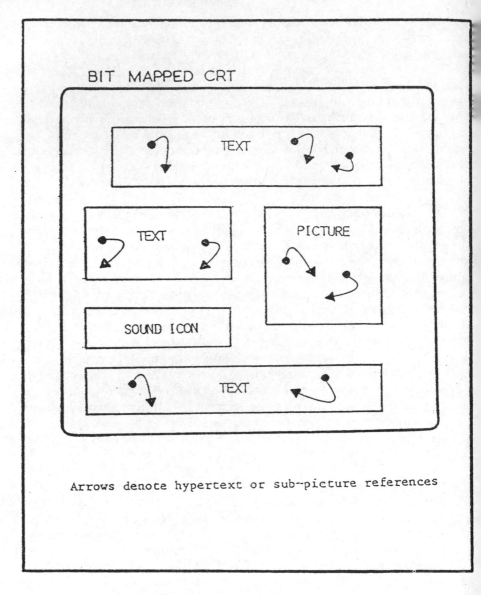

Figure 3.3 *Using reactive media*

a text segment) or picture component (within an image segment) the user is able to branch to related items of text (or pictures) that form part of a complex hypertext or hyper-image network. Of course, the creation of knowledge networks to support this type of interaction depends critically upon the availability of suitable media for the storage of large volumes of text, pictures and sound. In this context, optical media have an important role to play.

3.2.3 Optical media

Because of the capacity that they offer for storing pictures, sound and text, optical media offer a powerful resource for the fabrication of the type of multi-media CAL facilities that have been described in the previous sections of this chapter. Instructional designers often employ both disc and tape as a source of multi-media teaching materials. However, because of its manipulative inflexibility (and lack of robustness) tape is not used in any of the design studies described in the following section. Little more will therefore be said about this medium. Consequently, our attention will therefore be devoted to disc-based storage facilities – video disc and compact disc read only memory (CDROM).

Although many new developments are taking place continually, two basic optical storage technologies are currently being employed by instructional designers. The first of these is based primarily upon the analogue recording of video information while the other uses digital recording techniques. For pictorial information video disc currently offers the greater storage capacity. CDROM is used mainly for the digital storage of text and sound. A newly emerging standard, CD-I (Compact Disc – Interactive), also allows the storage of certain types of graphical information. Competing with CD-I is another recently announced standard called DVI (Digital Video Interactive). This is claimed to offer far more facilities for multi-media storage than are available with the CD-I standard. Of course, some conventional video disc systems can be used for the storage of both analogue pictures and digital data. For example, the video discs used by the United Kingdom's Domesday Project (Tapper, 1986a; 1986b) store over 24,000 maps (in analogue form) and a subset of the 1981 census data (in digital format). Unfortunately, a current problem with the hybrid storage approach is the development of an appropriate standard that will allow instructional resources to be used on different hardware configurations.

The interactive learning environments described in the following section rely heavily upon the use of optical video disc for their implementation. The motivation for using optical storage media and the multi-media instructional methodologies that they support stems from a number of important factors. Some of these are briefly outlined below.

Bandwidth considerations
One of the major advantages of using multi-media techniques for education is the extremely high communication bandwidths that can be achieved. These are attained by using multi-media communication strategies in which pictures, text and sound are optimally intermixed in order to achieve a maximally effective communication facility (Barker, 1987b; 1987c; 1987d). From the learner's point of view, in terms of knowledge uptake per unit time invested in study the multi-media learning method offers a very high return on investment.

Distance factors
There are many ways in which instructional materials can be transmitted

(over a distance) from those who produce them to those who wish to use them. Because of their very high communication bandwidth and robustness (see below) optical media offer an extremely useful method of disseminating instructional resources – provided appropriate workstations can be produced and suitable learning techniques developed. These topics are discussed in more detail in section 3.3.

Time factors

The effectiveness of any form of learning activity is significantly influenced by (1) the total time available, and (2) the way in which this time is allocated to the various learning units within a course. Because of its high audio-visual content, learning material based on the use of optical media can make best use of the total time available for course implementation; indeed, in some situations, it is often possible to reduce conventional instruction times quite significantly through the use of new media. Also, because of the ease of access to materials it is possible to organize highly flexible time slots for individual units within an overall course of instruction.

Cost effectiveness

Preparing learning resources using optical media can be an expensive process. Obviously, the overall cost will depend upon the type of material that is needed and the potential market for the final product. Provided there is a significantly large audience for the material that is produced then the use of optical media can be very cost effective. This has indeed been found to be the case with a number of large commercial organizations. Smaller organizations can also make their use of optical media cost effective provided they are able to use existing bespoke material (tailored to their particular needs) or can find what they are looking for within the rapidly expanding repertoire of generic resources.

Interactivity

Optical media allow the fabrication of visual learning systems that can be highly interactive. That is, the learner has a high degree of control over the material that is shown and the way in which it is presented. Although extremely high interactivity is possible (for individualized learning situations), optical media do not necessarily have to be used in this way. Indeed, many other useful approaches to instruction can be developed based upon relatively low learner participation (as is the case, for example, in passive CAL).

Versatility

Another attractive feature of optical media is their ability to allow the creation of very versatile learning systems that can be used for a wide variety of applications. These range from language development through science teaching to training in inter-personal skills and other management techniques. They also allow the use of many novel instructional methods that would not be easy to implement using other media. The technique of surrogation is one illustration of this (Barker and Manji, 1988b). It is used, for example, in the 'Interactive Science Laboratory' (Wiley, 1987) to enable students to conduct surrogate experiments that would be difficult or dangerous to conduct in a real laboratory. This technique can, of course, be applied in a host of other interesting ways – such as surrogate travel, conversation, exploration, gaming, and so on.

Realism

One of the most important objectives of any instructional facility is to provide the learner with experiences that are as close to real life situations as is possible. This is often achieved through the use of various types of simulation. The closer a simulation becomes to reality the more meaningful the educational encounter is likely to be. Optical media can provide high degrees of pictorial realism in a variety of simulation contexts. This realism derives not only from the effective use of pictorial form but also from appropriately designed and presented sound effects and, of course, through the use of value added imagery (a combination of computer graphics and video pictures).

Robustness

Many open learning situations necessitate the availability (to the learner population) of learning resources for substantial periods of time under demanding conditions that are not normally met within conventional classroom environments. Therefore, for many applications in which a high degree of utilization is anticipated, disc-based optical media offer a far more robust facility than does the use of tape-based storage. Of course, the major weakness of tape for the storage of sound and pictorial sequences) is its ability to stretch and even snap when subjected to excessive wind/rewind operations at high speed for considerable periods of time. Of course, none of these disadvantages are apparent with disc-based storage.

Usability

The question of the usability of storage media has to be addressed from a number of different angles. Three of the most important aspects that need to be discussed are (1) the ease with which educators can record on them, (2) the presentational features that each candidate medium is able to offer, and (3) the facilities available for updating and modifying recorded material. Of course, at present, disc-based optical storage media score highly only with respect to item (2). In contrast, within the context set by items (1) and (3) they are much less usable than are, for example, tape-based media. However, the ease with which (a) individual images (or sound segments) can be accessed, and (b) image sequences can be software edited and manipulated (for example, played in forward or reverse direction at various speeds) certainly makes optical disc storage a highly usable medium.

Cautionary remarks

The factors listed above provide considerable justification for the use of optical media within interactive learning environments. Of course, no claim is made with respect to the comprehensiveness of this list or of the degree of relevance of individual factors within particular application areas. Each potential application must therefore be considered on its own merit taking into account the items discussed in this section – where they are appropriate.

3.3 Interactive learning environments

The technogloies described in the previous section can be put together in a variety of different ways in order to produce new types of learning resource suitable for creating adult learning opportunities. Some of the ways in which this can be done are described in this section by means of a number of simple design scenarios. Each scenario involves the utilization of some aspect of either explicit or implicit computer assisted learning.

Within the types of instructional system that are described in this section the computer plays the role of system co-ordinator. It monitors the activity of the user and maps this behaviour on to an appropriate system response sequence. This will involve:

(1) analysing the responses made via the input devices (see section 3.2.2);
(2) selecting or generating an action plan containing details of what has to be done;
(3) activating the optical devices (CDROMs and video discs) in order to obtain the information and support material needed to carry out the action plan;
(4) initiating any ancillary computation that needs to be undertaken (for example, to support the technique of value added imagery), and
(5) presenting the final sequence of material to the user in conjunction with an appropriate control strategy.

Of course, the computer will also be the source of any 'intelligence' that the system shows – particularly, with respect to the use of adaptable interfaces, user models or sophisticated knowledge-based structures (Barker and Proud, 1987).

In the remainder of this section three design scenarios are presented. The first one outlines the use of optical media for the creation of interactive learning aids for use in exhibition centres and museums; essentially this illustrates the 'informatory' approach to CAL. The second scenario describes some approaches to the creation of electronic books; this embodies some of the many different techniques involved in the realization of 'exploratory' CAL. Finally, the third design study describes the use of optical storage technology within multi-media workstation environments that are designed to support 'instructional' CAL through the use of distance learning resources based on CDROM and video disc.

3.3.1 Exhibition centres
Exhibition centres, museums, art galleries (and other forms of multi-media extravaganza) offer important facilities in the context of creating adult

learning opportunities. Quite recently we have been involved in the design and development of a variety of educational 'public awareness' exhibits aimed at adult audiences. These exhibits have been designed to fit within the framework of exhibition centres similar to that illustrated schematically in Figure 3.4. In this figure the arrows represent the intended direction of flow of people through the various instructional routes contained within the exhibition centre. Within the exhibition system shown in Figure 3.4 three basic types of instructional facility are employed: theatre presentations, exhibits (such as posters, pictures, computer controlled displays and working models), and electronic books (see below). A variety of computer controlled multi-media aids are used within the theatres to produce many different types of special effect. The types of aid that are used include film, video and multiple slide projection techniques (Barker and Manji, 1987a; 1988a).

Many of the exhibits that we have constructed have involved the development of multi-media presentation facilities in which video discs and CDROMs have been used to store pictorial material, digital graphic overlays and high quality sound effects including conventional music, synthetic music and audio narrations. Both single user systems (based on booths and carrells) and facilities for multi-person audiences (based on multi-media theatres and showrooms) have been produced. Single user systems often allow greater degrees of interaction flexibility in that they can be made user-driven. This is more difficult in the case of group presentations wherein the locus of control usually resides with the computer rather than with the users. In the case of single user systems learner control is often accomplished by means of interactive touch screens. Naturally, this type of system embodies many of the principles (and benefits from the advantages) of active CAL. In contrast, however, because of the group dynamics and interactions involved, theatre presentations more resemble passive CAL since little audience participation is involved; that is, the audience has little control over the events to which it is subjected.

3.3.2 Electronic books

A number of different approaches have been used by various researchers for the production of electronic books. Some of these are discussed in greater depth elsewhere (Barker and Manji, 1988b). In this section the approach that we have been using is briefly described.

Our approach to electronic book fabrication is based upon the technique of surrogation. The use of 'surrogate books' based upon the utilization of new techniques for storing, accessing, retrieving and presenting information is a rapidly developing field of technology. The construction of our electronic books depends upon the inter-connection of a video disc player (for information storage), a TV monitor (for information display) and a concept keyboard (for dialogue fabrication). The arrangement of these components is illustrated in Figure 3.5.

In our system all user interaction takes place via touch operations made

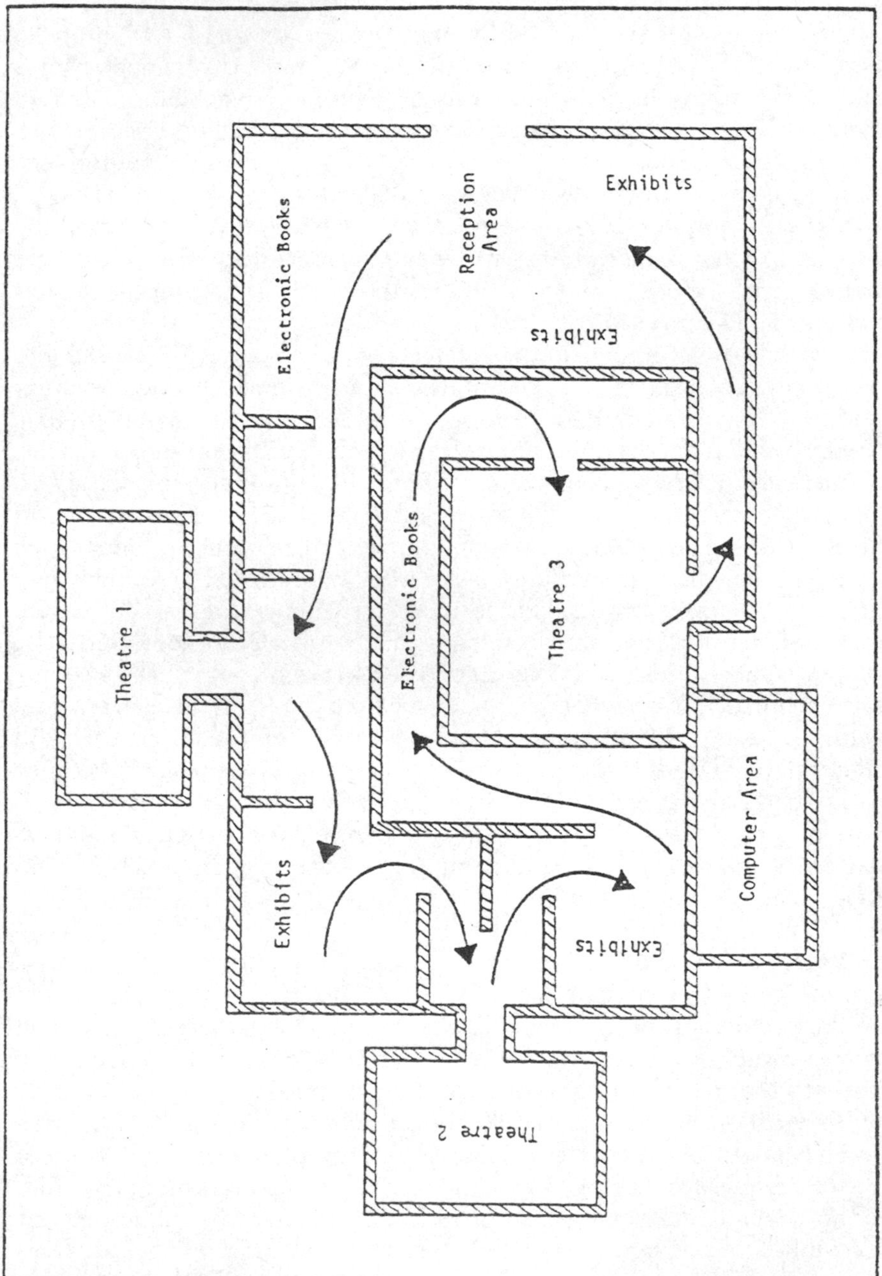

Figure 3.4 *Multi-media exhibition centres*

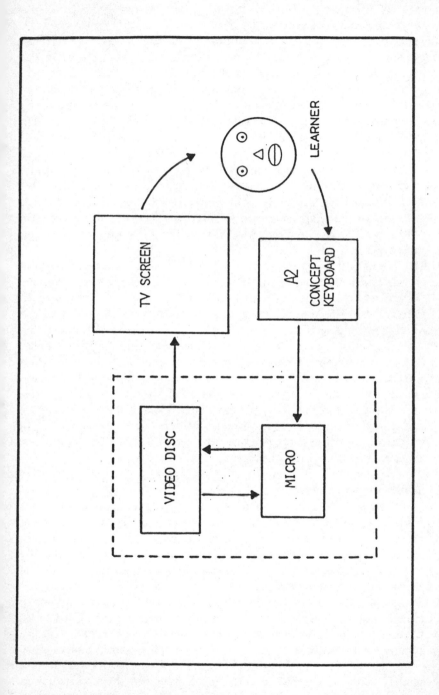

Figure 3.5 *Structure of an electronic book*

on the surface of the concept keyboard. In order to achieve this a thin cardboard overlay is required. An example of such an overlay is illustrated schematically in Figure 3.6. This pictorial overlay fits snugly on top of the surface of the concept keyboard. Its basic function is to provide the user with a choice of topics and control options. These topics correspond to the different segments of information stored on the video disc that forms the contents of the surrogate book. Selecting a topic (by touching an appropriate box on the paper-based overlay) corresponds to the selection of a particular chapter of a conventional book. Once a topic selection has been made, its associated sequence of video frames is presented on the TV monitor along with its title. At any instant in time, while this sequence of video frames is being viewed, the user can interact with the system to freeze a picture, go backwards or forwards one video frame at a time, restart (and hence, continue) from the present position within the chapter, repeat the whole chapter from the beginning, or exit the chapter. Each of these actions can be achieved quite simply by selecting the appropriate control functions from the overlay document lying on the surface of the concept keyboard.

The functions that the human-computer interface system presents to the user correspond to those one might perform while reading an ordinary book. These are (1) looking at the previous or next page, (2) continuing to read from the present page, (3) restarting again from the beginning of the current chapter, (4) selecting another chapter, and (5) closing the book. The choice of topics (or video chapters) that are contained in our present electronic book are mainly technology based – ranging from the application of laser technology for digital data transmission (using fibre optics) through to the design of sophisticated computer-based air-traffic control systems. Of course, there is no reason why the electronic book principle could not be extended to other subject areas. Indeed, we are currently involved in producing books devoted to the teaching of inter-personal skills, languages, cookery and various engineering topics.

3.3.3 Multi-media workstations

As has been suggested earlier in section 3.2.1, a multi-media workstation is one in which a wide variety of interaction devices is available for use in conjunction with the base microcomputer that is used for system fabrication. The exact subset of devices that is used will depend critically upon the nature of the educational objectives that are to be fulfilled and the particular learning/training tasks that are to be undertaken. Two examples of multi-media workstations are described below. One involves the use of multiple concept keyboards and a digitizer to support learning activities undertaken in conjunction with an expert system (Barker, 1988a); this is a prototype workstation that we have been developing within a laboratory environment (Barker and Manji, 1987b). The other workstation is a commercial system developed in the United Kingdom by a consortium involving the British Broadcasting Corporation (BBC), Acorn Computers Ltd and Philips Electronics; it is called the AIV workstation (AIV is an

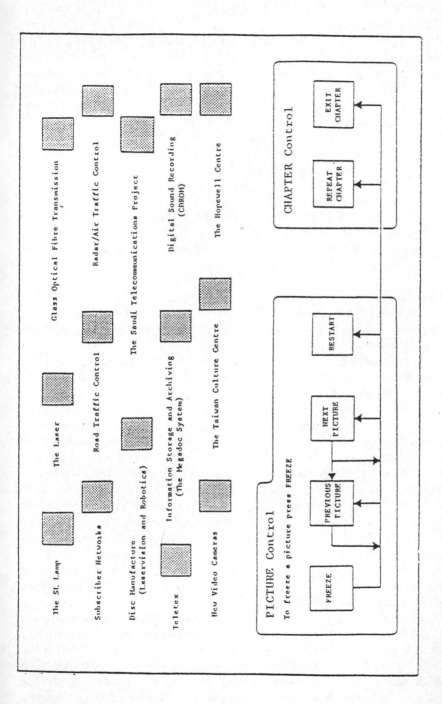

Figure 3.6 *Concept keyboard overlay document*

69

acronym for Advanced Interactive Video).

(A) Pictorial interfaces to expert systems
Within our multi-media workstation (shown schematically in Figure 3.7) three concept keyboards and a digitizer have been interfaced to the base microcomputer. In addition there is an audio unit (for sound effects) and a video disc player (for pictorial support). Users interact with the system by means of pointing operations made on the surface of the interaction devices. Upon these surfaces are mounted pictorial paper-based documents (also called device overlays) that contain collections of high quality coloured pictures arranged in the form of a matrix. The example shown in Figure 3.7 involves using an expert system to solve a bird recognition problem. The device overlays therefore contain pictures of birds, a map (for specifying locality information) and close-up pictures of claw and beak shapes. By means of a sequence of pointing operations made upon the overlays the user is able to specify the information available for problem solution. Where it is appropriate, bird calls, flight patterns and bird pictures can be retrieved from the audio unit and video disc, respectively.

(B) The Domesday System
One of the first commercially available advanced interactive video workstations developed on a large scale in the UK was that produced to support the BBC's Domesday Project (Tapper, 1986a; 1986b). The workstation is illustrated schematically in Figure 3.8. The system is based upon a BBC Master Series microcomputer and a Philips Laservision video disc player. Using a keyboard and/or a trackerball (or mouse), the user has access to a large number of maps, photographs, aerial views, textual descriptions, audio narrations, statistics, charts and moving video sequences. Because the AIV workstation has the ability to access such an extensive and varied database many spectacular visual effects can be achieved. For example, it is very easy for the user to retrieve a map of some particular urban area and then superimpose relevant data on top of it. It is also possible to compare and display data in various ways – typically, using either a bar chart or a pie chart format (depending upon the option chosen by the user). The workstation can also generate a very stable still-frame display and will permit the accurate overlaying and mixing of pictures with computer-generated data and graphics. Of course, all this is achieved by combining visual information with digital data. Earlier in this chapter this facility was referred to as 'value added imagery'.

The user interface to the Domesday system is based predominantly on the use of a trackerball which operates an on-screen pointer. This icon may be used to select from the horizontal menu bar (shown at the bottom of the CRT in Figure 3.8) or from a vertical menu; it can also be used to specify an area of interest on a map. The interaction with the system is therefore quite simple – the basic grammar being 'point and click'. Using the trackerball (and the keyboard for the entry of keywords or grid references), the Domesday workstaton allows instant access to all its maps, photo-

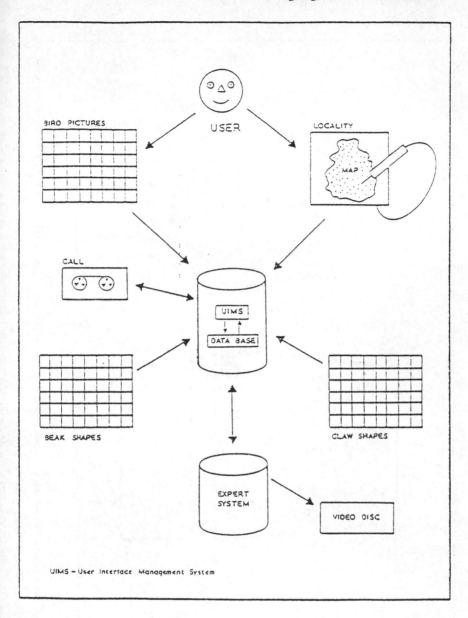

Figure 3.7 *Pictorial interfaces to expert systems*

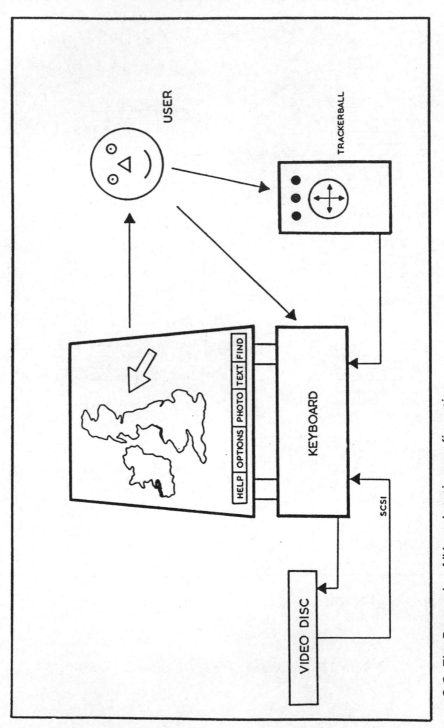

Figure 3.8 *The Domesday AIV workstation configuration*

graphs, aerial views, text, statistical charts and video sequences.

The Domesday system contains two optical laser discs. These are referred to as the National Disc and the Community Disc, respectively. The content of each of these discs is briefly discussed below.

The National Disc

The contents of the National Disc are organized by topic. There is a hierarchical structure of subject headings under which everything on the disc is stored. The disc contains information on the UK economy, culture, society, and its environment. There are about 9000 data sets on the disc; these can be accessed via keywords or by means of a CRT-based menu selection dialogue using the trackerball. In the latter case the information to be retrieved is located by selecting one of the four categories listed above and then specifying progressively more precise details (using the trackerball) to home in on the subject of interest. At each stage during the dialogue the system specifies exactly what is available as text, data or pictures on the subject that has been chosen. Alternatively, using keyboard entry, it is possible to use a keyword in order to directly access the data that is required. This 'discovery learning' aspect of the AIV system is illustrated by the Domesday Gallery (a visual index for the user) and by what are known as 'surrogate walks'. Some of the 20000 photographs on the National Disc are used to present a series of comtemporary environments: typical houses, a market town, a farm and a nature reserve.

The Community Disc

The Community Disc is based on Ordnance Survey maps; the information on the disc can all be accessed using these maps as pictorial menus. The user can move from map to map, either horizontally (going across the country on maps at the same scale) or vertically (by jumping to a map of another scale). At each level, text and photographs are available, including satellite views for the larger areas. The user can move through the system in four ways: (a) by entering a place-name, (b) by entering a grid-reference, (c) by specifying a keyword, and (d) by 'map-walking' using the trackerball.

The Community Disc contains about 150000 screen pages of text and 20000 photographs. The organization of the disc is based on a total of 24000 Ordnance Survey maps. As was mentioned above, these are arranged in six levels with text and photographs available at each level. Levels 0, 1 and 2 generally contain satellite and aerial photographs and text, whereas levels 3, 4 and 5 provide more detailed information ranging from community photographs, street maps to special feature photographs and floor plans of special sites.

The user can enter the system at any level. This can be accomplished by typing in a place name, a regional description, a grid reference, or by using the trackerball to move a pointer on the screen. At any level it is a simple process to move across the map, to access photographs (descriptions and/ or data) or to move to other levels either above or below the current one. Using the Community Disc it is also possible to perform interesting computational operations on the maps that are being displayed. For example, the user might choose to automatically compute the distance between two points on the map (either directly or by road) or calculate the area contained within a user defined boundary.

Potential applications for stimulating learning
The potential utility of the Domesday AIV system as a tool for the creation of learning opportunities is really quite enormous. It is our intent to study the utility of this system within a number of different learning contexts such as (1) its use as an open learning resource within libraries, musuems and other public places, and (2) its potential within the home environment (as an example of an electronic encyclopedia). Although at present the overall system would be too costly to consider for widespread use in the home, its potential within this context is clearly quite significant. Currently we are actively involved in evaluating the potential utility of the Domesday system as an adult learning resource within a polytechnic library environment (Hill, 1987). Although this work is not yet complete the results that have been obtained to date look quite encouraging.

3.4 New aproaches to learning

Over the last decade developments in electronics and computer science have produced a number of new and exciting technologies. In the context of educational design two of the most important of these are (1) low cost techniques for image storage, manipulation and presentation, and (2) new methods for facilitating human interaction with computers. The many technical developments that have been made in these two areas have made possible the creation of a variety of new types of instructional paradigm and the development of many novel types of learning metaphor. Together these developments can be used to create very rich learning environments for both young and adult learners. In this final part of this chapter two of the new learning paradigms will be briefly discussed: reactive media and surrogation. Two illustrative examples of new learning metaphors will also be outlined: 'scrapbooks' and 'shopping baskets'.

3.4.1 New paradigms
A learning paradigm is essentially a model or a generic concept that forms a basis for the development and production of new learning materials and resources. As was mentioned above, two very important paradigms in the context of designing multi-media workstations are the paradigms of reactive media and surrogation.

The reactive media paradigm is made possible primarily due to the new developments that have taken place in the technology of human-computer interaction. Such interaction may be accomplished through the use of a mouse, a trackerball, and (more importantly) digitizers, concept keyboards and touch sensitive screens. The latter types of device are important because they are able to give the user the impression that both paper-based and CRT-based text and graphics are able to react to demands made of them via pointing/touching operations. This type of effect has previously been illustrated in Figure 3.3 wherein touching text, pictures or sound icons on a bit-mapped screen could cause very interesting things to happen. Similar, but less versatile reactive encounters can also be created using concept keyboards and digitization devices.

The surrogation paradigm has already been briefly mentioned in earlier parts of this chapter. It is made possible through advances that have been made in the areas of image storage and image processing. Surrogation is the general term used to describe highly visual and interactive simulations. They are usually created using images (and image sequences) that are stored on a video disc or a CDROM; if need be these images can be processed and manipulated in various mays using appropriate image processing equipment – such as a special effects frame store. Surrogation has been quite widely used in order to generate highly participative interactive learning environments in a number of widely different situations. For example, it has been used to enable students to conduct experiments in a simulated laboratory (Wiley, 1987) and also to support surrogate walks and travel. This latter application of surrogation is discussed further in the following section.

3.4.2 New metaphors

A learning metaphor is essentially a teaching strategy that depends upon the creation of an analogy to a concept with which the learner is familiar. Two metaphors are briefly outlined here.

The first metaphor is called the scrapbook metaphor. Most people are familiar with the idea of collecting picture postcards and photographs and making notes about a journey or voyage that they have undertaken. Often such a collection of items is pasted into a scrapbook that can be shown to other people. We have been involved in developing electronic scrapbooks that emulate this type of activity using suitably designed multi-media workstations. The basis of this metaphor is the use of a video disc image store to enable the learner to undertake a surrogate journey. Through the use of icons, the learner is provided with a 'camera' and a 'notebook'. As the journey takes place, so the learner can take photographs of and make notes about the things that are seen. Later the 'film' in the camera can be developed and the photographs electronically mounted and pasted into a scrapbook; each photograph can be annotated with notes taken from the notebook. Fundamental to the operation of the metaphor is an underlying multi-media data base management system. For each learner, this holds details of the photographs that are taken and the notes that are made. Later, we hope to extend this metaphor to handle sound and animation – thereby providing emulations of an audio tape recorder and a portable video camera.

Our shopping basket metaphor is analogous to the scrapebook metaphor except that instead of taking photographs the learner participates in a surrogate journey in which objects are collected and placed in an electronic 'shopping basket'. This metaphor is being used in the development of a number of games such as a treasure hunt and a surrogate shopping expedition. The accurate implementation of this metaphor is more difficult than the previous one. Giving the learner the ability to select (and hence remove) objects from a screen image can require the solution of quite complex problems relating to picture composition and image semantics. Although we are some way from the complete solution of these problems, the use of the metaphor is not impaired provided its limitations are understood.

3.5 Conclusion

Education has to serve a multitude of technical, social and cultural learning/ training purposes. Many of these place significant demands on both educational technology and instructional design. This chapter has outlined a number of reasons why multi-media methods (particularly, those involving CAL) might be useful. The technologies needed to create various forms of interactive learning environment have been outlined and several design scenarios have been used to illustrate the approaches being advocated.

We believe that optical media can be used in conjunction with computer-based control systems to provide a variety of new types of multi-media learning environment. The design scenarios that have been described in this chapter merely scratch the surface of what is likely to be a plethora of new educational opportunities. The techniques that have been outlined can be used in a variety of ways to enable cultural development, rapid re-training in a variety of different skill areas, the stimulation of creativity, and for many more general educational purposes.

3.6 References

Barker, P.G., (1986). A practical introduction to authoring for computer assisted instruction. Part 6: Interactive Audio, *British Journal of Educational Technology*, 17(2), 110-128.

Barker, P.G., (1987a). Interactive learning systems for the 90s, paper presented at the symposium on Innovative Learning Systems and Technologies, Singapore Polytechnic, October 30th, 1987.

Barker, P.G., (1987b). *Author Languages for CAL*, Macmillan Press, London.

Barker, P.G., (1987c). A practical introduction to authoring for computer assisted instruction. Part 8: Multi-media CAL, *British Journal of Educational Technology*, 18(1), 25-40.

Barker, P.G., (1987d). Multi-media CAL, Chapter 13 in *Tutoring and Monitoring Facilities for European Open Learning*, edited by Whiting, J. and Bell, D.A., North-Holland/Elsevier.

Barker, P.G., (1988a). Expert systems in engineering education, *Engineering Applications of Artificial Intelligence*, 1, 47–58.

Barker, P.G. and Manji, K., (1987a). Device interfacing for multi-media CAL (Part 1), *Computer Education*, 57, 22-24.

Barker, P.G. and Manji, K.A., (1987b). Pictorial knowledge bases, 161-173 in *People and Computers III, Proceedings of the Third Conference of the British Computer Society's Human-Computer Interaction Specialist Group*, University of Exeter, 7th-11th September, 1987, edited by Diaper, D. and Winder, R., Cambridge University Press.

Barker, P.G. and Manji, K., (1988a). Device interfacing for multi-media CAL (Part 2), *Computer Education*, 58, 7-9.

Barker, P.G. and Manji, K., (1988b). New books for old, paper presented at ETIC '88 International Conference, Plymouth Polytechnic, April 1988.

Barker, P.G. and Proud, A., (1987). A practical introduction to authoring for computer assisted instruction. Part 10: Knowledge-based CAL, *British Journal of Educational Technology*, 18(2), 140-160.

Barker, P.G. and Singh, R., (1985). A practical introduction to authoring for computer assisted instruction. Part 5: PHILVAS, *British Journal of Educational Technology*, 16(3).

Barker, P.G. and Yeates, H., (1985). *Introducing Computer Assisted Learning*, Prentice-Hall, Hemel Hempstead.

Conklin, J., (1987). Hypertext: an introductory survey, *IEEE Computer*, 20, 9, 17–41.

Hill, M.A., (1987). Evaluation of the Domesday AIV system, MSc Dissertation, Department of Computer Science, Teesside Polytechnic, County Cleveland, UK.

Papert, S., (1980). *Mindstorms: Children, Computers and Powerful Ideas*, Harvester Press, Brighton.

Smith, R.B., (1986). The alternate reality kit: an animated environment for creating interactive simulations, 99–106 in *Proceedings of the 1986 IEEE Workshop on Visual Languages*, Dallas, Texas.

Tapper, R., (1986a). The Domesday Project – an educational review, *Journal of Educational Television*, 12, 197–210.

Tapper R., (1986b). The Domesday Project, *ASLIB Information*, 14, 160–161.

Wiley, (1987). *The Interactive Science Laboratory*, John Wiley & Sons, Baffins Lane, Chichester.

Chapter 4
CAL for Mathematics and Science Teaching

Yeow-Chin Yong
Ngee Ann Polytechnic

4.1 Introduction

Computer aided learning was first introduced over two decades ago. In 1960 the University of Illinois launched the PLATO (Programmed Logic for Automatic Teaching Operation) project with the goal of designing a large computer-based system for instruction. CAL was not widely accepted at that time because it was regarded as a potential threat to teachers. Furthermore, the use of mainframe computers for CAL courseware development was very costly.

In the late 1970s, microcomputers were introduced into academic institutions and attitudes towards CAL then suddenly changed. It became possible for universities, schools and even individuals to own a computer which could be used for educational purposes. Since then microcomputers have gradually become a standard part of most educational systems. They can be used as a productivity tool for teaching, learning, experimentation and administration. The cost of microcomputers has been continuously decreasing; at the same time their computing power has increased tremendously. Because of this CAL has slowly gained popularity as a means of augmenting traditional classroom teaching. The advantages of CAL over traditional methods of teaching are now widely recognized. Today, educators look upon CAL as a means of producing a new and improved form of education.

Unfortunately, the current status of computers in education does not reflect the many activities needed to fully implement and develop CAL systems. It is common to observe that many schools and institutions use microcomputers more as a tool to teach computer literacy and programming than as a device for computer aided instruction and/or computer managed instruction (Yong and Tan, 1988a). The main reason for this is probably due to the fact that most teachers still lack the confidence to explore the CAL approach. Alternative reasons might be a shortage of funds to provide facilities for full development and implementation, no strong institutional support for CAL, a resistance to new challenges, and no proper plans to incorporate CAL into course curricula.

In the past five years computers have significantly influenced the teaching and learning processes of mathematics and science. Undoubtedly, they will become the dominant educational delivery system of the future. Bork (1985), who is well-known for his work with computers in education, suggests that 'the computer is a means to an end' – the end being to assist all students to learn efficiently and effectively. It is now time for teachers to place greater emphasis on CAL as a supplement to traditional classroom teaching in order to enhance students' learning.

This chapter is intended to give a description of some of the experience gained by the author over the years that he has been involved with the development of CAL for mathematics and science teaching. Various attempts to implement CAL as a form of self-paced electronic remediation programme (to assist students who find difficulties in studying) are discussed. Diagnostic tests and CAL induction courses to validate the effectiveness of CAL are reported. Combining CAL with peer tutoring leads to an exciting pedagogic activity which can be used to enhance teaching and learning; some of our results of using this approach are tabulated. A pilot project on computer managed instruction is fully discussed. Finally, the creation of a model CAL laboratory is described. In summary, this chapter could best be used as a useful introduction for those educators who are preparing to investigate multi-media CAL as a means of spear-heading progress towards a new approach to education.

4.2 Why CAL?

In the process of classroom teaching, educators would like to see a constant flow of interaction between students and their teachers. The now out-dated scenario whereby a subject expert delivers subject materials and the learners merely assimilate facts and figures is no longer wanted. This is a one-way flow of 'donor to receptor' teaching activity which was practiced many decades ago and which should now be abandoned. Instead, students should be motivated and encouraged to approach their teachers in order to express their views on the subject being taught, to clarify any doubts that they have and to seek assistance in solving problems. A small class with a size of 10 students is ideal for this approach; such a classroom environment can promote closer interaction among learners and the subject expert. In addition, one-to-one coaching and personal tuition can be practiced without too much difficulty.

In practice, however, this situation is rarely realized. Schools and colleges usually maintain large class sizes with student populations ranging from 40 to 200 students per class. Teachers find great difficulty in getting to know all the students; furthermore, personal coaching is almost impossible. Teachers' work loads are usually heavy and each teacher might have to conduct lessons for more than four classes. Students may also have to compete for time in order to consult with their teacher. Moreover, students who are weak in any particular subject are usually too shy to approach their teacher because of an 'inferiority complex'. Such a predicament exerts pressure on teachers to find a more appropriate and practical way of improving the teaching environment.

Another problem faced by teachers is the ratio of good students to slow learners in any given class. Students do not learn at the same pace; this imposes an extra burden on teachers – who must consequently adjust and balance their teaching strategies accordingly. It is therefore imperative to adopt a new methodology in order to fully exploit the potential of computer technology to overcome such academic 'bottle-necks' Yong (1988).

CAL is viewed as a practical solution to the above problems (Yong *et al*, 1985). It provides the opportunity for students to study at their own pace and to review subject materials repeatedly until they master their contents. Therefore, this approach is extremely useful for students who suffer from any form of inferiority complex or who are too shy to approach teachers or even peers for assistance. Through interaction with computers, students can revise the subjects being taught, consolidate the skills involved in problem solving and undertake self-tests to ensure their total understanding of the subject matter. By incorporating a classroom administration facility into the CAL system, the progress and learning behaviour of students can be recorded and monitored. Teachers can therefore be kept informed about the progress of weak students; it also serves as a check-list for teachers to 'fine-tune' their teaching programs.

4.3 The CAL development process

As far as this chapter is concerned, CAL refers to the use of computers as 'teaching tools'. In a typical teaching situation a computer is used to deliver instructional material to a student; it then presents questions in increasing levels of difficulty. The computer responds at a rate determined by the correctness of the learner's responses. In short, the computer allows controlled learning paths and repeated review of materials. It also closely monitors the progress of the learner. Based on this definition, CAL materials can be designed and developed in order to support many different modes of learning. These include problem solving, simulation, games, inquiry, drill and practice, revision, testing and so on (Chuah *et al*, 1987). In order to use these approaches to learning a variety of different types of courseware is needed.

Currently, there is a growing repertoire of commercially available courseware. Unfortunately, for a variety of reasons commercial courseware produced by software houses has often been severely criticized. Indeed, evaluations of this courseware have been very much less than enthusiastic. Generally, teachers are usually not satisfied with the objectives or the instructional design of commercial courseware. It is therefore imperative for teachers to develop in-house instructional material that will meet the requirements of their own curricula. If a strong belief in the utility of CAL is cultivated within an organization, then enthusiasm, optimism and momentum can be gathered – thereby spear-heading the in-house development of CAL methods.

During the development process an attempt should be made to capitalize on the potential of teachers who have instinctive knowledge of the ways in which a topic might be taught to a student (Yong and Tan, 1988b). It is only teachers who can ensure that sound pedagogical procedures are followed when designing the courseware. Throughout the whole process of development, emphasis should be on team work. This necessitates the writing of courseware, the coding of software and the evaluation of the CAL materials by team effort. Only a very simple organizational structure is required to ensure optimum utilization of the available physical and human resources. Figure 4.1 illustrates a simple model for an effective and productive courseware development unit. The organizational structure consists of three main working groups: production, evaluation and planning, and laboratory development and resource provision. The production manager is responsible for courseware and software production to meet the target planned by the co-ordinator. Usually a realistic time frame for one-hour of CAL material would be 300 man-hours. A single unit of CAL material would normally be allocated to a three-member team consisting of a subject expert, a programmer and an evaluator.

The evaluation/planning manager is responsible for arranging evaluations of the courseware and software to ensure that its production adheres closely to the guidelines embedded in four basic design principles. These principles involve the utilization of (a) good man-machine interaction, (b) learner control of the learning process, (c) good material organization, and (d) well-planned graphic display designs. Each of these is discussed in more detail in section 4.4. The manager also plans the diagnostic testing that is used to validate the effectiveness of the CAL materials that are produced.

The laboratory development/resource manager undertakes the task of providing computer hardware support and setting up laboratories for student use and staff development work. The manager also keeps an inventory of the software developed and the authoring tools used by production group members.

During the development process, teachers and students are invited to respond to a series of surveys that are intended to provide feedback on CAL production. Student input is extremely valuable and the professional judgement of teachers is imperative. The feedback that has so far been obtained in our work indicates that CAL has successfully changed the conventional teaching of mathematics and science (Yong *et al*, 1985). It reflects a strong need for CAL to be incorporated into mathematics and science curricula.

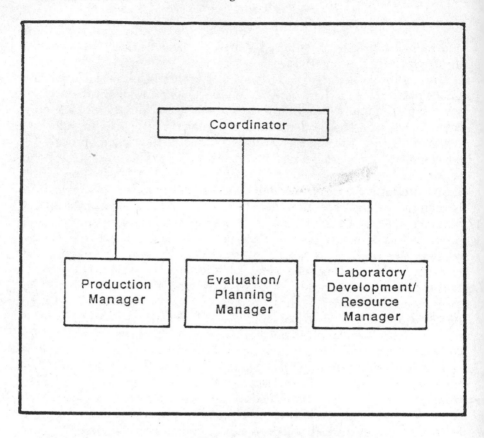

Figure 4.1 *Team organization for CAL projects*

4.4 Design principles for effective courseware

A computer offers a two-way communication medium which is well suited for individualized learning and instruction. However, sophisticated skills are required in order to develop effective instructional materials. When developing courseware teachers must realize the need to make observable improvements in teaching methods. Otherwise, an item of computer courseware will be just like a chapter of a textbook. It will simply provide a costly page-turning facility. Quite a proportion of the commercially available CAL material is of this nature. The potential and good features of the computer are not fully explored and utilized. There is what we would like to call a 'deficiency' in such courseware. Shortcomings of this type can result in a loss of confidence in the acceptance of CAL materials for classroom teaching.

CAL courseware production is an activity demanding time, effort and resources. Much like the development of a large computer program, a cost effective CAL lesson depends on proper planning and design. Based on our experience in CAL development, we present below four basic design principles which can be used to produce effective and pedagogically sound courseware (Yong and Tan, 1988b). The four principles deal with man-machine interaction, learner control of the learning process, material organization, and graphics display design.

4.4.1 Man-machine interaction

The success or failure of CAL courseware depends very much upon how friendly it can be made. Any piece of courseware that requires a great deal of memorization in using specific keys on the keyboard will certainly scare away learners. Similarly, the sight of row after row of instructions appearing on the CRT screen of a video display unit will also discourage them.

A CAL lesson which simply requires its user to press the return key or space-bar in order to obtain the next page of information is equally bad. The vital role of the computer as a two-way communication tool is greatly reduced and the CAL program (being just a page-turner for lecture notes) is considered as non-interactive.

Man-machine interaction emphasizes learner participation by promoting the learner's ability to initiate actions called 'events'. The computer then interprets these events and then responds appropriately. In other words, the computer system is expected to be event-driven and the learner's responses should be to the creation or removal of displayed information. In order to achieve good man-machine interaction in CAL software, the following suggestions are made:

(a) use menu-driven lessons;
(b) echo all inputs from the learner on the CRT screen;
(c) ensure rapid computer response to the learner's input; and,
(d) ensure that suitable remarks or comments appear on the CRT screen in order to encourage and attract the attention of the learner.

4.4.2 Learner control of the learning process

From the point of view of learner control, there are three major shortcomings of much of the conventional courseware that has been used in the past. These shortcomings are itemized below.

First, it is quite common to observe that many CAL programs do not allow the learner to control his/her own pace of learning.

Such programs often impose severe restrictions on the learning process. For example, by setting a time limit for the display of each screen-full of information these programs attempt to control the speed at which students learn.

Second, a common feature of effective learning is the need for the periodic review of material that has been previously presented. Unfortunately, many CAL programs do not permit this.

Third, some CAL programs require the input of an answer to a question to match exactly with the correct solution. Because such programs usually cater for only one input they prevent the learner from exploring other feasible solutions.

The above shortcomings represent quite common deficiencies of a large proportion of currently available courseware. Of course, when writing instructional programs that embody learner control it is imperative that these shortcomings are avoided.

CAL courseware writing differs significantly from classroom lesson preparation. Indeed, at every stage or step in a lesson extra effort is needed in order to provide a learner with control over his/her learning progress. In order to promote this the following guidelines should be considered:

(a) no attempt should be made to force a student to leave a lesson if he/she fails to respond to a question or is not following the lesson material;

(b) always provide alternative pathways that allow the learner to revise the lesson or proceed to another learning unit which is a pre-requisite for the lesson being studied;

(c) always try to provide a computer managed testing facility that gives the learner a score and an achievement rating before allowing progress to be made to the next stage of instruction;

(d) for any given question allow the learner to have a minimum of three attempts and provide appropriate hints and tips after each attempt; and

(e) allow learning to proceed at the learner's own pace but keep a record of the learning time so that the student can be kept informed of the time he/she has taken; feedback should then be provided to the student which compares his/her time with the class norm for the learning unit.

4.4.3 Materials organization

In order to produce good CAL courseware many organizational factors have to be considered. As was mentioned above, these factors make courseware writing very different from traditional classroom lesson preparation. Based upon our experience we believe that the most important factors to consider when organizing the materials for a CAL lesson are:

(a) deciding upon the courseware modes to be used;
(b) choosing the learning approaches to be adopted;
(c) allocating the timings for each CAL lesson;
(d) selecting the presentation format to be adopted;
(e) specifying the nature of the target audience; and
(f) overcoming the limitations of the authoring tools that are to be used.

4.4.4 Graphics display design

Computer graphics has a vital role to play in CAL courseware. Effective courseware requires adequate pictorial presentation in order to arouse the learner's interest in learning and to capture his/her attention. Many authoring tools now have quite powerful facilities to enable courseware developers to design graphic displays very easily – compared to the use of programming languages. Some approaches to pictorial interface design are discussed later in Chapter 7.

It is important to realize that too many static graphic displays are not effective. Graphics with animation, enlargement, overlapping of colour pictures and superimposing of graphs will definitely enhance the learner's ability to learn. An interactive (and participative) graphics display facility in which the learner has the flexibility and opportunity to build up a graphic image as he/she inputs data is a most desirable facility to have.

4.5 Validation of the effectiveness of CAL

For many educators the effectiveness of CAL has always been a concern. This is particularly true for those who are about to embark upon a CAL project themselves. Of course, one of the best ways to validate the effectiveness of a CAL program is to seek direct feedback from the teachers and students themselves. From the survey that we conducted (Tan, Yong and Tan, 1987), the feedback from both teachers and students was positive and encouraging. Teachers were convinced that CAL served the purpose of assisting weak students with their studies. Furthermore, they were also very excited over the students' willingness to attend the CAL lessons. Students thought that the CAL materials held their attention, maintained their interest and provided them with viable learning paths to master the subjects previously taught by their teachers.

Of course, a quantitative measure is needed in order to substantiate any qualitative findings. Therefore, we conducted an experiment in diagnostic testing using a CAL induction course. The experiment was used to validate the effectiveness of CAL and at the same time search for a mathematical model which could be used to identify and rectify areas of difficulty encountered by the students. The tests also served as an 'early-warning' indicator which would enable us to reduce the failure rate during the first year of study.

The procedure for the experiment is depicted in Figure 4.2 (Tan, Yong and Tan, 1987). Two tests were conducted, one prior to the CAL induction course and the other following it. The induction course was designed to serve as a supportive environment for discovery learning and also provide a quick revision (and basic grounding) in mathematics and science. Four hundred students were invited to form a sample for the experiment. They were divided into two groups; both groups were given a pre-test in mathematics and science under the same conditions and using the same test items. After the pre-test, group I took the CAL induction course whereas no computer contact was provided for the group II students. This group of students used the prescribed text book and teaching materials in a traditional way. They were required to do self-study; however, their teachers were available for consultation.

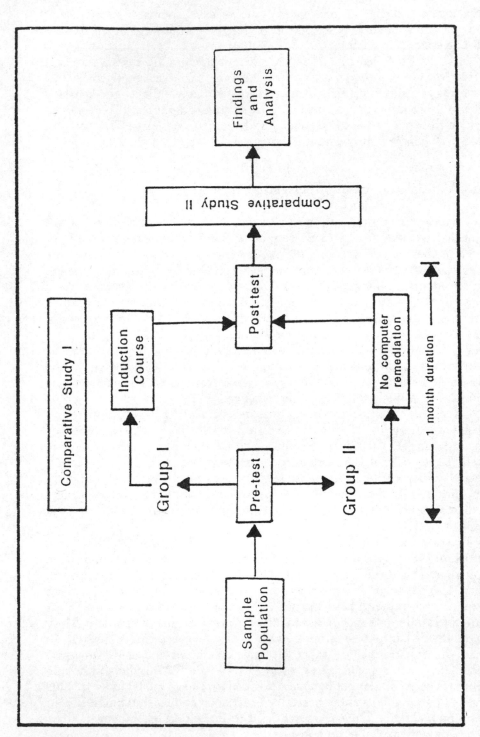

Figure 4.2 *Experiment to validate the effectiveness of CAL*

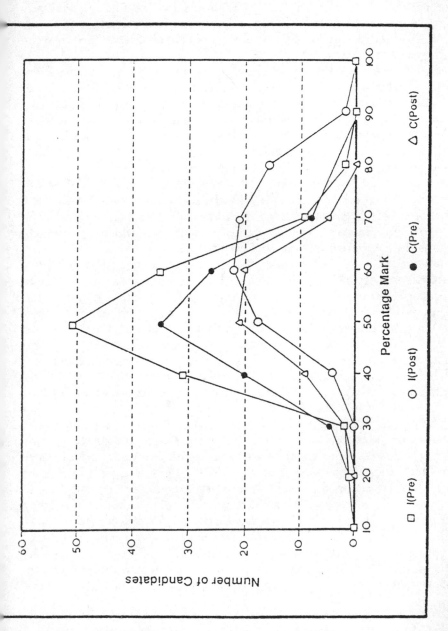

Figure 4.3 *Results of CAL experiments*

A post-test was carried out one month later in much the same manner as the pre-test. The format of both tests was multiple-choice questions. Comparative studies were carried out to determine if there was any significant improvement in performance of the students before and after the CAL induction course and also any significant differences between the two groups after the two tests.

Analysis was based on simple hypothesis testing (Tan, Yong and Tan, 1987). The findings are summarized in the graphs presented in Figure 4.3. The diagram shows that the difference in mean scores achieved by the two groups in the pre-test is not significant. But it is interesting to note that the two groups gained in mean score after taking the post-test. Group I, which had undergone the CAL induction program, developed a significant improvement in the mean score of 11.9 per cent. Moreover, the failure rate was reduced from 64.9 per cent to 27.5 per cent (an improvement of 37.4 per cent). The results also indicate that there is no significant gain in mean score for group II which attended the traditional induction program. The gain in score is merely 1.5 per cent and the failure rate which is marginally reduced by 5.8 per cent, remains relatively high.

A second experiment was conducted in order to determine how effective the CAL programme was compared with conventional teaching. A similar procedure was used. Group I undertook the CAL induction course and group II attended classes conducted by a group of teachers. In their teaching, the teachers based their courses on the same material as was used in the CAL courseware. Both groups of students achieved significant improvement in the mean score. The CAL group achieved 11.8 per cent while the teachers' coaching group reached an improvement of 13.9 per cent in the mean score. The failure rate for the CAL group reduced by 22.5 per cent while the other group reduced by 36.5 per cent.

The graphs in Figure 4.3 show the attendance of the students in both groups dropped after the pre-test. Such a situation is expected as the experiment was carried out on a voluntary basis. However, the inference from the experiment shows that the enabling technology is a significant factor that influences the results and serves as an important milestone in the new era of education. The second experiment suggests that CAL may not replace teachers in teaching. Nevertheless it is a new and effective way of providing students with self-study facilities and of providing assistance for those students who are experiencing difficulties with their studies. The effectiveness of CAL is validated and it is a particularly useful way to supplement the teaching of mathematics and science.

4.6 CAL, Tutorial and Peer Tutoring – an integration

A new exciting teaching activity which we have been exploring is the integration of CAL, Tutorial methods and Peer Tutoring. The aims of this activity are to provide students with more CAL practice, to conduct on-the-spot quantitative classroom assessment, to keep a close watch on students' progress, and to promote closer interaction between the teacher, peer tutors and weaker students (Yong and Tan, 1988a).

Our approach requires teachers to conduct tutorial classes in the CAL laboratories. Each student is allocated a workstation and is required to undergo quantitative classroom assessment (QCA). This involves computer managed testing in order to assess the ability and understanding of the students in the subjects being taught by the teachers. Immediate feedback on student performance is shown on a CRT monitor. This gives individual students the results of their assessment. The teacher also receives a detailed report of the students' performance; this report also indicates the level of achievement of the class as a whole. Students who fail to score at least 70 per cent of the available marks are recommended to book additional computer time in order to revise the material that has been taught in the tutorial. This remedial CAL is undertaken at a time which is most suitable for the individuals concerned.

After the QCA has been conducted, the teacher will identify the better students and appoint them as peer tutors. These tutors are required to assist fellow classmates in moving on to the next stage of the teaching programme (the problem solving sessions). Peer tutoring is therefore conducted with the peer tutors 'guiding and assisting' their classmates in solving problems which are generated by the computer. The teacher will however monitor the learning progress of the class. Peer tutoring in the context of primary school teaching has been described in some detail by Barker *et al* (1987).

In order to get some feedback from the students an evaluation survey was conducted. The majority of students agreed that CAL, Tutorial and Peer Tutor integration leads to:

(a) an opportunity to quickly assess their understanding of the subject being taught;
(b) an opportunity to master particular topics and learn at their own pace using an open learning environment;
(c) a more flexible approach to the assimilation of different levels of subject matter;
(d) sharing of experience and knowledge of a topic with fellow classmates; and
(e) an increase in personal confidence.

4.7 Computer managed instruction

During a learning process instructors have to (a) manage instructional delivery, (b) monitor student behaviour, and (c) assess and record students' progress. Of course, each of these functions could be implemented using a computer system. Such an approach is commonly referred to as Computer Managed Instruction (CMI). A comprehensive CMI environment should perform the following basic functions:

(a) the organization and administration of both the instructional and the testing materials;
(b) management of both the instructional delivery and the testing process; and
(c) the provision of data collection and analysis facilities.

Many situations arise in which stand-alone microcomputers cannot meet all of the above requirements. For example, the administrative system used for monitoring purposes requires that each computer is able to send monitoring information to a central point. There is therefore a requirement for having the micros connected together. Fortunately, because of advances in technology and the falling cost of computing resources this is now possible. Indeed, a local area network (LAN) can now be used to provide a CMI environment for many simultaneous users. Such an environment is extremely useful because each learner can access the central files which store the CAL courseware and the test items that are to be used for group instruction.

Of course, the choice of the LAN must be appropriate for the teaching and learning environment concerned. In our work we have used an Attached Resource Computer network system (ARCnet). It uses a distributed star topology and a token-passing access scheme. Using a network with these features permits a less error prone CMI environment to be achieved once the network is properly configured. We discuss our configuration in more detail later.

The basic elements of a CMI system suitable for mathematics and science teaching should consist of (1) a network operating system, (2) CAL courseware (produced in-house),(3) a bank of test items, (4) an administrative system, and (5) a presentation facility. In our system the presentation facility is actually the 'lesson driver' that is used to deliver the instructional materials. It has the ability to support learner/computer interaction and gives learners control over their own learning processes. The learner may use a combination of English language and simple commands in order to interact with the system. The functions of the administrative system include data capture, report generation and course administration. Access to the system is by different levels of password. The system that we have implemented is discussed in more detail in the following section.

4.8 A model CAL laboratory

Traditionally, minicomputers and mainframe systems have been used for the implementation of CAL, CMI and related types of learning environment. The time-sharing facilities and the enormous computing capability of these computers are ideal for such applications. However, the cost per hour of learning on these machines is normally far too high for most institutions. Of course, the cost of developing instructional materials must also be considered, as must the issue of software portability and hardware maintenance.

4.8.1 Microcomputers for CAL
The evolution of microcomputers (and their associated software) have provided many educators with hopes and promises of a low-cost, individualized, self-paced learning environment. Unfortunately, as we discussed

above, stand-alone microcomputers are not able to provide a total CMI environment unless they are complemented with either a time-sharing or a networking facility. Whether the learning environment takes the form of a classroom or a laboratory, these facilities are inevitably required in order to support the sharing of instructional resources and peripheral devices, and to provide educational management (Tan and Yong, 1988).

Ergonomic factors also play an important part in providing an effective learning environment. Hence, the design and planning of a conducive and effective CAL environment should consider not only the learning tools, but also the physical setting of the environment.

We believe that a CAL laboratory for mathematics and science teaching should be able to accommodate each of the following activities:

(a) the provision of diagnostic testing and induction courses;
(b) electronic remediation and testing;
(c) computer managed instruction;
(d) the integration of CAL, tutorials and peer tutoring; and
(e) in-house courseware production.

Microcomputers are able to support each of the above activities. A laboratory equipped with 25 workstations (networked together) has been found to provide a suitable environment for our CAL work. Some of the factors that we had to consider when setting up our CAL laboratory are briefly discussed below.

4.8.2 The inter-connection of workstations

When designing our CAL laboratory we had to select a method of linking our workstations together. Two possibilities arose: use of a centralized time-sharing system or use of a distributed networking facility. The function of each of these approaches is to achieve resource sharing and increased utilization of the devices that are available. The two approaches differ in that in the former the microcomputers are used as 'dumb' terminals that are attached to a more powerful central resource whereas in the second approach all micros have equal status and operate autonomously. As we mentioned earlier, we choose a network approach.

By definition a network extends over some small or large geographic region. In contrast to a wide area network (WAN), a local area network covers only a limited geographic locality – typically a single building or a college campus. Such a facility is therefore adequate for the requirements of CAL. As most of our commercial courseware (and that developed in-house) runs in a DOS (Disk Operating System) environment, a DOS network system was selected for use in our system. The DOS network is also able to support the common administrative and presentation systems which provide the CMI environment.

4.8.3 The physical setting of the CAL laboratory

As well as good laboratory management, it is important to realise that a well-designed laboratory setting will promote and enhance a student's interest in learning. A 'conducive' environment can stimulate self-study and encourage students to work quietly and independently with minimum supervision from teachers. Of course, each student should be assigned a workstation that is located in a suitably designed area of the laboratory. Appropriate operating instructions for the workstation must also be provided.

Design considerations for the physical layout of the laboratory must also take into account the various activities that are likely to take place within it. Typically, these will include briefing, individual or small group consultation; quantitative classroom assessment, and peer tutoring. It is usually not possible to conduct these activities in a conventional computer laboratory setting. Therefore, a new concept in CAL laboratory design was envisaged. Our idea combined the function of a regular classroom setting with that of a conventional computer laboratory. The physical arrangement that we envisaged is shown schematically in Figure 4.4.

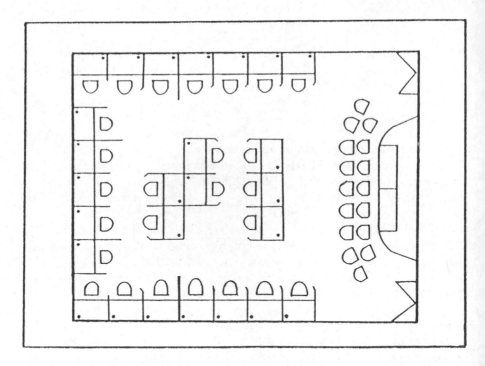

Figure 4.4 *Organization of a model CAL laboratory*

4.8.4 System configuration for the CAL laboratory

The basic configuration of the CAL laboratory that we use for mathematics and science teaching consists of 25 workstations, 4 file servers, a high-speed printer and an external tape backup unit. These units are connected together using an ARCnet network system through a distributed star topology (Novell, 1987). Figure 4.5 shows the basic system configuration.

The four file servers each have a hard disk (of capacity 60 Mbyte) and are fitted with 2 Mbyte of main memory. By connecting these in the way shown in Figure 4.5 we are able to attain an equal distribution of the servers' load (about six to seven workstations per server) thereby achieving optimum system performance. All servers and workstations are based on Intel 80286 microcomputers.

4.9 Future directions

As computers continue to influence teaching and learning processes, CAL will gradually become the dominant educational delivery system of the future. However, it does not follow that the role of teachers will be subsumed. Indeed, it is anticipated that teachers will be expected to play a more prominent role in the design and organization of interactive learning materials.

It is not surprising to learn that today's educators are doubtful about integrating CAL and CMI into classroom teaching. Usually, their common concerns are the effectiveness of CAL, the time needed to develop materials, and acceptance of CAL by teachers and students. In addition, lack of expertise and confidence can also hinder CAL development. Ways of sustaining and increasing interest in CAL are also important factors to be considered.

CAL development is undoubtedly a difficult process. Nevertheless, the significant impact of computer technology on our lives will continue at an ever-increasing rate. Education cannot escape this impact. It is therefore time for teachers to consider greater innovation in their teaching (especially of mathematics and science) through the use of CAL methods. Dedication, willingness, proper planning and structured working groups are key factors for success in achieving this goal.

CAL offers new avenues by which students can explore the experimental nature of mathematics and science. Through CAL students can acquire the skills involved in observing, exploring, forming intuitions, making predictions, testing hypotheses, conducting trails and controlling variables (Baird, 1986). Teachers must now play a new role with respect to the ways in which students receive new information, the ways in which they process it and the ways in which they are assessed. In this context it must be emphasised that CAL and CMI provide teachers with immediate and accurate diagnostic information. The quality of teaching and learning can therefore be significantly enhanced.

New and improved generations of microcomputers (with substantially increased speed and memory) will make effective CAL programs easier to develop and simpler to use. New tools based on expert systems technology are emerging. It is therefore envisaged that the programmed-instruction approach to CAL will be replaced by one involving extensive use of artificial intelligence. The artificial intelligence approach involves studying the ways

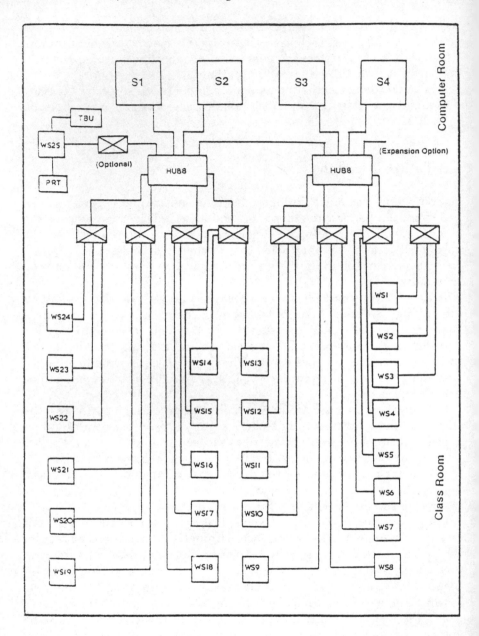

Figure 4.5 *System configuration for the CAL laboratory*

in which effective teachers actually teach their particular subject. Computer programs are then developed which will emulate the behaviour of these teachers. Such an approach will, in the long term, make a major contribution to CAL.

The need for computers in mathematics and science is indispensable. Teaching science and mathematics depends on the resources that can be made available. Emphasis must be on students doing science and exploring mathematics for themselves. Today, it would be hard to concieve of mathematics and science education without the benefit of computers. The use of computers should, therefore, be aimed as an aid to the understanding of the theoretical and conceptual processes of science. The applications of computers (in the form of CAL) certainly meets these requirements.

In conclusion, the author wishes to quote Hooper's views on CAL used in education (Hooper, 1987):

... there are two categories of claims relating to the use of CAL which are put forward by practitioners themselves. The first category relates to those functions of computers that could not, in common sense terms, be performed by other media (including the human teacher). The second category relates to functions that the computer can perform but that can also be performed by other media (either singly or in combination) such as teachers, books or video tapes.

Hooper's study supports the great value of CAL in mathematics and science teaching. It is therefore imperative that we encourage the full development and implementation of CAL for teaching in these areas.

4.10 References

Baird, W., (1986). The influence of computers and informatics on mathematics and its teaching, *Journal of Computers in Mathematics and Science Teaching*, Winter 1986/87.

Barker, P.G., Lees, J. and Docherty, D., (1987). Flexible learning in a multimedia environment, 123-128 in *Aspects of Educational Technology, Volume XX: Flexible Learning Systems*, edited by F. Percival, D. Craig and D. Buglass, Kogan Page, London.

Bork, A., (1985). *Personal Computers for Education*, Harper and Row, New York.

Chuah, C.C., *et al*, (1987). *CAL: Promise, Potential and Performance*, background working papers, Teaching and Learning Advisory Unit, Univ. Science, Penang, Malaysia.

Hooper, R., (1987). Computers in science teaching – an introduction, *Computers in Education*, 2, 1-7.

Novell, (1987). *LAN Evaluation Report*, Novell Inc., Orem, Utah.

Tan, B.T., Yong, Y.C. and Tan, H.G., (1987). *Validation of the Effectiveness of CAL as a Form of Remediation*, Proceedings of Educomp'87 Conference, Kuala Lumpur, Malaysia.

Tan, H.G. and Yong, Y.C., (1988)., A model laboratory for CAI, 340-359 in *Proceedings of the Australian Computers in Education Conference*, Perth, Australia.

Yong, Y.C., (1988). Computer aided instruction in mathematics, paper presented at Professional Development Day Conference, Humber College, Toronto, Canada.

Yong, Y.C. *et al*, (1985). The CAI way to assist weak students, paper presented at Singapore National Quality Control Circle Convention (Public Sector).

Yong, Y.C. and Tan, H.G., (1988a). Educational computing program: implementation and development of computer aided instruction in mathematics and science, 1-11 in *Proceedings of the International Conference on Computers in Engineering and Education*, Singapore.

Yong, Y.C. and Tan, H.G., (1988b). Design principles for effective courseware production, paper accepted for publication in the *Journal of The Educational Computing Association of Western Australia*.

Chapter 5
Electronics Teaching – A Multi-Media Approach

Geoffrey Reynolds and Ken Meierdiercks
Singapore Polytechnic

5.1 Introduction

Singapore is one of the countries that is racing to be an 'Electronic Nation'. One that will use computers to link people and nations together. It is a government priority to actively encourage the use of computers in business and to push for a population that is computer literate.

Singapore is a highly industrialized country of 2.6 million people distributed on a small island that measures 42 km by 23 km. The island is located at the tip of Malaysia. Singapore is one of the busiest ports in the world. It has no other natural resources except its people and the sea. The nation therefore has to become a technological stronghold in order to survive. Singapore thus realizes the importance of securing a position in the 'electronic future' that information technology is making possible.

The institutions of higher education in Singapore are playing their part in preparing for this electronic future. Most of the students in the tertiary level are in engineering departments. Apart from the teacher training institute, the tertiary level of education is provided by four establishments. Of these, two are polytechnics, another is a technical university, and the fourth is the National University of Singapore (a comprehensive university).

At the elementary and secondary levels computers are entering the classrooms in greater and greater numbers. The Curriculum Development Institute of Singapore (CDIS) is actively involved in developing CAL materials for use at these levels. At present there are two schools which have been set up with computer laboratories (in conjunction with vendors) in order to test out processes and materials. Computer use at this level provides tutoring, drill and practice activities, and computer literacy courses. The computer at this level is not used as a tool.

At the tertiary tier, computers are used primarily as tools to solve engineering problems. However, outside of the computer language courses (BASIC, Fortran, Pascal and so forth) computer software is rarely used to teach a subject or to help students learn with drill and practice programs.

Effort is now being made in the tertiary institutes to develop Computer Aided Education (CAE) and CAL materials. A fairly comprehensive review of the current status of CAL in Singapore has recently been presented by Barker (1988). Some of this CAL activity is also further described in this book in Chapters 4, 6 and 11.

As well as the government's encouragement, increased activity in developing CAE software springs from the availability of low-cost microcomputers, greater research effort, a general increase in the public's computer awareness and, most importantly, a growth in the number of computer/education enthusiasts who just 'tinker around'. For example, Mrs Lau Yuen Kit of Singapore Polytechnic's Electronics Department has produced an extremely useful CAL program on binary numbers; she has developed this working at home on her own computer.

Technology progresses at a very rapid pace. Sometimes, a problem is not recognized until the means to solve it are at hand. For example, we certainly didn't know that we needed to be in another place in such a hurry until the automobile and airplane were invented. Now that the computer is here we need to solve the problem of using it to teach. In the remainder of this chapter we describe an experiment that we have undertaken in order to investigate the potential utility of multi-media CAL for electronics teaching.

5.2 CAL in electronics teaching

Computer assisted learning in one form or another is being used quite extensively for the teaching of electronics (Barker and Manji, 1988). Henderson (1988), for example, describes the use of a computer-based simulation package (called ASP) for teaching processor fundamentals. This system runs on a minicomputer and makes extensive use of graphics. At the microcomputer level, the LabVIEW system (which is briefly described by Barker *et al* in Chapter 7) is an example of a sophisticated interactive desk-top engineering package that can be used to enable students to design laboratory instruments and then simulate their behaviour. Snowden (1988) also describes a microcomputer-based interactive teaching package called INCA. This package can be used for DC and steady-state AC analysis of linear electronic circuits. Video disc systems for electronics teaching are also starting to become commercially available. The Wiley Science Laboratory Discs, for example, contain sections for teaching various aspects of AC circuit theory (Wiley, 1987).

Given that there is potential for CAL in electronics teaching it was decided that some attempts should be made to use this technique to help teach this subject at Singapore Polytechnic. Before describing the approach that we adopted it is important to describe the background to our problem and the way in which our interest in multi-media CAL arose.

Most of the 15 lecturers from the Electronics and Communications Department of Singapore Polytechnic (who offered an Electronics course to the second year Mechanical Engineering students) accepted the way the course had been structured and slotted it into their time-tables. As far as they were concerned there didn't seem to be a better way to teach this basic electronic course to 800 Mechanical Engineering students each year.

One lecturer, however, being familiar with competency based education methods, thought there might be a better way and began talks with the Polytechnic's instructional designer. The designer knew about video tapes, computers in education and modular course construction. Having knowledge of various educational delivery systems and strategies, he was able to 'shake out' the problem, so to speak. It was simply this: given the various educational means at our disposal, could we design a course that was more effective and efficient for both the department (as represented by the lecturers) and the learners?

5.2.1 The anatomy of the problem

In order to enable the reader to gain an understanding of the task we were undertaking, this section provides a summary of the details of the problem that faced us when we began to design our multi-media course.

(a) *Subject:* Electronics for Mechanical Engineering Students (16 topics);
(b) *Population:* 800 students per year (divided into 20 groups of 40 students each);
(c) *Staff:* 15 staff to provide the lectures, the tutorials, and the laboratories;
(d) *Schedule:* 2 hour lecture per week, 2 hour tutorial every 2nd week, 2 hour laboratory every 2nd week;
(e) *Resources:* Identical class and lecture notes for all classes;
(f) *Evaluation:* Two end-of-term tests of three comprehensive electronic questions and a final end-of-course examination;
(g) *Intangibles:* It was felt by some staff that the mechanical engineering students were not particularly interested in the subject because it was outside of their declared major: mechanical engineering. Naturally, there was more pressure on them to achieve in the mechanical mainstream.

5.2.2 The experiment

Three instructional activities that help students learn are: information gathering, solving problems with paper and pencil, and solving problems using laboratory devices and equipment.

These correspond to the lecture, the tutorial, and the laboratory, respectively. In order to include each of these activities, a multi-media course design was constructed that used video tapes, paper modules, staff tutors and computers.

For the experimental course the 10th and 11th topics of the 16 topic course was selected for use. The topics concerned were: Topic 10 – Integrated Circuits and Topic 11 – Number Systems. The group involved in the CAL teaching contained 40 students (one section of the 120 students in one lecturer's class). This group was used as the experimental group while the other 80 students continued as in the past and were considered to be the control group. The three sections which made up the class of 120 were assigned randomly to the lecturer by the registrar.

5.2.3 Multi-media resources

In this multi-media teaching experiment a number of different types of resource have been used. Some details of the various resources employed are given in this section.

The paper module

The paper module (or workbook) is made up of the usual class notes. These contain subject information, data references, and instructions. The latter are quite extensive and include descriptions of how to travel through the course materials, practice examples, and mention of other available resources. Students are encouraged to add their own notes and observations to this material. The workbook is very much like a textbook in purpose, and we expect that it will eventually find a place on the student's professional reference shelf. It is given out in sections that are assembled as the student progresses through the course. Eventually, it will form a small book. A specially designed loose-leaf binder is given out to help the student file each section. In the future we hope to be able to benefit from Desk Top Publishing in order to make these booklets more attractive and thereby more digestible for the student.

Video tapes

The principal lecturer involved in the course made seven video tapes of his lectures covering Topic 10. The material was the same in both video and live lectures. The taping was done in a studio without any formal preparations – such as shooting scripts, rehearsals or involved graphic display. A white-board was used for diagrams and real apparatus such as IC chips, meter readings and electronic equipment were shown – for the most part in a 'tight' close-up. Some graphic titling was edited in later. Because of the proficiency of the lecturer the video taping was usually done in one session (and quite often in one take) only holding the tape on pause to move equipment around, or to add to the diagrams on the white-board. Using this approach eight lecture hours were completed in 80 hours. Because the titling and summary titles were edited in after the taping, more time was spent in editing than was anticipated, or needed.

Computer aided learning

In order to use CAL methods some instructional software had to be prepared. The PC/PILOT author language (Washington Computer Services, 1985) provided the framework within which to create computer programs that followed on from each of the video tapes. These gave the students a chance to practice what they had seen and to get some idea of how they were doing. Essentially, these involved drill and practice with feedback. Circuit diagrams were drawn using the PILOT Graphics Image Editor (GIE) and then transferred to PC/PILOT.

The basic logic embedded within the CAL programs is illustrated in Figure 5.1. Each student has four chances at getting the right answer for the question before being moved on to the next question. After each wrong

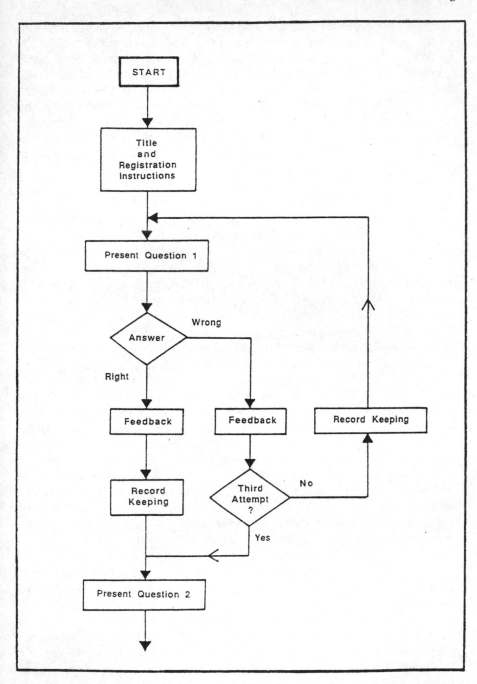

Figure 5.1 *Basic control logic underlying the CAL programs*

answer the program provides hints on how to arrive at the correct answer. At the conclusion of the computer generated drill and practice exercise, the student is shown by the final screen in the CAL program how many questions were answered correctly on the first attempt and how many were right altogether. A print-out is then produced and is given to the instructor; this shows how many tries the student made for each of the questions on the test. Using this print-out as feedback, the lecturer can evaluate the validity of the questions as well as the effectiveness of the video presentation. In other words some fine tuning can be accomplished.

5.2.4 The learning procedure

At the commencement of the course all of the students (120), met for their first lecture on Topic 10 of the Electronics for Mechanical Engineers course: Integrated Circuits. The group that was chosen to be the experimental group (40) was told not to come to any more lectures. Furthermore, they were told that they would be given special instructions when they met for the first time that week in their tutorial. No attempt was made to avoid the Hawthorn effect (Rowntree, 1982). It was more important that the experimental group was told that it was an experiment and they were expected not to share their materials, videotapes, or computer programs with the control group – for fear of contamination of the results.

The basic learning procedure for the experimental group involved a self-paced strategy similar to that depicted schematically in Figure 5.2. Members of the experimental group were given the paper-based modules and an explanation of the learning procedure to be followed. The modules have colour-coded sections; one colour for procedural instructions, another for examples and a third for information/instructional pages. Students were given only the section of the workbook that would compose the part of the next 'lecture'; this could then be inserted into the notebook-holder which was provided. At the end of the section of instructions and examples, the students were instructed to go to the library in order to view the video tape corresponding to the reading matter in the module. The library has over one hundred video tape recorders in the Learning Resources Centre.

The library used a simple form in order to check that the correct video tape was given to the student, and not one that might be well ahead of his/her preparation.

After viewing the video tape, the student was instructed to gain access to a microcomputer in the computer applications centre (Singapore Polytechnic has over one thousand microcomputers) and to do the computer practice test. The results of the test are passed along to the lecturer (Mr Reynolds) responsible for the course. The students then met with Mr Reynolds on an individual basis in order to discuss the results of the computer test and any problems that they might have had with the learning materials. A sensitive teacher can, at this point, enrich the student's education by careful questionning based on the computer test results and by his/her own experience and depth of knowledge. There is

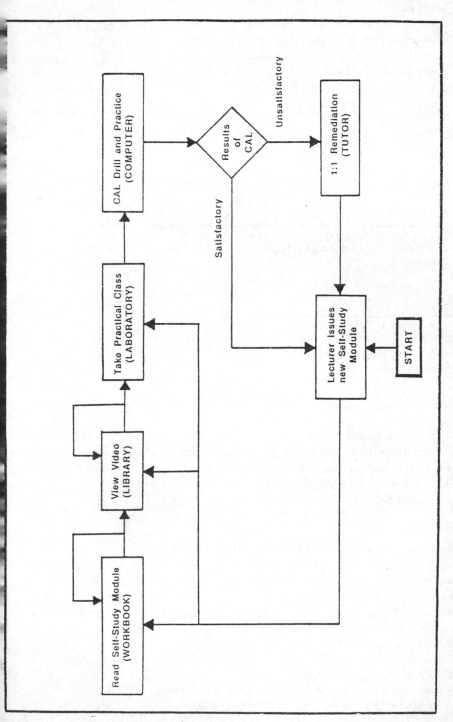

Figure 5.2 *Self-paced strategy for the Linear Integrated Circuits topic*

here a chance to interact with the student, and hence, to individualize education.

After an individual tutorial session the student is given another module, along with any resources that the instructor thinks might lead to the student travelling on the path to success.

From the description given above it is easy to see that the process cycle for the learning operations looks like this:

INFORMATION	-paper module section	given out at tutorial
	-video tape of lecture	viewed in the library on individual VCR's
PRACTICE	-computer program	to practice solving problems and test understanding
TUTORING	-individual tutoring	for diagnostic and prescription, including the next module hand-out

The only schedule that the students are given is the time by which a unit has to be finished in order to begin the next unit and take the end-of-term test. Times that the students could meet with the tutor for their individual sessions are announced, the most prominent one being their scheduled formal tutorial.

5.2.5 The results

Two instruments were used to evaluate the learning programme (a) a student survey, and (b) the end-of-term test. All of the 40 students responded to a survey that was conducted at the end of the course but not all answered all of the questions on the questionnaire. Briefly, and putting aside responses that pertain to the mechanics of the systems, such as availability of equipment, helpful people at the centres, scheduling and such, the results of the survey are as follows:

WORKBOOKS: (paper modules)
    Reading level: (32) just right
    Need improvement: (15) yes
                                            (18) no
    How can they be improved?   (More examples)

VIDEO:

Watched on individual bases	(29) yes
	(4) no
Number of times viewed same tape	(15) once
	(17) twice
	(3) three times

Did you 'pause' or 'replay' any of the
sections?   (34) yes.

Which sections?
(Those with diagrams.)

Which did you prefer video tapes?   (33)
                or going to lectures?   (1)

Why?
(Replay feature, better view of
demonstrations, done at own pace,
private.)

How can video tapes be improved?
(Make videos 30 minutes, give
questions and worked examples.)

COMPUTER AIDED TUTORIALS:

Were the programs 'user friendly?	(30) yes
	(1) difficult
On average, how many times did you run the same tutorial?	
	(15) once
	(15) twice
	(2) three times
	(1) four times
Were the tutorials	(11) easy
	(21) just right
	(1) difficult

Compare the computer tutorial with the
classroom tutorial:

Computer tutorials	(6)
Classroom tutorials	(25)

Why?
(Classroom more challenging; presence of
tutor if help is needed while doing problems; more interaction.)

TOTAL PROGRAM:
The main source of my learning the materials was …
    Video 1st, Computer 2nd, Print 3rd
    (This was the main pattern of responses.)
Comments: (generally positive, with 'Hope that it will continue'
commonplace. Negative comments expressed: difficulties with
facilities, 'put Computer Centre nearer Manufacturing
Department' being typical.)

5.2.6 Academic achievement

The end-of-term test given to all 120 students showed no significant
difference in achievement between the standard classroom teaching
process and the self-paced, electronically aided, experimental group.

The results are comfortably like results from similar adventures into the
new paradigms of learning even when we use the yardstick provided for us
by the incumbent paradigm: it should at least give us pause to wonder.

5.3 Future plans

The study revealed that changes were needed to the resource materials, principally the CAL component.

The lack of challenge and interaction reported by students were largely the result of the multiple-choice format and the predictability of the questions (if the student needed to repeat the tutorial). Also the student was normally given only one question on any learning objective.

In spite of the difficulties the CAL component will once again be tried but in a slightly different format.

Multiple choice questions will be reduced to a minimum and when an incorrect response is given the student will be presented with a succession of hints as well as remedial problems before being tested again on the same objective. Random presentation of the questions should eliminate any predictability in the CAL program.

5.4 Conclusions

Generally the favorable student response to the self-paced learning package suggests their interest in this concept of a different learning methodology. However, further experimentation is needed into the correct blend of materials and the nature and format that these materials must take, particularly the CAL component.

It is anticipated that this experimental work in self-paced learning will eventually provide students with an alternative learning method that can be run in conjunction with the conventional teaching classroom format – so giving students a choice as to their preferred methods of learning.

No doubt a CAL component will be part of this multi-media package providing a vehicle for cost-effective and efficient dissemination of knowledge and skills to future Singaporean technologists.

This year all 120 students will be using the revised package for the unit on Integrated Circuits. One small step for the Polytechnic; one large step for the learner.

5.5 References

Barker, P.G., (1988). Computer assisted learning in Singapore, *British Journal of Educational Technology*, 19(3), 193-201.

Barker, P.G. and Manji, K.A., (1988). Multi-media CAL techniques for the teaching of electronics, paper submitted to *Engineering Applications of Artificial Intelligence*.

Henderson, W.D., (1988). *Animated Simple Processor: A CAL Package for Teaching Processor Fundamentals*, Newcastle Upon Tyne Polytechnic, Newcastle Upon Tyne, UK.

Rowntree, D., (1982). *Educational Technology in Curriculum Development*, pages

199-200, Second Edition, Harper and Row, London.

Snowden, C.M., (1988). *Interactive Circuit Analysis Package*, John Wiley and Sons, Chichester, UK.

Washington Computer Sevices, (1985). *PC/PILOT Language Reference Manual*, Version 4.0, Washington Computer Services, Bellingham, Washington, USA.

Wiley, (1987). *The Wiley Interactive Science Laboratory*, John Wiley and Sons, Chichester, UK.

Chapter 6

Training of Deck Officers – Electronic Navigation Simulator

R F Short
Singapore Polytechnic

6.1 Introduction

Seafaring is a profession in which man ventures into a hostile environment and confronts physical danger. The navigation of ships is hazardous and the consequences of failure to maintain those standards required by 'the ordinary practices of seamen' can be very heavy indeed. Ships are very fragile when pitted against great natural forces. They must be handled with great skill. If not, they founder, capsize, break up, strand, burn and collide. Despite this, men will always venture forth upon the sea to trade, to travel, to fight and to relax.

Seafaring is also a profession in which enormous responsibilities are frequently placed upon the man in charge of the ship, the master. By law and by custom it is the master who is responsible for the ship and her crew and fault on his part can, in addition to causing death and destruction to that over which he has authority, injure others, damage other property and severely pollute the marine environment. The modern cost of maritime casualty is clearly indicated by the cost of the stranding of the tanker 'Amoco Cadiz' in 1978, which is likely to exceed S$6 billion. While others are also implicated – maritime casualties are seldom simple affairs – at the time of the casualty one man, the master, was in the critical position of authority whereby his decisions determined the outcome of the chain of events that, in this case, led to disaster.

The crew of a ship are engaged to assist the master in the execution of the heavy responsibilities arising out of the operation of the ship. Deck officers assist with the navigation and maintenance of the ship and with the cargo handling. Engineer officers assist by ensuring that power is provided for the propulsion and other requirements of the operation of the ship. Radio officers assist by ensuring that the ship can communicate with other ships and with the shore. These officers are in turn assisted by other members of the crew.

It is in the navigation of the ship that the greatest potential for accident exists and it is therefore necessary to ensure that the deck officers are thoroughly trained in all aspects of navigation, collision avoidance and ship handling. The theory of these important skills has usually been taught in shore-based classrooms, while the practice has been acquired on the job at sea. Real practical competence is acquired by putting theory into practice and experiencing the outcome. It is when the deck officer has to navigate through hazardous coastal waters in restricted visibility, or when he must interact with several other vessels in a collision avoidance situation, that his appreciation of these complex navigational situations and of his significant role in determining their successful outcome is developed. He acquires a sensitivity for the situation that leads to responsible and effective control. The amount of practice is however limited by the very fact that it is being done as part of the navigation of the ship and nothing should be done which may hazard the safety of the ship and her crew or the safety of others. It has therefore been difficult for the deck officer to obtain experience in dealings with stressful situations prior to actually encountering those situations.

While there is no doubt about the usefulness of analysing demanding navigational situations, as has long been done as part of the training of deck officers, even when diagrams and models are used it is not adequate preparation for dealing with the real situation when it does develop at sea. Individuals do not know how they will react until tested by reality. In this respect, the training provided by the maritime training centres has fallen short of the training needed adequately to prepare the deck officer for many of the navigational and collision avoidance situations that he will have to deal with at sea. Even the most thorough classroom analysis cannot really convey the dynamics of a navigational situation.

6.2 Electronic navigation instruments

The use of electronic navigation aids on board merchant ships has developed rapidly in recent years. Prior to the 1939-1945 War, only the electronic depth-finder (echo-sounder) and the medium-frequency radio direction-finder were in use and then usually only on the larger ships. The war provided the impetus for the rapid development of radio direction and ranging (radar) into a functional navigation aid of the greatest importance and for the invention of electronic hyperbolic navigation systems which enable ships and aircraft to fix their position without terrestrial or celestial observations. The earliest of these included the Decca Navigation System, which provided fixes of considerable accuracy up to 250 miles off the coast of North West Europe. This was followed by Loran, which provided long range fixing, but of a lower accuracy. More recent years have seen the introduction of the worldwide coverage provided by Omega and by the use of navigation satellites (Satnav).

Although the introduction of radar provided the most useful aid for coastal navigation and collision avoidance in restricted visibility, the number of ship collisions that were occurring in congested waters, despite the use of radar, gave rise to great concern over the ability of the navigator to handle the heavy flow of information coming from the radar. Consequently, by international agreement, the very advanced automatic radar plotting aid (ARPA) was developed and is now being compulsorily fitted on board the larger merchant ships.

The bridge of a typical modern ship is likely to be fitted with the following instruments:

(a) True and Relative Motion Radar for navigation in the proximity of land and for collision avoidance;
(b) Automatic Radar Plotting Aid for collision avoidance through electronic analysis of target movements detected by the radar;
(c) Decca Navigator for accurate position fixing up to 250 miles from land;
(d) Loran C for position fixing on the high seas, particularly in the Northern Hemisphere;
(e) Omega and Satnav for position fixing on the high seas;
(f) Echo-sounder for determining the depth under the keel of the ship, when over the continental shelf; and
(g) Radio direction finder for position fixing in the proximity of land and also for determining the direction of another vessel transmitting a radio signal.

Although traditional methods of classroom instruction are adequate for explaining the principles and theory underlying the operation of these instruments, they are far from adequate in developing the comprehensive appreciation of the instruments and their limitations that is necessary to ensure that the deck officer can utilize them to the full in complex navigation and traffic situations.

6.3 Electronic navigation simulation

The development of maritime training simulators in recent years has been a major step in overcoming this deficiency in maritime training and, while experience in handling dynamic situations on a simulator can only be considered as complementary to sea experience, it does introduce a welcome degree of realism into the classroom situation. There are five arguments for using simulation in the training of deck officers. Each of these is briefly discussed below.

1. A simulator is safe; students can be taken through exercises that would be completely inadmissable in the real world; emergency and near-disaster drills can be repeated until the correct response becomes almost automatic; 'ships' can be allowed to run aground or to collide in Singapore Straits; wide experience of navigational crises can be compressed into a week long course.
2. It saves money; a simulator may be expensive but it is still cheaper to buy than a ship – and much cheaper to run.
3. It saves time; the computer puts the participants into the training area straight away and there is no need for transport by ship.
4. Simulator conditions are completely under control; if the instructor wants restricted visibility, a strong tidal current and two ships in the fairway, he puts them there – precisely designed exercises can thus be set up.

5. Conditions are exactly repeatable, so that an exercise can be replayed from any chosen point in order to drive home a particular lesson.

Simulators are playing an increasingly important role in many aspects of maritime training. The use of radar, particularly in collision avoidance, has been taught by means of radar simulators since the late 1950s and, in more recent years, this simulation has been extended, to include other electronic navigation instruments. Liquid cargo handling and machinery contol room simulators have also been introduced.

The training of deck officers for merchant ships has been an important function of Singapore Polytechnic since it opened its doors to students in 1958. Electronic simulation was introduced in 1972 when UNESCO presented the Department with a radar simulator that was able to simulate the radar displays on three ships. This was very good but this limited simulator was replaced in 1983 by a comprehensive marine navigation simulator which, in addition to simulating the latest radar equipment installed on merchant ships so that four 'own ships' could be navigated independently, also provided realistic simulation of all the other electronic navigation instruments in common use at sea.

In choosing the equipment, thorough consideration was given to the technology in use, its reliability, the ease of obtaining software, the feasibility of future upgrading, the provision of maintenance services in Singapore, price, delivery and installation. After carefully vetting equip-ment manufactured in Britain, Germany, Japan and Norway, the most suitable was found to be that manufactured by RACAL-SMS Ltd of Surrey, England.

6.4 Simulation equipment

The Racal MRNS 9000 Marine Radar and Navigation Simulator is installed in air-conditioned and sound-proofed rooms on the top floor of Teaching Block 7, well away from normal student traffic. The simulation complex is divided into two rooms: (1) The Ship's Bridge Simulation Room (T734), and (2) The Electronic Navigation Systems Room (T735).

The layout of these rooms is shown in Figure 6.1. A brief description of the equipment contained in each room is presented below.

6.4.1 The bridge simulator room
This room contains the following equipment: (a) central processing unit, (b) four booths, each representing a ship's navigating bridge and containing various electronic navigation aids, (c) an instructor's facility, and (d) a debriefing area.

Each of these items is briefly discussed below.

The Racal-SMS System MRNS-9000 CPU with its associated software provides the simulation for the 4 own ships, 48 manoevrable targets, 500 fixed targets, the coastlines and the data readout for the electronic navigation aids available within the playing area.

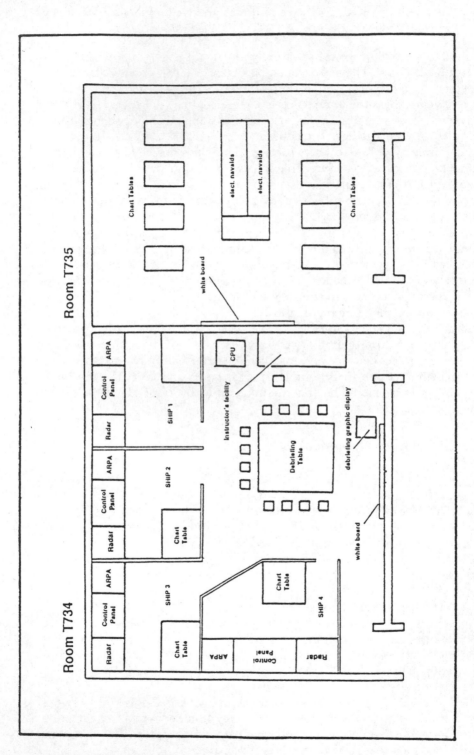

Figure 6.1 *Layout of the rooms in the simulation complex*

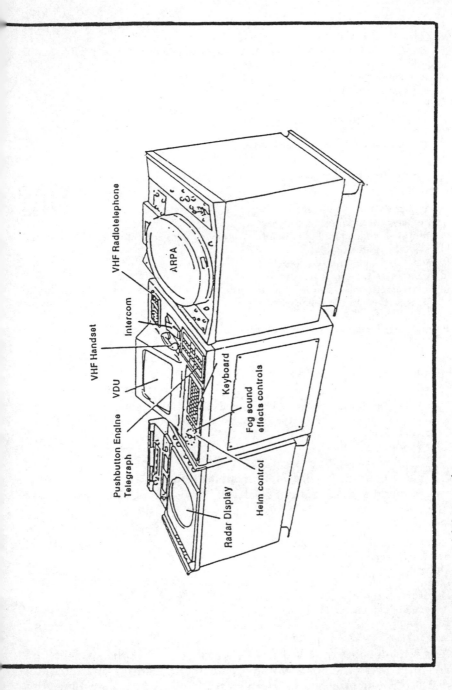

Figure 6.2 *Students' 'own ship' console*

Each sound-proof booth (see Figure 6.2) represents the navigation bright of a ship and contains:

(a) a VDU for the display of the parameters set for the ship and the data readings from the electronic navigation aids;
(b) a keyboard for the student to set the ship's parameters and to respond to faults;
(c) a helm control for manoeuvring the ship;
(d) an engine telegraph for controlling the ship's speed;
(e) fog signalling apparatus;
(f) simulated VHF radio communications;
(g) intercommunications equipment;
(h) a radar display; and
(i) an Automatic Radar Plotting Aid (ARPA)

The instructor's facility (see Figure 6.3) consists of:

(a) a graphics display unit, an alpha-numeric VDU and a 9 inch radar display – these are used for monitoring exercises;
(b) two keyboards to facilitate the preparation, running, monitoring, recording and playback of exercises;
(c) simulated VHF radio equipment;
(d) intercommunications system;
(e) two cassette tape recorders – one to record VHF conversation and the other to provide the input of the pre-recorded VHF conversations between traffic in the area;
(f) a matrix dot printer which provides hard copies of the graphics display on the VDU page.

The debriefing area contains:

(a) a large table for the display of charts and other nautical publications;
(b) a graphics display repeater for viewing the recorded exercises;
(c) a whiteboard; and,
(d) an OHP.

6.4.2 The Electronic Navigational Systems Room

The instruments in the adjacent Electronic Navigational Systems room are as follows:

Automated Radar Plotting Aid (ARPA)
Satellite Navigator
Omega
Loran C
Decca Navigator Mk 30
Automatic Radio Direction Finder
Echo Sounder

These instruments are linked to Own Ship 1 so that the readouts are correct for the position of Own Ship 1 at any time during an exercise. A visual display unit provides the parameters of Own Ship 1 at any time. Also provided are charts and other nautical publications and appropriate furniture.

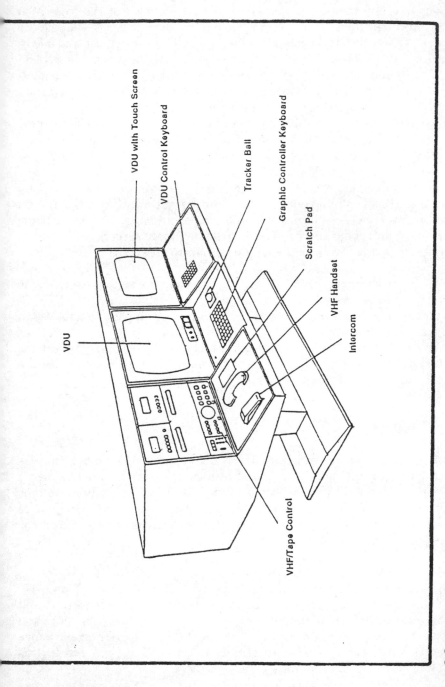

Figure 6.3 *Instructor's console*

6.5 Operation

Essentially, the trainees are required to navigate each of the four 'own ships' through the selected playing area. Four playing areas – Singapore Straits, Dover Straits, Lisbon and Chesapeake Bay – are in use and a fifth playing area – Malacca Straits – is being developed. The navigation is blind in that there is no view from the bridge and the trainees are dependent upon the information provided by the radar and other electronic navigation instruments. Each exercise requires safe navigation, including the avoidance of collision with other ships. The instructor can introduce new dangers or otherwise modify an exercise as he wishes. There is also a quadraphonic sound system for the simulation of fog and manoeuvring signals.

The simulator enables the instructor to require the trainees to navigate any of the following ship types: coaster, fast ferry, cargo, fast cargo, roll-on roll-off, container, medium sized tanker, laden and light very large crude carriers, liquified gas carrier. The instructor has 40 targets (other ships, navigation marks) available and he can also introduce clutter effects due to wind and rain.

The instructor uses his VDU and keyboards to prepare an exercise. He can create a new exercise or simply modify an existing one.

Prepared exercises are stored on floppy discs and completed exercises can be recorded for replay.

The real instruments in the adjacent Electronic Navigation Systems (ENS) Room are used to familiarize the trainees with the operation of the most widely used electronic navigation instruments.

6.6 Courses

The installation of the ENS simulator and linked instruments room has enabled the Department of Nautical Studies to offer realistic and highly effective training in the use of all of the electronic navigation systems normally found on board merchant ships. The courses that are briefly described below are now being provided for the training of deck officers for Singapore's merchant fleet.

6.6.1 Navigation control course
The most senior officers undergo two weeks (60 hours) of intensive training in the navigational control of a ship while transitting and manoeuvring in hazardous and congested waters, such as Singapore and Dover Straits. The use of radar and ARPA in effective collision avoidance work is emphasized. About 70 senior officers will be exposed to this training in the next 12 months.

6.6.2 Electronic navigation systems course
Watchkeeping officers undergo five weeks (150 hours) of basic training in

the principles and use of radar and the other electronic navigation aids, prior to obtaining their first certificate of competency. The use of the simulator and the instruments room ensures that the trainees see these aids clearly demonstrated in the operational condition and are given the opportunity to acquire practical experience in their use while navigating various types of ships. This course is also intensive and heavy demands are placed upon the trainees. About 120 officers will undergo this training during the next 12 months.

6.6.3 Other courses
The simulator is also used for:

(a) providing upgrading training in plotting techniques, coastal navigation and collision avoidance for officers of the Republic of Singapore Navy;
(b) providing Pre-Sea cadets with an appreciation of the use of radar and other electronic navigation aids;
(c) providing realistic risk of collision situations for Home- Trade officers taking the Radar Interpretation and Plotting Course; and
(d) providing the upgrading training necessary for servicing officers to revalidate their qualifications.

6.7 Conclusion

The MRNS 9000 electronic navigation systems simulator used by the Department of Nautical Studies is the most advanced marine navigation simulator in the region and enables the Department to provide its deck officer trainees with realistic training in the use of the latest navigation instruments fitted on board merchant ships. The teaching staff and the ship's officers attending the courses offered by the Department in preparation for sitting the certificate of competency examinations conducted by the Marine Department are the direct beneficiaries of the foresight of the Polytechnic in ensuring that the best of equipment is provided for the training of Singapore's ships' officers. Effective use of this equipment will help to ensure that the ships are navigated in accordance with the highest standards necessary to protect safety of life and property at sea and to preserve the marine environment.

Chapter 7
Pictorial Interfaces

Philip Barker, Karim Manji and L.K. Tsang
Teesside Polytechnic and The Lee Wai Lee Institute, Hong Kong

7.1 Introduction

There is an old proverb, possibly Chinese, which claims that 'a picture is worth 10,000 words'. Although it is difficult to justify this claim on purely computational grounds, some evidence to support it has been presented (in the context of problem solving activity) in a paper by Larkin and Simon (1987). There is also some evidence to suggest that for certain types of cognitive activity (such as category matching) the time taken to understand pictures is less than the time needed to understand words (Potter and Faulconer (1975). These findings would suggest two possible important outcomes with respect to the utility of pictures as a communicative resource. First, that pictorial forms offer a high bandwidth mechanism of communication. Second, that pictures and images may be easier to assimilate than text and other forms of the printed word. Because of their importance as a communication aid this chapter is concerned with the use of both conventional paper-based images and electronic imagery for initiating and developing instructional human-computer dialogues. Further descriptions and discussions of the relative merits of images as a communication mechanism have been presented by Adams (1987), Kindborg and Kollerbaur (1987) and Barker (1989).

Before discussing pictorial communication in more detail it is important to understand the role that books have played as an instructional resource. Through the printed word, books have always been the mechanism by which the results of human endeavour have been documented for posterity (Barker, 1986). As a learning resource conventional books have many attractive features: they are portable, easy to produce and relatively low cost. However, they also have many limitations. Because they are essentially static objects, they are not in any way interactive. Furthermore, they cannot easily be updated and they are not able to adapt or modify their behaviour dynamically in order to meet the particular requirements of individual users. Some of the limitations of conventional books were aptly summarized by the remark that Alice made prior to embarking on her adventures in Wonderland':

'And what is the use of a book,' thought Alice, 'without pictures or conversation?'
Lewis Carroll (1865)

Due to the limitations of conventional books many attempts have been made to fabricate new types of book using the various media that are now emerging from developments being made by research into new storage technologies. Frequently, the term 'electronic book' is used to describe developments in this area. As we shall discuss later in this chapter, pictorial interfaces play an important role in the development of such books.

The concept of an electronic book was introduced many years ago in a paper authored by Goldberg (1979). This paper outlined some early research that was conducted at the Xerox Park Learning Research Centre towards the realisation of new types of learning resource. Known as the 'Dynabook' concept this work envisaged a new type of highly portable reactive learning resource capable of supporting text, sound and animation. Many of the ideas embedded in this research are at last starting to appear in the portable personal computer systems that are now becoming available commercially. The concepts and ideas embedded in the Dynabook are also of significant importance with respect to the new types of optical and electronic book that are currently gaining significant popularity (Yankelovich *et al*, 1985; Weyer and Borning, 1985; Conklin, 1987; Marchionini and Shneiderman, 1988). We have been exploring the possibility of using low-cost electronic books in order to provide interactive learning environments within which to implement informatory and exploratory computer-based learning (Barker, 1987; Barker and Manji, 1988a; 1988b). Our approach to the realization of these books is described in more detail in the following sections of this chapter.

7.2 Types of pictorial interface

Prior to any discussion of the nature of our electronic books we need to describe the various types of pictorial interface that are presently used to facilitate human communication with computers. Currently, there is much interest in the use of pictures as a communication medium – both for the output of information to users (via computer graphics) and for its input from them (using image and picture analysis techniques). One appealing aspect of the use of pictures as a communication medium is that (in contrast to text) they offer a highly parallel mechanism for information transfer. For this reason, as we have suggested in the previous section, they provide a relatively high bandwidth communication facility. Furthermore, there is a growing volume of evidence (Barker and Skipper, 1986) to suggest that graphical communication methods based upon the use of such facilities as windows (Norman *et al*, 1986), icons (Gittins, 1986) and comics (Kindborg and Kollerbaur, 1987) can provide powerful and efficient mechanisms for the facilitation of human-computer interaction.

The general role of a pictorial interface is illustrated schematically in

Figure 7.1 (Barker, Najah and Manji, 1987). This diagram depicts the idea of human-computer communication taking place through the medium of either static images, reactive images or time varying dynamic (possibly highly animated) imagery. By reactive, we mean that the content of the images changes as a result of human interaction with them. In Figure 7.1 the expression 'multi-dimensional time varying ...' refers to the idea of having a system containing one or more screens each of which may be segmented in various ways. The information contained within each of the various screen segments may be static, reactive or time varying.

A variety of techniques is available for generating pictorial forms on a screen. This screen may take the form of a CRT, a plasma panel, or an opaque surface such as that of a digitizer, graph plotter or laser printer.

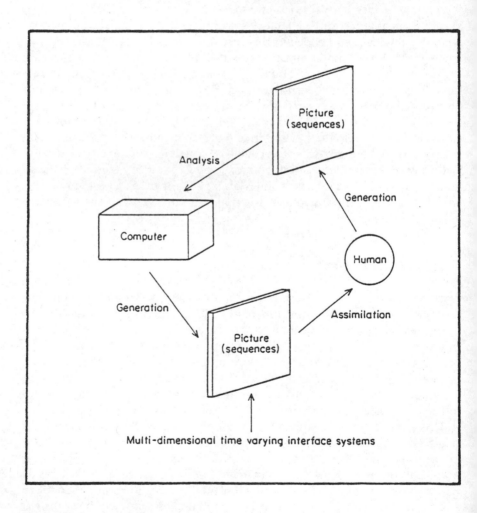

Figure 7.1 *The function of pictorial interfaces*

Once an image has been produced many different kinds of technology and device are available to facilitate human interaction with it. Some of the more popular picture production methods and interaction devices to support human-computer communication through the medium of pictures are listed in Table 7.1. The various technologies represented in the two columns contained in this table can be combined in many different ways to facilitate pictorial communication with a computer.

Table 7.1 *Techniques for image production and interaction*

Image Production	Interaction Devices
Computer graphics	Touch screens
Video images	Light pen
Image projection	Mouse
Photographs	Tracker Ball
Diagrams	Digitiser
Sketches	Concept keyboard
Gestures	Sonic glove
	Joy Stick

The nature of the various interaction devices, techniques for using them, and their relative merits are described in more detail elsewhere (Barker, 1989 – this book also documents appropriate descriptions of the various image production methods listed in Table 7.1).

The peripheral devices listed in Table 7.1 can be interfaced in various combinations to an appropriate base microcomputer in order to produce a variety of different types of interactive instructional workstation. Some examples of workstations that employ pictorial interfaces have already been described previously in Chapter 3. Therefore, in the remainder of this chapter we concentrate on how these devices can be used for the production of new types of electronic book (Barker and Manji, 1988a; Manji, 1988).

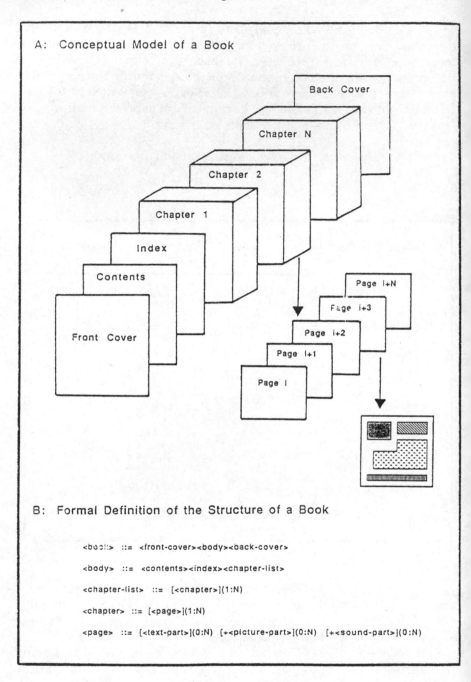

Figure 7.2 *The logical structure of a book*

7.3 New books for old

A book may be informally defined as being a corpus of textual or graphical material that is logically subdivided into chapters. Chapters are, in turn, divided (both logically and physically) into pages. Pages may contain just text, sound or pictures; alternatively, they may embed a combination of each of these communicative forms. Pages are normally numbered sequentially and an index is provided that enables the rapid and effective location of the material that is embedded in particular sections of the book. The logical structure of a book is depicted schematically in Figure 7.2. It is possible to represent the structure of a book of this type quite precisely, in mathematical terms, by means of an appropriate formal notation (Barker and Manji, 1988c). Such a definition is presented in Figure 7.2.

The above logical description of a book makes no mention of the medium that is used for its publication – that is, its physical structure. However, it assumes that the medium selected for its fabrication may be used to encode text, sound and graphic forms and that no distinction is made between any of these mechanisms of communication. The above description would therefore fit a conventional book (that is printed on paper) but it could also be construed to include the other forms of book that were introduced in the previous section. Books that fit the description given above but which depend upon the use of other media for their realization are often referred to as 'surrogate books'. A variety of different media might be used for the fabrication of such books: floppy discs, hard discs, optical storage facilities, and so on. In this chapter, we shall be primarily concerned with surrogate books that are based upon the use of optical discs (both video and CDROM) for their construction. Three basic types of surrogate book will be described: static picture books, moving picture books and multi-media books. The first and second of these are used primarily to support informatory computer assisted learning. The third is used to provide interactive learning environments to support exploratory CAL within particular target domains. Further details of each of these approaches to CAL are given elsewhere (Barker, 1987).

7.3.1 Static picture books

A static picture book is essentially a collection of pictures that are logically/ physically associated with each other for some particular purpose. For example, they may share a common attribute or they may, as a group, be needed in order to perform some specific teaching function. The conceptual model that a user requires in order to use a static picture book is illustrated in Figure 7.3. In this example the book just consists of a front-cover, a collection of static pictures and a back-cover (Manji, 1988). Such a book could be fabricated in a variety of ways: using paper-based images (in the form of a conventional workbook), by means of static images taken from a video disc or CDROM, or by using high-speed, real-time computational graphics. One limitation of the static picture book shown in Figure 7.3 is its lack of chapter structure (Noble, 1988). However, giving the book a chapter

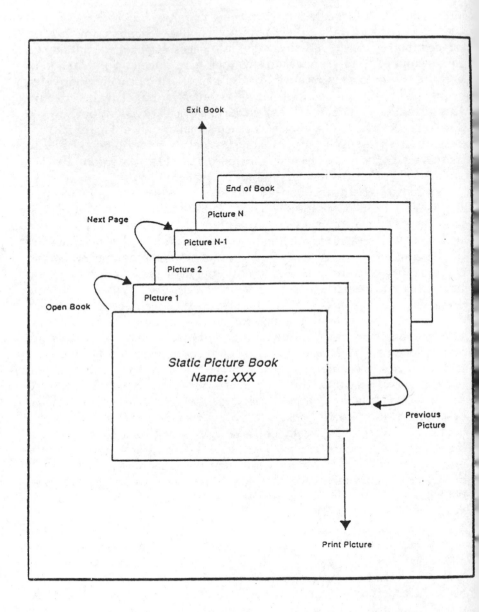

Figure 7.3 *Conceptual model for a static picture book*

structure would not be difficult; this would then allow collections of static images in a common theme to be brought together. For example, a static picture book on the theme of 'animals' could consist of individual chapters containing pictures of cats, dogs, birds, and so on.

It is important to note that in order to manipulate the pages contained in a static picture book various control options need to be made available to the user. These are denoted by labelled arrows in Figure 7.3. These control options can be embedded within menu structures that are either associated with the overall book or which operate on particular pages of the book – depending upon how it is designed. Some of the ways of implementing end-user book manipulation operations are described in more detail elsewhere (Manji, 1988).

7.3.2 Moving picture books

A moving picture book is one which contains animated images rather than static pictures. These animated images may be produced by computational means or by retrieving them from a suitable storage medium such as video disc or CDROM. In the latter case images are presented to the user in rapid succession in order to create the illusion of movement at slow, normal or high speed – depending upon the rate of image display.

The conceptual model that a user requires in order to use a moving picture book is illustrated in Figure 7.4. Like the conceptual model for a static picture book, the model for a moving picture book also contains a front-cover and a back-cover. Between these covers there exists a chapter structure similar to that depicted in Figure 7.2. Each chapter consists of an image sequence dealing with some particular topic or theme. If need be, a 'section' and/or 'sub-section' structure could be super-imposed within the chapter structure.

As can be seen from Figure 7.4, various control options are available to the user in order to allow him/her to manipulate the contents of the moving picture book. For example, particular image sequences can be selected and played; while a chapter is being viewed, images can be 'frozen' on the screen and examined in detail. Once an image has been frozen its preceding or succeeding image can be examined; alternatively, full-motion viewing (forwards or backwards) can be re-instated.

7.3.3 Multi-media books

As its name suggests, a multi-media electronic book consists of text, sound and images that are brought together in any desired combination in order to produce a particular instructional effect. The page layout of this type of book is illustrated schematically in Figure 7.2. In this diagram, the shaded areas within the sample page represent various contributions from the different textual, sonic and graphical communication channels that the author has elected to use. The way in which this type of page structure is represented in a bit-mapped CRT screen has been previously illustrated in Figure 3.3.

As well as containing static images, a multi-media book may also contain

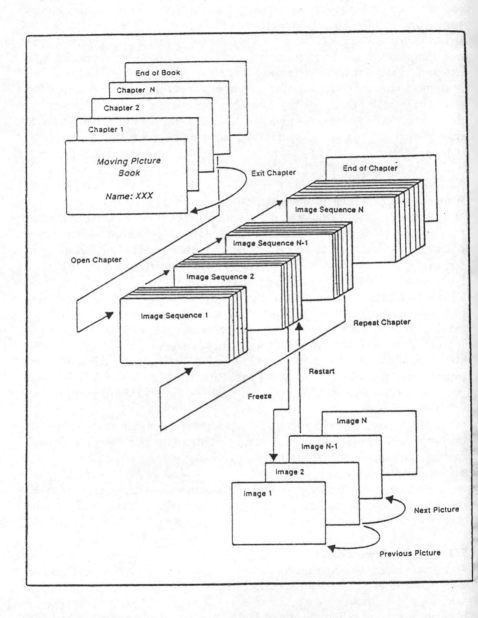

Figure 7.4 *Conceptual model for a moving picture book*

animation effects and moving pictures. The way in which these effects are produced is discussed in more detail in Section 7.4. An important tool for organizing the layout of pages is a window management facility (Barker, 1989). This enables a CRT screen to be segmented in various ways with each window performing a different function. For example, one window may contain some text, a second may contain a static image and a third window might be used to present a full-motion movie display. Of course, sound cannot actually 'be seen'. Therefore, as well as the sound narrations that accompany other windows, additional sonic effects can be produced through the use of icons which, when touched or selected with a mouse, cause their associated sound effect to be produced.

In many types of electronic book it is convenient to regard a page of the book as being composed of a base image to which are added contributions from various overlays (Barker and Singh, 1985). Such an arrangement is illustrated schematically in Figure 7.5. The overall page, as the user sees it, is therefore composed of the sum of the contributions from each of the 'logical screens' that is available. Of course, each contribution can be turned on or off or can be changed in various ways under program control. An 'overlay manager' is therefore a useful facility for organizing and controlling the structure and composition of multi-media books that are built using the overlay model. Further details of this type of facility are given elsewhere (Manji, 1988; Noble, 1988).

7.4 Some authoring techniques

Creating the types of electronic book that have been described in the previous section involves three basic activities: first, bringing together the multi-media information that the book is to contain, second, linking this information together in various ways, and third, designing appropriate interfaces that will enable users to access and manipulate the stored information. A variety of different types of authoring facility currently exists to enable these three activities to be undertaken with varying degrees of ease and efficiency. Some of these, such as HyperCard, PROPI and PC/PILOT are briefly discussed in Chapter 13. The remainder of this chapter is therefore devoted to providing an overview of some of the various methods that are currently used for creating pictorial interfaces for use within interactive multi-media CAL systems of the type described in the previous section.

7.4.1 Creating static pictures
Within a CAL system the most obvious way of generating both CRT-based and paper-based images is through the application of some sort of graphics programming facility. In order to cater for this requirement, many conventional computer programming languages are able to call upon libraries of graphics routines that can be used to generate a variety of different types of pictorial form. In contrast, some languages (such as

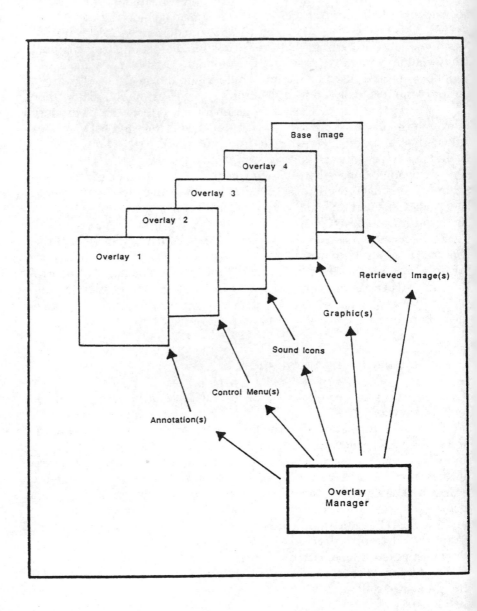

Figure 7.5 *Logical screen structure for a CRT display*

BASIC) allow the programmer to achieve similar effects through extensions that have been made to their built-in command sets. Some author languages and authoring systems also have their own built-in graphics primitives. For example, PC/PILOT makes available a 'turtle graphics' facility; this is a set of primitive commands that control the position and movement of an imaginary CRT-based turtle. This turtle draws coloured lines and shapes as it moves about the screen under program control and PC/PILOT also provides facilities for creating and manipulating 'sprites' – thereby enabling simple animation to be created.

Unfortunately, the above approach to producing pictorial interfaces requires the designer to acquire quite sophisticated programming skills. This is not always desirable or indeed necessary since other ways of producing pictorial interfaces are available. One particular alternative approach is to use some form of picture creation package that allows designers to generate images interactively either on a CRT screen or by means of a high resolution digitizer. Depending upon the type of pictorial interface that is to be produced two basic types of package might be employed. The first type involves using a library of simple graphic forms (that are resident on a magnetic disc or a CDROM) from which the designer can select and copy image components; these can then be assembled into the desired CRT screen image. The second approach involves using a drawing or sketching package that allows users to produce free-hand pictures on a CRT screen using a stylus or a mouse.

Of course, an even simpler method of producing pictorial interfaces is to use some form of image acquisition facility that enables (a) existing paper-based artwork to be entered into the computer, or (b) images derived from a video camera or TV broadcast to be entered into the computer system and processed in various ways. Low-cost image scanners are now available that enable images on paper to be scanned very rapidly and then stored in digital form inside the computer. Video images can also be easily and rapidly digitized and then stored in digital memory. Once the images are available in digital form within the computer they can be modified and processed in different ways using a variety of sophisticated techniques. Typically, they can be 'touched up' (using a pixel-level editor) or they can be 'cut up' in various ways in order to produce image segments. Subsequently, these image segments can be 'pasted' into different parts of a CRT display screen in order to produce quite sophisticated pictorial interfaces.

Figure 7.6 shows some examples of the sorts of pictorial interface that it is possible to generate using the types of technique that were described above. These interfaces were produced using an interactive instrument design and teaching package called LabVIEW (National Instruments, 1987). LabVIEW is an acronym for Laboratory Virtual Instrument Engineering Workbench.

Figure 7.6A shows the front-panel of a simple function generator. The on/off status of the instrument, the type of waveform that it generates, and the frequency/amplitude of the waveform are all controlled interactively by means of cursor selection operations. This involves using a mouse

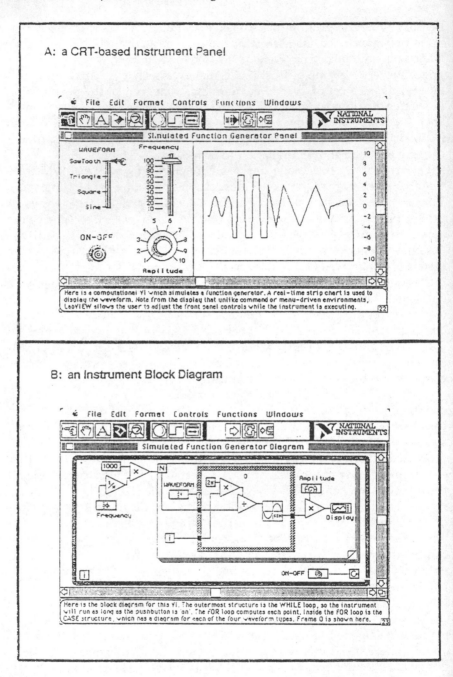

Figure 7.6 *Pictorial interfaces to a CAL package*

C: Front Panel for a Voltmeter

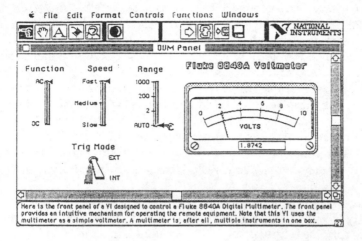

Here is the front panel of a VI designed to control a Fluke 8840A Digital Multimeter. The front panel provides an intuitive mechanism for operating the remote equipment. Note that this VI uses the multimeter as a simple voltmeter. A multimeter is, after all, multiple instruments in one box.

D: Front Panel for a Spectrum Analyser

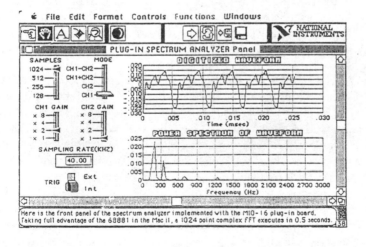

Here is the front panel of the spectrum analyzer implemented with the MIO-16 plug-in board. Taking full advantage of the 68881 in the Mac II, a 1024 point complex FFT executes in 0.5 seconds.

Figure 7.6 *Continued*

to move a cursor around the CRT screen and then 'clicking' the mouse button in order to make a selection. In Figure 7.6A the cursor takes the form of a 'hand' that is currently pointing to the SawTooth option of the waveform menu. As the instrument operates a real-time strip-chart recorder (shown on the right of the instrument panel) is used to display the nature of the signal being generated. The electronic block diagram for this instrument is shown in Figure 7.6B. This diagram is produced using the various tools and constructs available from the horizontal menu bars that run along the top of the CRT screen.

Two further examples of simulated instruments that have been created using the LabVIEW package are illustrated in Figures 7.6C and 7.6D. The first of these shows the front-panel of a digital voltmeter while the second shows the panel for a two-channel spectrum analyser. Through pictorial interfaces of the type shown in Figure 7.6 it is possible to create quite 'realistic' simulations of electronic instruments at relatively low cost.

7.4.2 Creating animation

A variety of ways exist for creating simple animation effects. One of these, the use of sprites, was briefly mentioned in the previous section. Essentially, a sprite is a graphic object that can be moved around a CRT screen under program control. Normally, in a typical animation, many sprites would be simultaneously active – each contributing to the overall pictorial effect. Unfortunately, producing animation using conventional programming techniques is much more difficult than producing static images. Appropriate animation tools are therefore required in order to remove the need for any complicated programming. One such tool, called VideoWorks (Hayden Software, 1985), is illustrated schematically in Figure 7.7.

VideoWorks enables as many as 24 different graphic objects (or sprites) to be animated simultaneously. It also caters for sonic effects using a special sound effects channel. Through a range of graphics tools (such as CheapPaint and Quick-Draw) it allows the creation of artwork for inclusion in animations. Editing facilities are also available (using the score window – which is described below) to allow animation sequences to be manipulated in various ways using 'cut' and 'paste' operations.

VideoWorks allows the pictorial interface designer to use two basic types of animation technique: real-time recording and frame-by-frame animation. In the first of these, a particular object to be animated is dragged around the screen using a mouse; as the object is moved about the CRT its position is recorded and the motion of the object can then be 'replayed'. Frame-by-frame animation involves creating an individual frame of animation (containing its component objects), recording the frame; changing its composition in order to create a new frame, recording the new frame, and so on. VideoWorks also provides an 'in-betweening' facility which allows the designer to specify the starting and ending positions of a sprite and the number of frames needed to describe its movement across the screen; the intervening frames are then filled-in by the VideoWorks

A: VideoWorks Control Panel and Windows

B: Using a Pre-defined Library of Images

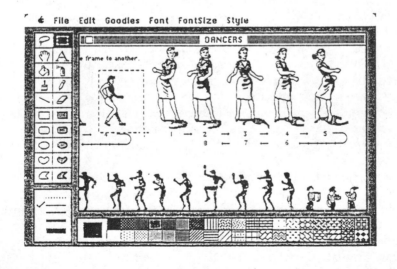

Figure 7.7 *Tools for producing animation*

program. A range of tools is available to support the operations involved in using each of the above approaches to creating animation. Some of these tools are illustrated in Figure 7.7A.

Figure 7.7A shows the basic VideoWorks control panel and some of the windows that it provides in order to allow users to create and control sequences of animation. The control panel is located in the top right-hand corner of the screen. It provides the same types of control functionality that one might expect to find on an ordinary video cassette recorder. Along the top (going from left to right) there are buttons for rewind, single-step backwards, stop; single-step forwards; play forward; add; and repeat. The add button allows animation sequences to be inserted at selected locations in a score (by pushing subsequent frames to the right). The repeat-key can be used to cause the animation to run in an endless loop by automatically re-starting the display from frame 1 upon termination. Going from left to right, the second row of switches/indicators perform the following functions: control of stage (or screen) colour (black or white); setting of the on/off status of the sound track; display and specification of the play-back speed (frames/second) using the horizontal slider-bar; and the provision of a frame number indicator. On the right of the control panel is a channel indicator/selector (a 6 x 4 matrix of small squares) that indicates which animation channels are currently occupied and currently active. Beneath this grid of squares are two numbers (the range indicator) that denote the beginning and ending frame numbers of the selected animation sequence.

Along the bottom of the screen shown in Figure 7.7A is the horizontal menu of 'cast members' that are used in a particular animation. There can be up to 256 members. These are organized into four banks (labelled A, B, C and D) each containing 64 members (8 rows of 8). In Figure 7.7A the cast contains some static images of a frog and a plant. The currently selected image is always shown surrounded with a bold black square frame. After selection an individual cast member can be dragged onto the 'stage' using the mouse and then animated using the techniques described above. The animation sequence represented in Figure 7.7A is intended to depict two frogs hopping across the CRT screen from left to right. Normally, when the animation is running, each of the windows and the control panel would be made invisible.

The cast members in an animation can be generated using four basic methods: by using the CheapPaint easel, by means of Quick-Draw primitives (shown on the extreme right of the cast members menu), by using an external graphics package such as MacPaint and then importing the images into VideoWorks, and by using a pre-defined library of graphics images. This latter approach is illustrated schematically in Figure 7.7B. In this diagram the selection tool (shown high-lighted in the second column of row 1 in the vertical menu bar) has been used to select an image component from an artwork library – a male dancer stepping backwards. This image component (which is surrounded by a broken rectangle) can be copied into a VideoWorks CheapPaint easel and then stored at an appropriate location in the cast member menu. It can then be used as a normal animation character.

The final window illustrated in Figure 7.7A is the score. It contains all the information that the author needs in order to edit animation sequences in a variety of different ways. Each column represents one frame of animation and each row represents one channel – there are 24 video channels (labelled A through X) and, at the top, one sound channel (labelled with a loudspeaker icon). The priority of a sprite is determined by the value of its channel letter – later letters denoting higher priority. When sprites pass each other on the screen these in later channels pass in front of those in earlier channels. Sound effects can be introduced into the score by making selections from the Sfx menu option (see the top right-hand corner of the screen) and entering appropriate cues in the sound-track channel. Depending upon the way in which the display switches are set (these can be seen in the top left-hand corner of the score window) each of the two rows that compose a channel provides information about cast members and other aspects of the animation – such as relative movement, the Efx mode selected, the origin of cast members and so on. The Efx (special effects) menu options are used to specify the way in which two images interact with each other when their paths cross on the screen.

Packages such as VideoWorks represent very powerful authoring tools for the creation of animated pictorial interfaces to multi-media CAL software. Their utility lies in the fact that they can substantially reduce the amount of effort needed to produce professional animations for use in an instructional context. An example of the way in which simple animation can be used to improve the effectiveness of a human-computer interface (and hence, the quality of learning) is illustrated in the CRT screen dumps presented in Figure 7.8. These represent the status of a chess board during a student's interaction with a CAL package for learning how to play chess (Hayden Software, 1984). During the game the student moves the chess pieces around the CRT-based board using a mouse-driven cursor dialogue. This involves moving the cursor over the chess piece that is to be moved and then dragging the item to its new location. The moves made by the computer are recorded and displayed in the window depicted in the top right-hand corner of the screen. The window beneath this is used to indicate the program's move search performance for the current and previous moves. Within this interactive game a variety of parameters can be set in order to select the level and speed of the game.

7.5 Conclusion

This chapter has attempted to demonstrate the importance of pictorial interfaces to CAL courseware. Two basic types of interface have been considered: those composed of static images and those that consist of dynamic/reactive moving pictures based upon the use of animation

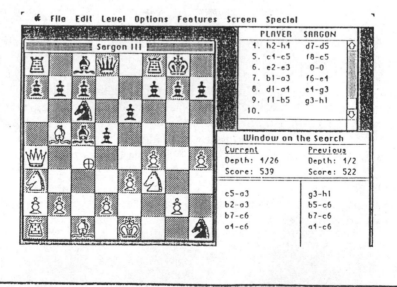

Figure 7.8 *Tools for producing animation*

techniques and various sorts of image store. Because of the extremely high communication bandwidth associated with pictorial interfaces they can be used to create a variety of new types of interactive learning resource. Collectively, in this chapter such resources have been referred to as 'electronic books'. Three basic types of electronic book have been briefly described: static picture books, moving picture books, and multi-media books. Some techniques for authoring electronic books have been outlined – particular emphasis being given to the use of static images and the creation of animation. Several examples of quite sophisticated pictorial interfaces have also been presented in order to illustrate their potential and their ease of use.

7.6 References

Adams, D.M., (1987). Communicating with electronic images: transforming attitude, knowledge and perception, *British Journal of Educational Technology*, 18(1), 15-21.

Barker, P.G., (1986). Video discs in libraries, *The Electronic Library*, 4(3) 166-176.

Barker, P.G., (1987). The potential of optical media for creating adult learning opportunities, *Bulletin Leren Van Volwassenen*, 20, 165-180.

Barker, P.G., (1989). *Basic Principles of Human-Computer Interface Design*, Hutchinson Education, London.

Barker, P.G. and Manji, K.A., (1988a). New books for old, paper presented at ETIC '88, Plymouth Polytechnic, to appear in *Programmed Learning and Educational Technology*, Kogan Page, London.

Barker, P.G. and Manji, K.A., (1988b). Paradigms, metaphors and myths for interactive learning, paper submitted to the British Computer Society's HCI '88 Conference, University of Manchester.

Barker, P.G. and Manji, K.A., (1988c). The use of formal methods for the specification of human-computer dialogues, paper presented at the Formal Methods Workshop, Teesside Polytechnic, 18th-19th July, 1988.

Barker, P.G., Najah, M. and Manji, K.A., (1987). Pictorial communication with computers, *International Journal of Man-Machine Studies*, 27, 315-336.

Barker, P.G. and Singh, R., (1985). A practical introduction to authoring for computer assisted instruction. Part 5: PHILVAS, *British Journal of Educational Technology*, 16(3), 218-236.

Barker, P.G. and Skipper, T., (1986). A practical introduction to authoring for computer assisted instruction. Part 7: Graphic Support for CAL, *British Journal of Educational Technology*, 17(3), 194-212.

Carroll, L., (1865). *Alice's Adventures in Wonderland*, modern version (1986) Puffin Books, London.

Conklin, J., (1987). Hypertext: an introduction and survey, *IEEE Computer*, 20(9), 17-41.

Gittins, D., (1986). Icon based human-computer interaction, *International Journal of Man-Machine Studies*, 24, 519-543.

Goldberg, A., (1979). Educational uses of a Dynabook, *Computers and Education*, 3(4), 247-266.

Hayden Software, (1984). *SARGON-III – The Ultimate in Computer Chess*, Hayden Software, Lowell, MA.

Hayden Software, (1985). *VideoWorks Reference Manual*, Hayden Software, Lowell, MA.

Larkin, J.H. and Simon, H.A., (1987). Why a picture is (sometimes) worth ten thousand words, *Cognitive Science*, 11, 65-99.

Kindborg, M. and Kollerbaur, A. (1987). Visual languages and human-computer interaction, 175-187 in *Proceedings of the British Computer Society's HCI '87 Conference*, University of Exeter, 7-11th September, 1987.

Manji, K.A., (1988). Pictorial communication with computers, draft PhD thesis, Teesside Polytechnic, County Cleveland, UK.

Marchionini, G. and Shneiderman, B., (1988). Finding facts versus browsing knowledge in hypertext systems, *IEEE Computer*, 21(1), 70-80.

National Instruments, (1987). *LabVIEW Users' Guide*, National Instruments, Austin, Texas, USA.

Noble, B.J., (1988). A user interface management system for electronic books, MSc dissertation, Teesside Polytechnic, County Cleveland, UK.

Norman, K.L., Weldon, L.J. and Shneiderman, B., (1986). Cognitive layouts of windows and multiple screens for user interfaces, *International Journal of Man-Machine Studies*, 25, 229-248.

Potter, M.C. and Faulconer, B.A., (1975). Time to understand pictures and words, *Nature*, 253, 437-438.

Weyer, S.A. and Borning, A.H., (1985). A prototype electronic encyclopedia, *ACM Transactions on Office Information Systems*, 3(1), 63-88.

Yankelovich, N., Meyrowitz, N. and van Dam., A., (1985). Reading and writing the electronic book, *IEEE Computer*, 18(10), 15-30.

Chapter 8
Satellite Broadcasting

Gareth Jones
Teesside Polytechnic

8.1 Introduction

Satellites are becoming an increasingly popular way of transmitting educational material from one location to another (Christian-Carter, 1988; Oklahoma State University, 1988). The basic ideas underlying a satellite transmission system are illustrated schematically in Figure 8.1 (Barker and Steele, 1983; Barker, 1986). This diagram depicts the use of a satellite in order to fulfil two basic functions (a) the bi-directional electronic inter-connection of geographically remote sites (via suitable ground stations), and (b) the uni-directional dissemination of instructional programs (tele-software) via a broadcasting agency. Because of their future potential importance within education this chapter is intended to provide a brief outline description of satellites and some of the ongoing educational projects in which they are used.

The word satellite is derived from the French, meaning 'attendant body'. Very simply a satellite is a transmitting and receiving device situated above the earth. According to Long (1982) there are three main types:

(1) Point-to-point satellites that relay messages from one large relay station to another. These use expensive ground stations.
(2) Distribution satellites that operate on a higher frequency and generate more power. They relay information from large earth transmission stations to cable or broadcasting stations.
(3) Direct broadcast satellites (DBS). These have the power to broadcast information from the earth into inexpensive receiving terminals. One important characteristic of these satellites is their ability to bypass broadcasting and cable stations and serve institutions as well as individual homes. They are therefore well suited for use in distance learning.

Satellites are normally situated in one of two orbits above the earth. The low orbiting satellites circle at around 1000 km in a polar orbit covering the whole globe a number of times each day (they take on average about 100 minutes). They are used mainly for remote sensing of the land, sea or atmosphere. The high orbiting satellites, on the other hand, are in what is known as a geosynchronous orbit. In other words they appear to be

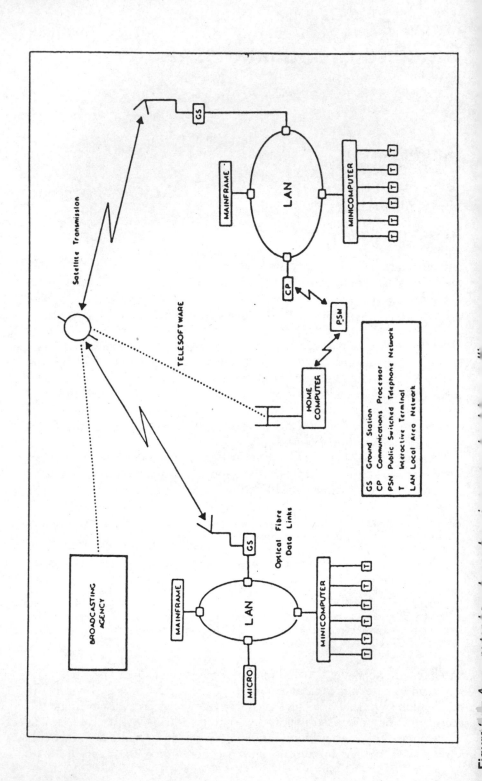

stationary with respect to the spinning earth. They must be launched to 35,900 km where their speed is about 21 km per second. For example, there are five such spacecraft spaced together evenly around the equator viewing weather conditions on a global basis (Reynolds, undated). These are the satellites that are used for transmitting and receiving information and cover a particular area all of the time. This area is known as a 'footprint'. For the Olympus satellite, which is the major concern of this chapter, the footprint is shown in Figure 8.2. All DBS should be in geosynchronous orbit otherwise the receiving and transmitting stations would need to be realigned constantly.

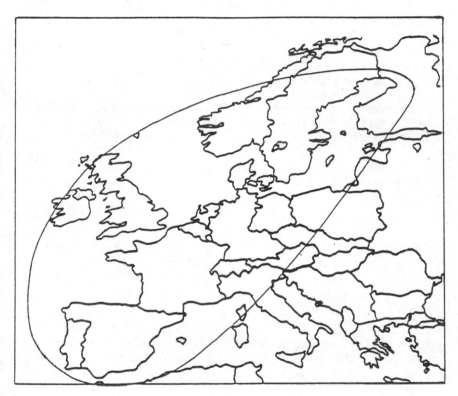

Figure 8.2 *The Olympus footprint*

8.2 Educational uses of satellites

There are four main uses of satellites in education (OLS News, 1988) namely (1) remote sensing, (2) data transfer, (3) broadcasting, and (4) videoconferencing.

Remote sensing refers to the observation of the earth from a distance via satellite, in particular, weather patterns. Such satellites can also be used for transferring data (for example, voice transmission), interrogating databases – as with the ERIC database, electronic mail, and computer conferencing.

Most people associate communication satellites with either surveillance or with broadcasting. At the moment there are two ways of receiving satellite broadcasts. Firstly, by being connected to a cable network. Secondly, by posessing a TVRO (TeleVision Receive Only) system. With the former, an earth station receives the broadcast from the satellite transmission via a large dish, which is subsequently fed into a fibre optic cable and is then received in the home. About 250,000 people are able to receive broadcasts in this way in the UK (*OLS News*, 1988).

For viewers not on the cable network the only alternative at the moment is a TVRO system. Such systems have a number of drawbacks (*OLS News*, 1988):

(a) they can cost between £800 – £1500;
(b) planning permission is required since the receiving dish that is needed is over 0.9 metre in diameter;
(c) the dish must be aligned accurately with the horizon – which is very difficult to do in an urban area or a wooded and mountainous region; and
(d) the dish must be fixed securely (motorized systems are available at extra cost).

However, with the advent of the new medium-to-high powered satellites (which provide direct broadcast) the prospect of receiving high quality broadcasts in the home becomes more of a reality. The size of the receiving dishes can be smaller (between 0.4 and 0.9 metre) and therefore do not need planning permission. Again, dishes will need to be motorized for accuracy of alignment. Up to now the major problem has been the lack of agreement over transmission standards. At the moment there are three types of standard used in Europe: (1) PAL (conventional TV), (2) D-MAC (Multiplexed Analogue Components), and (3) D2-MAC.

The MAC system has been specifically developed for the DBS satellites and provides improved quality of both sound and picture over the conventional PAL system of transmission. The MAC standard was accepted by the UK government as being the standard to adopt for UK satellite broadcast services (Cain *et al*, 1983). The problem is that there are currently two MAC standards. At the present moment D2-MAC seems to be the standard that is currently being favoured (*OLS News*, 1988; ESA, 1987a) although SES (the company running the Astra satellite) have compromised by saying that those using the 16 channels of Astra will be able to use all three standards.

The main advantage of adopting the D2-MAC standard is that there are more microchips available which are compatible with it. However, it is not as good as D-MAC since it only carries four sound channels (D-MAC carries eight hi-fi channels). It is possible that in the very near future microchips will be on sale to cope with both systems.

The main advantage in chosing a MAC standard transmission system is that a receiving station can receive broadcasts from the extensive overspill which will occur in many countries (ESA, 1987b; Pattie, 1987). However, the real problem will not be in the transmission systems used, but in unscrambling encrypted transmissions (*OLS News*, 1988). There are two reasons for encrypting broadcasts (as indeed data): firstly, some information will be confidential to closed user groups, and secondly, in order for the providers to cover costs and provide revenue. The fourth use of satellites in education is for videoconferencing or teleconferencing. This can be carried out at the moment via existing low powered satellites but the cost is prohibitive to education (OLS News, 1988). Not only is there a need for additional powerful uplinks in addition to the DBS receiving equipment, but, there are controls over these uplinks. Any UK group wishing to use this facility must first approach either British Telecom or Mercury. There are also other problems, such as the absence of encryption, technical standards, and the problems of copyright.

8.3 Satellites in education – some examples

Reference has already been made to some of the problems and possibilities for satellites in education. This section will address these issues with reference to some experiments that have already been conducted or are now taking place in selected parts of the world.

8.3.1 Australia

Australia took the decision to have its own communications satellite in 1979 (Gough *et al*, 1981). At the time there was some anxiety felt since it was thought that decisions on the system would be taken not on the basis of public interest but on the basis of technology. Gough *et al* suggested there should be adequate consultations and immediate action on the following considerations:

(a) Number of channels?
(b) Frequencies?
(c) Dedicated or shared channels?
(d) Charging for non-commercial users – full, discounted or nominal?
(e) Audio, visual or both?
(f) Two way or one way video?
(g) Controlled centrally?

They further stated that any decisions taken would have a considerable effect on the users' opportunities. Furthermore, it was suggested that the non-commercial user needed:

> ... a one-way video channel ... two-way audio channels using frequencies which permit the use of low-cost earth stations. Channels could be shared with other non-commercial users and charges should be heavily discounted or nominal.

Long (1982) has also addressed the issues of satellites to facilitate distance learning. He suggested that:

> Adult educators should be aware of the capacity of satellites, linking computers, to provide information networks of staggering size and complexity.

He does, however, temper this with caution and states that it is not a panacea, but could be very useful in facilitating learning particularly at a distance. He suggests a number of roles that satellites might play within education, these included their ability to bridge geographical distance between learners, support distance learning programs, bring experts together, stimulate non-traditional learning, facilitate computer assisted learning, provide learning and cultural networks, stimulate the storage and retrieval of knowledge, co-ordinate national education campaigns and enhance the quality of access to education.

Again it is emphasized that a communication satellite can provide two-way audio for teleconferencing, data channels to permit the use of computer assisted learning and a facsimile reproduction service. Long (1982) points to a number of difficulties, namely (a) the rising cost of software, (b) the preparation of suitable sofware, (c) the linking of hardware to existing systems needs planning and thought, and (d) satellite broadcasting requires extensive co-operation (Dean, 1985).

Gough *et al* (1981) concur with Long (1982) by stating that careful planning and collaboration with industry is essential. He does, however, point out that for the non-commercial user time is only provided because a satellite has surplus capacity. For the student, Gough *et al*, (1981) believe that:

> ... the planned and proper use of satellite and computer technology will actually enhance the educational experience of the student both by individualizing and personalizing it and by allowing students easier and more effective access to staff

However, some notes of caution are offered:

> ... performance of technology has not always realized its promise

> and ... technology fails most often when understanding of its appropriate uses is inadequate; when insufficient attention is paid to the development of the neccessary support and software systems; and when the users are not fully consulted about their needs.

The satellite system for Australia became operational in 1986 after many interruptions (Dean, 1985). It was planned to provide radio and television to remote parts of the country and to poor reception areas as well as voice, data transmission services, and an improved telephone system (Pritchard, 1980). Prior to the introduction of alternative systems of delivering television broadcasts, the sole provider was the Australian Broadcasting Corporation. With the introduction of a satellite system state specific programmes have been eliminated and funds for production and acquisi-tion of programmes have been cut (Dean, 1985). Up until 1985 only two states had been successful in providing a service (Victoria and Western

Australia). With tertiary education the picture is not so promising. Dean comments:

> ... although there is a high degree of enthusiasm for the use of television ... there is uncertainty as to the extent of future participation in a satellite based service.

The satellite system (AUSSAT) has no firm plans for permanent education services. However, the satellite debate has given rise to a number of issues (White, 1987):

(1) new communications technologies are being seen as integral to the delivery of educational services;
(2) a re-appraisal of existing communications services (telephone) is taking place; and
(3) AUSSAT's two tier price tarif (20 per cent discount for educational users).

The first of these issues might well have encouraged educational planners in Australia to evaluate their communication system needs – be they satellite based or not (White, 1987). A number of developments have occured which may be used to illustrate this. Two of these are briefly discussed below.

(A) Student-tutor communication in radio tutorials
This project which began in 1983 is based at Murdock University and the University of Western Australia. The system uses existing broadcast transmitters. A simple technical device (known as Subsidiary Communications Multiplex Operation) allows the use of existing broadcast transmitters to send a second programme along with the main FM broadcast (Barret, 1987). This allows the students to phone the tutor and the second allows the students to interrupt the conversation, but not to speak to each other. They found that students talked more, more students participated and talked for longer periods.

(B) School of the Air and AUSSAT
The School of the Air (SOTA) commenced in 1983. SOTA has been described as the 'Australian response to the educational needs' of children in remote areas (Kitt, 1987). Australian educators believed that satellite technology would somehow solve the problems encountered by isolated learners.

The Queensland Education Department above all recognized the problems encountered by those disadvantaged learners and accepted an offer to participate in a research project using the Australian satellite system. Their terms of reference were:

(a) to develop further the concept of the use of the satellite for SOTA;
(b) to introduce enhanced services through the integrated use of the satellite;
(c) to develop cost estimates; and
(d) to outline an evolutionary introduction of satellite services.

The researchers recognized that the introduction of new communications systems would require 'fundamental changes to the organization of services' and that it would be inappropriate to preserve existing services. Further, that any new designed system should take account of the needs of the learners (Kitt, 1987). They also recognized that a decentalized system would 'overcome the problems of distance learners'.

The family in the trial group will be supplied with a fully interactive satellite earth station which will allow for two way audio and receive only television (TVRO). The system will also be capable of data exchange and the process of paper making by the Primary Correspondence School in Brisbane will be transfered to SOTA possibly through the use of personal computers.

8.3.2 China

One of the most exciting projects recently reported in the literature is project 'Clear Skies'. This is a computer-based training project using Canadian technology to teach a first year honours course in computer science at East China Normal University in Shanghia. It may well become one of the world's largest open learning systems with a satellite based delivery facility with many hundreds of receiving sites across East China (Godfrey *et al*, 1987).

Software engineering principles have been applied to the 'design and production of cost- and time-effective courseware'. A new concept – CBT implementation engineering – covers the 'systematic process by which large scale CBT courseware is integrated into a specific learning environment'. This project has been tested in British Columbia and has proved to be successful. One of its major advantages is that different types of computers can be used.

The main objectives of the project was to see if courseware created for one country could function in a different educational and telecommunications environment and in another language.

At the end of 1985 three ICON workstations and one fileserver were installed at the Institute of Modern Educational Technology in Shanghai to deliver the course in question. Early in the following year seven workstations and a second fileserver were installed. A third network was planned for downtown Shanghai; this was connected to the other two networks via telephone and microwave links. According to Godfrey (1987), 'such networks could be located in a number of places across China, with each network being able to receive new courses and updates via satellite'. If the project is successful then it may form the first stage in the CBT teacher training programme in Shanghai.

8.3.3 Indonesia

Within Indonesia a distance education satellite system (SISDIKSAT) is being used to provide higher education via satellite. This project involves the linking of ten universities and the Directorate General of Higher

Education with a two channel audioconferencing network.

One of the problems facing Indonesia is that about 400,000 students apply to government institutions of higher learning and only 18 per cent of them can be accepted. The remainder either look for places in the private sector, try again , or give up altogether. In 1984 the Indonesian Open University (IOU) was set up to provide higher-level training for those unable to obtain a place, or to attend because of the vast distances involved – the Indonesian archipelago is about 3,000 miles long (Johari and Willard, 1986). The IOU uses the satellite audioconferencing system that is outlined below.

Based on the Papala B1 satellite SISDIKSAT uses two dedicated voice channels and a four-wire ground telephone system. One audio channel is used for audioconferencing while the second is used for facsimile, private telephone conversations, telewriting (via a graphics system), and as a backup audio channel. The system is low cost and line noise has been overcome by the installation of a gating system between classrooms and the central telephone exchanges at each site.

The main purpose of the link is for 'course sharing, seminars, audioconferences, information exchange and demonstrations' (Johari and Willard, 1986). Its main activity is in course exchange, particularly to identify courses that are greatly needed and courses they feel they are capable of delivering. Training programmes are also held on the techniques necessary for teaching via satellite. It offers courses to students, enrollments for which have increased rapidly (Johari and Willard, 1986). Each course is allotted two hours a week for instruction to students and one half-hour for meetings between the local tutors and the lead teacher. Because Indonesia spans three time zones the satellite system is used for 70 hours per week.

Johari and Willard offer a number of suggestions:

(a) long-term planning for satellite communication is essential – particularly for ensuring the quality and stability of telephone lines;
(b) equipment should be chosen in such a way that there are staff, time, money and skills available to support it; fax and graphics were more vulnerable to problems than audio;
(c) always pay more attention to 'software' than to 'hardware';
(d) group co-ordination and organization at the centre is vital;
(e) system has been very good for in-service training of staff; and
(f) there must be staff trained in the use of interactive audioconferencing in order to train other staff and to show its capabilities.

The three national projects described in this section illustrate the wide variation in the use of satellites in education. Many other problems and possibilities have been encountered through a review of the vast amount of literature relating to satellite broadcasting. Some of these will be explored in the next section which deals with a new European satellite (Olympus) and its proposed educational projects.

8.4 The European initiative

The Olympus satellite is scheduled to be launched at the beginning of 1989. It is a large communications satellite developed by the European Space Agency (ESA) in order to meet the requirements of the 1990s. These requirements include a need for high-power direct broadcast satellites. The first of these, Olympus-1, has been designed as a technology demonstrator. It is the world's largest and most powerful civilian three-axis-stabilized communications satellite (Pattie, 1987; ESA, 1987b).

General descriptions of the potential of Olympus have been given elsewhere (Christian-Carter, 1988; DELTA, 1987). The remainder of this section therefore concentrates on three issues: its technical specification, gaining access to it, and some examples of how it will be used.

8.4.1 Technical details

Olympus will have an in-orbit mass of 1.5 tonnnes and will be capable of generating up to 3.6 kW of electric power from its solar arrays which measure over 25 m from tip to tip (Pattie, 1987). The main difference between Olympus-1 and other communications satellites are the frequency bands used for transmission. It will use the higher frequency bands where competition and interference is less than at lower frequency band levels. It will operate in the 12/30 GHz band, experimenting in areas such as videoconferencing, videophone services, satellite switching, and a direct European television broadcast service. These high frequency bands are not as simple to use as the lower frequency bands (ESA, 1987b). For example, in periods of heavy rain atmospheric attenuation is so severe that, in order to achieve high standards, there appears to be only two solutions. Firstly, to have two antennae spaced several kilometers apart so that one or other would always receive reasonable reception, and secondly, to have many more earth stations, say, in every town.

The Olympus-1 has two DBS channels, one for Italian use and the other open to applicants from the rest of Europe. This is the channel available to educational users and is capable of simultaneously transmitting a wideband video signal (pictures and sound), a data stream, teletext, and about five audio channels (ETA, 1987). The DBS payload consists of two on-board transponders, the transmitters of which are tuned to three television channels. These have a capacity of 27 MHz each and are connected to two transmitting antenna on board the satellite. By combining the beams of both antenna it is possible to cover most of the European community. Signals to be used in these channels are sent up to the satellite by means of one or more earth stations or uplinks. A third antenna on board the satellite is dedicated to the reception of these signals (Gressman, undated).

The MAC transmission standard refered to earlier in this chapter has been developed to transmit combinations of moving, still, colour, and black/white pictures, sound and data. These can be combined into one complex signal. Sound and data are transmitted in packets of digital messages which can be arranged in a flexible manner, with the result that when there is no broadcast the transmission channel can be filled with data so that flow of data can be as great as 10 to 20 megabits per second. The equipment that is available for transforming these messages is the same as required for television programmes.

All transmissions will take place between the hours of midnight and 14.00 hrs and will be aimed at a very large number of receiving points either direct to the home, by community antennae or cable. Initially, there will be two uplink stations one at Redu (in the Belgium Ardennes) and the other a road transportable station which can operate anywhere within the Olympus receiving area. The providers of materials will be responsible for delivering the material in an electromagnetic form to the uplink stations (ESA, 1987b). This material can be sent directly or recorded on, say, magnetic tapes or cassettes. The formation of a proposed European Satellite Users Association (EUSA) would help to coordinate these functions.

Figure 8.3 shows the communication chain for the transport of materials (both audio and video) from the producer to the satellite uplink station. This material could be transported by either postal courier, microwave, cable or satellite circuits. The most important point to note is that each system will vary in its performance and that systems of delivery will vary between each country.

It is not the intention of ESA to provide any production facilities as these are seen to be the responsibility of the producers themselves (ESA, 1987b). As for the automatic recording of programmes, the MAC Packet standards (according to Gressman) 'contain the necessary provisions for programme identification'. The MAC Packet can also descramble programmes exclusively dedicated to a restricted category of users.

Depending upon whether they are domestic users or institutional users, receivers of programmes will need different equipment. Less sophisticated equipment is required by the former. The types of equipment needed is as follows:

(a) domestic users will require: receive-only antenna, a MAC standard receiving system, a television set, teletext, a VCR, an additional telephone and a printer;
(b) institutions will need: a receive-only antenna and also a receive/transmit antenna for broad-band reception and narrow-band transmission, a MAC standard receiving system, a television set, a separate sound decoder, an amplifier and a loudspeaker, teletext, a VCR/VTR, a sound recorder, a printer, an additional telephone, videotext, telex, telefax, and a microcomputer.

8.4.2 Access to the satellite

The Olympus satellite will be available to educational establishments for at least five years on a free basis. Each individually proposed experiment has initially been give two years with the possibility of an extension for an unspecified period of time (ESA, 1987a). However, each individual institution has to cover the other costs which include the costs of video production and transporting the tapes to the uplink stations as well as all the administrative costs which can be very high (ETA, 1987).

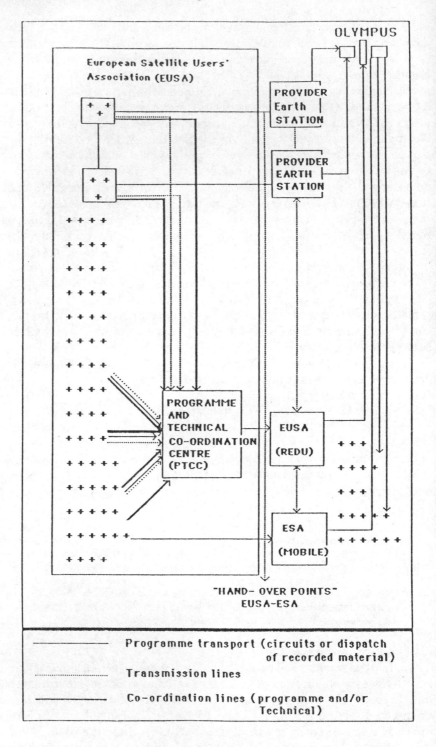

Figure 8.3 *Communication chain for the transport of materials*

All types of institutions were able to apply for time on the satellite for demonstration and experimentation. These included Education Authorities/Departments dealing with primary, secondary and tertiary education, institutions such as Polytechnics and Universities, and industrial establishments. Applications for time on the Olympus had to be finally submitted by April 1987. A total of 63 organizations were allocated time on the DBS payload. In addition to this, a total of 255 organizations were identified as being active supporters (ESA, 1988a).

About half the applications were for distance learning proposals. Satellite communication systems such as Olympus can offer opportunities to develop many new learning modes. At the same time existing institutional frameworks must be altered to accommodate these new learning modes if they are to make any impact in the quest for student autonomy in learning. Past experiments have largely had little impact on student learning modes since the structure of the educational system has not changed to accommodate it (Duke, 1988). According to Duke, it is crucial to employ satellite technology to explore the possibilities of modifying present provision and practices in order to:

(a) accommodate a greater degree of individualization of learning patterns;
(b) offer extensive elements of independent learning;
(c) offer supplementary and complementary schemes of distance learning; and
(d) to broaden conditions for access to tuition to extend openness of opportunity.

Experiences in other countries have shown that this is possible (see section 8.3). What is not known, in many cases, is how successful these experiments have been since most of these are recent. In my opinion, Europe cannot look to the experiences of the USA since cost structures are different. However, only recently the UK user groups for the Olympus project were presented with a possible list of industrial sponsors. Duke suggests that for any service to develop commercially it must have seed funding from some source.

It is worth mentioning here that it is not only the Olympus programme that seeks to stimulate innovation in education throughout Europe. There are at least three others:

(a) COMETT – one of its aims is to 'encourage links between universities and enterprises to improve professional and vocational training, and to train trainers using multi-media distance learning techniques';
(b) DELTA – whose main aim is to 'develop education and training by applying new technology'; and
(c) PACE – whose main aim is to 'support continuing education for engineers and is sponsored by international high technology companies and already delivers some of its courses by satellite' (ESA, 1988b).

Both PACE and COMETT have been granted some time on the Olympus. The organization acting for COMETT is Heriot Watt University in Edinburgh. This organization intends to demonstrate the concept of delivering advanced, high level, distance learning educational videotape in order to ascertain its effectiveness, whether live audio is practicable, and to see what the potential problems and the advantages and disadvantages of this method of delivery are.

Because of their common interests there is a need for close collaboration between each of these groups.

8.4.3 Proposed Olympus demonstrations/experiments

There were 82 proposals for the two telecommunications payloads. Seven of these were for education and training. The main interest of educational users of Olympus is to use the DBS payload to reach a large number of reception points (ESA, 1988a). The ESA has allocated about 40 per cent of all channel hours to the distance learning groups. Special liaison contractors were employed in order to find potential users of the satellite and to help them make their plans and to prepare submissions to the ESA. This procedure was necessary because very few potential users knew of the Olympus project or, for that matter, the potential of satellite communications (ESA, 1988a).

To date there has been very little documented information on the proposals that have been made. Therefore, what follows is a brief summary of some of the proposals that were accepted by the ESA in December 1987. The information below has been obtained from two sources (ESA, 1988a; 1988b).

It is important at this stage to mention that those wishing to use the Olympus for the transmission of data were requested to make a separate application for time. Data transmission can be a valuable adjunct to the delivery of video signals and can also be transmitted independently of the video signal (ESA, 1987b). The Olympus will use the new MAC standard for television signals (see section 8.2 above). It allows the digitization of television signals at data rates of up to 20 megabits per second. They will be received by a new generation of television set. The MAC television channel includes a channel for sound and data which can carry an effective rate of 750 kilobits per second or more. This is equivalent to the delivery of 300 pages of A4 text information per second.

Some 3000 hours a year will be available for education, with the UK user groups being allocated about a third of this. Nine other countries were allocated time. These were Belgium, France, Greece, Ireland, Netherlands, Norway, Spain, Sweden and West Germany. The 20 UK organizations that have been allocated time on the DBS payload by the ESA will experiment in areas which include distance learning, medical education, foreign languages and media studies.

Birkbeck College and Guys Hospital
This group will collaborate with the Universities of Paris and Geneva and the Max Plank Institue of Psychiatry in Munich to 'compare and transfer psychiatic and psychological expertise to professionals across Europe'. The topics will include the control of drug addiction and its relation to the spread

of AIDS, employment rehabilitation, and therapeutic skills.

This project will use video tapes of patients, superimposed text and graphics relating to test results and four multi-language audio channels. Since this will be a closed user group material will be encrypted.

SPACE

Satellite Programming for Adult Continuing Education (SPACE) is an umbrella group based at the Department of Extra-Mural Studies at London University. Its main aim is to 'demonstrate the use of satellites to promote health and well-being, together with professional and occupational education for adults'. Initially, it will only use one-way video, but eventually hopes to incorporate live feedback sessions using audioconferencing. There are many subgroups within this umbrella group, such as the Mental Health Film Council, Churches in Space and Coastal Zone Management. Both Birkbeck/Guys and SPACE hope to use the Live-Net optical fibre teaching network. Live-Net is an acronym for London Interactive Video Network (Farmer, 1988).

Clwyd TVEI Centre

This project has three main objectives. First, to experiment with international distance and open learning at secondary, tertiary and in-service education levels. Second, to use the satellite for transmitting local knowledge to provide English medium material relating to ordinary life, and thirdly (as a by-product) to provide a real market for students pursuing courses in video studies.

The Electronic University (Norway)

This group which is organized by Rogaland Mediesenter will produce programmes on offshore safety and health. These will also include petroleum exploration and production and the North Sea project. Of particular interest here is the hope that the Olympus project will develop into the proposed North Sea University.

Direct Business Satellite Systems Ltd (DBSS)

This company plans to demonstrate the concept of message broadcasting; this will include data, text, and voice. Messages will be sent via terrestial lines to a computer, encrypted, and then broadcast overnight. These messages would be received by one of DBSS's 'black boxes', then retransmitted to a computer, a fax machine or an audio recorder. The receiving equipment would be the normal DBSS equipment with a D-MAC standard system. The cost of the so called black boxes would be about £200.

EUREKA

The UK's Independent Broadcasting Authority, together with Bosch (Germany), Philips (The Netherlands), Thomson (France), and Thorn EMI

(UK) hope to develop a high definition television (HDTV) that is compatible with MAC. The screen will have over 1000 lines and will have a much broader shape of picture.

8.5 Conclusions

In this chapter an attempt as been made (a) to explore the educational potential of communication satellites, (b) to describe some experiences in satellite use from various parts of the world, and (c) to outline the European satellite initiative (Project Olympus). The Olympus satellite is to be launched in 1989 and will create considerable interest from the point of view of educational uses of satellites. Some details of this satellite have been presented and some of the experiments planned for the first two years of the project have been briefly outlined. The European community has made very little use of satellites for educational purposes compared with other nations such as the USA, Australia and India. This could be attributed to ignorance of the potential of such facilities but is more likely to be a consequence of the costs involved and the uncertainty of financial returns. The Olympus satellite has aroused considerable interest in the UK, particularly for activities that are 'experimental and developmental in nature allowing users to assess and evaluate the potential of satellites as an aid in the learning process' (Christian-Carter, 1988). It is significant that many of the proposed experiments on the Olympus will be concerned with exploring its potential for the delivery of distance learning (ESA, 1988a). It must be stressed here that the cost of involvement in satellite delivery of distance learning courses is still unknown and that collaboration between institutions, organizations and industry is essential if objectives are to be realized.

8.6 Bibliography

Barker, P.G., (1986). The changing face of computers in education, 29-31 in *National Electronics Review*, Volume 21, edited by C. Daubney, National Electronics Council, London.

Barker, P.G. and Steele, J,W., (1983). A practical introduction to authoring for computer-assisted instruction. Part I: IPS, *British Journal of Educational Technology*, 14(1), 26-45.

Barrett, J., (1987). Student – tutor communications in radio tutorials, *Programmed Learning and Educational Technology*, 21(4), 333-335.

Cain, J., *et al*, (1983). The implications of cable and satellites for social action and educational broadcasting, *Media Project, A Seminar Report*, BBC, London.

Christian-Carter, J., (1988). Satellites in education: a UK perspective, 251-257 in *Proceedings of ECCE '88, IFIP European Conference on Computers in Education*,

24-29 July, Lausanne, Switzerland, edited by F. Lovis and E.D. Tagg, North-Holland, Amsterdam.

Dean, T., (1985). Educational television and the satellite, *Media Information Australia*, 38, 103-105.

DELTA, (1987). Chapter X: Satellite-based Open Facility for Testing (SOFT), 351-409 in *Development of European Learning through Technological Advance – Initial Studies*, Commission of the European Communities, DG-XIII, Brussels, Belgium.

Duke, J. (1988). *Olympus in Perspective*, pages 1.1-1.11 in ESA (1988a).

ESA, (1987a). *Olympus Satellite Data Seminar Report*, Paris.

ESA, (1987b). *Olympus Satellite Users' Guide*, Issue 2.

ESA, (1988a). *Olympus, Education and Training in Europe*, A Seminar and Workshop on ESA Olympus Satellite for Education and Training in Europe, Avignon 13-15th April.

ESA, (1988b). *Olympus Satellite Newsletter*, No.1.

ETA, (1987). *Background Notes on Olympus*.

Farmer, M., (1988). Live-Net in education, *Computer Bulletin*, 4(3), 30-32.

Godfrey, D. Gong, S. Hart, R. Koorland, N. Smit, S. Project 'Clear skies': teaching computer science by computer based training and electronic messaging in China, *The Computer Journal*, 30(5), 469-474.

Gough, J.E., Garner, B.J., Day, K.D., (1981). Policy issues in planning for distance education using a domestic communications satellite, *Distance Education*, 2(1), 23-38.

Gressman, R., (undated report). European Institute of the Media.

Johari, R.A. and Willard, D.S., (1986). Higher education via satellite: The Indonesian Distance Education Satellite System, *International Review of Education*, 32(3), 325-330.

Kitt, J., (1987). Schools of the Air and AUSSAT: issues in planning, *Programmed Learning and Educational Technology*, 21(4), 318-323.

Long, P., (1982). The communications satellite as educational tool, *Convergence*, 15(1), 45-55.

Oklahoma State University, (1988). *Learning by Satellite, Arts and Sciences Teleconferencing Service*, Oklahama State University, Oklahoma, USA.

OLS News, (1988). Open Learning Focus: Satellites – A Life-line for Open Learning?, June.

Pritchard, C., (1980). Satellite race: Canada has inside track in bidding for Australia's $375 million project, *Financial Times of Canada*, October 20th.

Pattie, N., (1987). Thirty years of space communications, *Journal of the the Royal Television Society*, Sept/Oct, 243-248.

Reynolds, R., (undated). *Using Satellites in Education*, Griffen and George, pamphlet.

White, P.B., (1987). Australian educational communications in the satellite age: introduction, *Programmed Learning and Educational Technology*, 21(4), 307-309.

Chapter 9
Instructional Television for Continuing Education

Robert W. DeSio
National Technological University, USA

9.1 Overview

In the US over 60 billion dollars is spent annually by industry for training and education of employees. Continuing education has become an integral part of corporate strategies and in effect is a national strategy. Many corporations have built mini-campuses and universities have extended their missions in delivering courses to industry. The use of new communication technologies such as satellite transmission of live courses is being employed to minimize time away from the job. Today, this new partnership between higher education and industry uses the technology itself in fulfilling the education needs in a technology driven world. This paper gives specific examples of the use of instructional television both by industry and universities.

9.2 Background

The main characterization of the world today is one of change. At the center of this change is technology and it is creating profound impact on every human being on this planet. Technology is the primary driver and at the same time result. In this world of dynamic change and knowledge explosion, continuous life-long learning has become a dominant theme and is becoming an integral part of the personal human strategy. In this process, technology itself is playing a fundamental role in reaching out and bringing the best of education from many varied sources over great distances thanks to the marvels of computers and communications. No source is too remote and no learner is too isolated to fulfill the needs that we have for continuous education. In this chapter, I am going to discuss some of the exciting uses of educational technology – highlighting what is going on in the United States especially in the sensitive areas of higher technical education.

Experts tell us that as a result of the knowledge explosion, the learning that has taken place during the last 45 years is equivalent to that which took place during the prior 450 years. If we project that into the future, the past 45 years of learning will be comparable to what occurs during the next four and a half years. For those in technical areas the half life phenomena is a very real thing and the ultimate result is technical obsolescence, if education throughout one's professional life has not become a way of life. As a result business, industry, government and the military are preoccupied with finding educational solutions to meet the needs of their technical professionals.

As indicated earlier, change is the primary factor and cause which drives the quest for new knowledge. However, there are other important environmental factors which are worthy of mention. They would include international competition, specialization, and the growing interdisciplinary nature of the world today. The biggest educational challenge we have is to educate horizontally, professionals who are highly skilled vertically, in their specialized disciplines. Finally, with all this change, the product life cycle from invention to design, development and manufacture is getting shorter and shorter. This constant churning aggravates the needs for more and more education, to stay current with the state of the art.

In the United States the implications to industry are great. Continuous education has become an integral part of corporate strategies and is no longer relegated to the lower priorities of the company. In the past, the primary role the corporation played was in training its personnel to do the job. Such training centered on specific skills. Education, which was really generic and of strategic importance in a career sense to the individual was obtained in universities and other sources of learning before one was employed. Today, the vision and view is that education and training must continue on throughout professional life and is an integral part of the job. No longer does one separate the job from training and education, they go hand in hand. At the same time training and education should be delivered as much as possible to the individual's workplace so that there is minimum impact to the job. This is where educational technologies come to play, closing the physical distances so that the logical educational distances are mere microseconds away. The role of satellite communications in providing live, interactive education from great distances to the engineer in the laboratory becomes obvious. Experts have placed the annual education and training expenditures by American industry in excess of 60 billion dollars which is greater then all 3600 universities and colleges combined. This is a tremendous price but vital to the corporate goals and strategies.

There is another significant phenomena. Much of the education is being provided by the corporations themselves using their own technical professionals. This is the same generic education that might come from university campuses but the corporations have opted to perform themselves. There are good reasons for this when it does occur. In some cases corporate labs may be ahead of universities and be in a better position to teach the knowledge learned. This is especially important when one considers shorter product cycles and keener international competition. This in no way obviates the fundamental role that universities are playing in serving the needs of industry and business. In fact it is because of this that partnerships between industry and universities are becoming such a popular theme since both have tremendous dependencies on each other.

9.3 Instructional television

The use of educational technologies, such as instructional television (ITV), has been a primary vehicle for delivering education to working professionals. It is consistent with the intent to provide education as part of the job while minimizing time away from the job. ITV has many components and includes videotape courses, videotapes augmented with tutors and courses delivered live by microwave or over long distances via satellite transmission. In many cases the courses are produced in live 'candid' classrooms with local students present and then videotaped and/or exported over the airways. If the courses are live there is one way video from the classroom and two way audio between the source classroom and the remote students. This enables the remote students to ask questions and participate as though they were physically in the classroom. In effect, the walls of the classroom encompass all locations participating. In the industrial classrooms if a course is being taken with videotape and tutor, the tape is stopped every four to five minutes and the tutor facilitates the discussion of what was covered. This approach was pioneered by Stanford University in a Master's program for professionals at Hewlett Packard. It has been proven to be one of the most successful methods of education.

The role and mission of universities in America has been extended to include continuous education for part time students. This is a very significant factor and, as was mentioned before, forms part of the living partnership between higher education and industry. Many are working towards undergraduate or advanced degrees while others may be taking courses strictly for vitality. The university community has been true pioneers in the use of ITV dating back to the early 1960s.

The GENESYS system at the University of Florida in 1965 was one of the first to use microwave transmission of graduate courses from the campus to North American Space Agency (NASA) employees and contractors in Orlando, Florida. Between 1965 and 1972, over 250 professionals earned master's degrees taking live courses without being present in the campus classrooms.

Stanford University had tutored videotape graduate courses as well as graduate courses transmitted live by microwave to professionals at their work locations, in the San Francisco area. This pattern repeated itself at universities throughout the United States with each school focussing on part-time graduate students in their particular locale utilizing ITV and all it's different forms.

In 1976, a consortium of these schools was established to operate as a non profit entity on a national basis, providing over 350 videotape courses in engineering areas on a lease basis to professionals in industry. The Association for Media Based Continuing Education for Engineers (AMCEE) has since grown to 33 universities with over 550 videotape courses in the critical engineering and technology domains.

9.4 The National Technological University

With the dynamic progress in communications and computer technology and the cost effectiveness in employing these technologies there was spontaneous growth as more universities expanded their missions to the continuous learners by means of ITV. The most exciting and creative development was the establishment of The National Technological University (NTU) in 1984. The NTU's total mission is dedicated to technical professionals sponsored by their companies working on advanced degrees in five different disciplines. These degree programmes are in electrical engineering, computer engineering, manufacturing systems engineering, engineering management and computer science. There are 24 universities in the consortium and the vehicle for providing the courses is ITV with satellite transmission.

Each one of the 24 universities will have uplinks, so that courses can be delivered live from their classrooms to students at their industrial classrooms. There is voice feedback to enable active participation by the remote students. Currently, 15 of the universities have uplinks and in the Fall 1987 semester there are 75 graduate courses being offered. There are 120 downlink locations receiving the courses in industry, government and military locations. This semester, there are over 1200 course registrations. The faculties are made up of the faculties of each of the participating universities. As the individual courses are completed, NTU accumulates the credits and awards the degree; it has received full accreditation and there have been two graduating classes. NTU uses a transponder on GSTAR1 and by splitting the transponder, operates on two channels 20 hours a day. One channel is dedicated to the degree programmes and the other primarily to non-credit short courses and seminars. These short courses are offered in leading edge technological areas such as superconductivity with the lecturers coming not only from universities but also from industrial research and development labs. The very nature of NTU facilitates bringing together the best in education, especially in interdisciplinary and new areas that might be impossible to achieve at an individual university. It is a living example of universities working together in a co-operative way, with their partners in industry, government and the military. The NTU is exploiting the technologies using electronic mail and conferencing, to bring the remote students closer to their instructors and by providing open office hours over the satellite network, for students to interact with each other and the faculty.

As universities have expanded their scope of activities to corporate classrooms, so have corporations constructed state of the art mini campuses employing all the latest in computer communications technology. In many cases these companies are offering their own generic graduate level courses using their own professionals as instructors. This occurs primarily in new advanced areas where a company may be ahead of the university in a given area of technology. Because of the urgency, competition and critical timing, courses are offered locally without turning to the universities. When this does occur, industry has an obligation to help higher education position itself so universities can teach in these new important areas.

As indicated, there have been many 'state of the art' campuses built by industry. Many have established corporate education satellite networks so that the campuses can reach out to students at remote labs and plants. Texas Instruments, Motorola, Hewlett Packard and Aetna Insurance are all model examples.

9.5 The Thornwood Centre

The IBM Corporate Technical Institute (CTI) at Thornwood, New York will serve as a more detailed example of what is currently happening. This 285,000 square foot building houses four technical institutes each with its own professional faculty. Adjunct faculties from universities participate actively in the teaching. There are 12 classrooms each with a six inch raised floor to facilitate reconfiguring the room with PCs and other equipment. There are 250 dormitory rooms with PCs in each room enabling students to communicate throughout the facility or out over the IBM world wide electronic network (VNET). There are over 700 PCs in the facility which includes a 300 seat wired auditorium, library, laboratories, computer center and breakout rooms. The building is wired for voice, video and data point to point throughout the facility. The CTI is the uplink node for a digital satellite education system with instructional material going ultimately to 23 labs and plants in the United States. There are two candid classrooms for delivering courses and of course videotaping can go on concurrently. The signal is compressed and encrypted at the uplink node. Again, the VNET electronic mail system allows the remote students to interact with faculty at the Thornwood location.

9.6 Conclusion

There has been a tremendous growth and acceptance of ITV as a cost effective way to provide education of the highest quality. In effect the student has an open catalogue of course opportunities that can be delivered to his or her location no matter how remote the provider. This provides the potential to pick and choose the best whether from university or corporate sources. It might even be looked upon as a distillation process with the survival of the fittest and best education. One can envisage the linking together of corporate satellite networks with university networks so that industry can also provide leading edge courses, seminars and lectures to their professional peers on university campuses. We then will have the fulfillment of a true partnership which is essential in this world where change is such a dominating force. And in no way should we constrain our thinking to one nation or country. This is truly an international world and the potential opportunities to use these technologies in bringing us closer together in communicating, learning, and sharing is but a moment away.

Chapter 10
Knowledge Engineering for CAL

Philip Barker
Teesside Polytechnic

10.1 Introduction

Over the last decade or so the use of computers for the implementation of teaching and learning processes has grown substantially. This growth has taken place both within academic establishments and in commercial/ industrial environments (Barker and Yeates, 1985). Within the United Kingdom developments in the academic utilization of computers for learning have taken place at all levels of the curriculum: in primary schools (Russell, 1985), in secondary education (Watson, 1987), and at the tertiary level – within colleges and universities (Barker, 1987a; FEU, 1987). This growth of application within the UK has been paralled by similar developments in other European countries (Leiblum *et al*, 1986; Whiting and Bell, 1987) and, of course, in the USA (Bork, 1987), Canada (Gillies, 1986; CSIT, 1987) and Japan (Terada *et al*, 1985).

Fundamental to the successful utilization of computers for teaching is the preliminary process of instructional design (Romiszowski, 1981; 1982; Barker, 1988). Primarily, this design activity is concerned with the specification of pedagogic processes that achieve particular teaching and learning objectives. The design process commences with an initial needs analysis and a formal requirements specification. These are then used to guide the formulation of instructional blueprints (or plans) that can be used to realize the pedagogic objectives that are embedded within the formal requirements specification. The instructional design process involves a number of different phases. Three of the more important of these are (1) the specification and organization of the content of the various learning units that compose a course of instruction, (2) the selection of appropriate presentation/delivery strategies for the different learning units, and (3) the creation of suitable assessment metrics that will allow (a) the learner's current states of knowledge to be assessed and (b) the extent and effectiveness of skill/knowledge transfer to be gauged. This chapter is primarily concerned with items (1) and (2) although some aspects of item (3) are also discussed in the context of deriving student models.

Sometimes, a special name is given to the second of the instructional design phases listed above; it is often called 'media selection'. In a multi-media learning environment many different types of resource are likely to be used. Many of the advantages, disadvantages, merits and limitations of conventional media (such as books, lectures, instructional television, and so on) are well known and have been extensively documented in the literature. One of the major criticisms of most of the 'mass' knowledge dissemination techniques based upon the use of conventional media is their inability to cater for the individual needs of particular learners or learning situations. Earlier in this section considerable emphasis was given to the important fact that there is a growing utilization of the computer as an instructional resource. One of the major reasons why computer-based interactive learning systems are becoming so popular is the potential that they offer for overcoming many of the limitations inherent in the use of conventional media. This is particularly true in the context of the individualization of instruction. A second major reason for the growing popularity of computer-based study is the active nature of the learning/ training methodologies that CAL techniques are able to provide.

The pedagogic success of an interactive learning facility is critically dependent upon the way in which it is designed and used. A successful design will undoubtedly require the development of instructional software (courseware) that is adaptable to the needs of individual users. In addition, through the appropriate use of multiple media (Barker, 1987b), this courseware must also be stimulating and pedagogically effective. In this chapter we discuss the importance of knowledge engineering techniques in the context of the design of courseware for the support of highly interactive CAL activity.

10.2 Knowledge-based CAL

Knowledge may be conveniently regarded as the collective total of human experience. This important commodity exists in many different forms. Some examples of the more common and well-known of these are factual, procedural, conceptual, instinctual, experiential and documented. Because of the wide variety and significant volume of knowledge that exists taxonomies and schemata are often needed (Christiansen, 1987). These may be used to structure and organize knowledge into more manageable sub-divisions. From the point of view of knowledge based CAL, an extremely useful way of sub-dividing knowledge is into knowledge domains (Barker, 1986; Barker and Proud, 1987). A domain is simply a segment of some larger knowledge unit (called a universe of discourse) that has been identified and isolated for some particular purpose. Implicit in this statement is our definition of a universe of discourse as an aggregation of knowledge domains according to some unifying theme. Within a domain smaller epistemological units can be introduced. Two important ones are concepts and topics. As we shall discuss below, concepts and topics may be aggregated and inter-linked in various ways in order to produce different views of a learning domain.

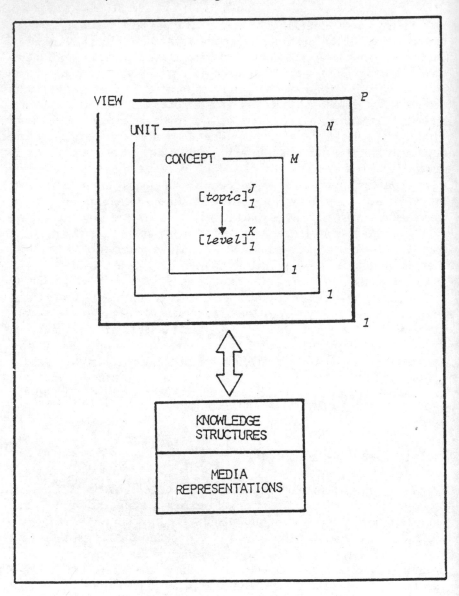

Figure 10.1 *Views of a learning domain*

Our basic approach to knowledge-based CAL is summarized schematically in Figure 10.1. This diagram depicts how knowledge structures and media representations must be made to support multiple views of learning units that are composed of various concepts and topics that may be taught at a variety of different levels. The pictorial notation used in the upper part of Figure 10.1 is intended to express the fact that any given learning domain is likely to consist of a number of student views [1..P]. These views will reflect the different backgrounds and current knowledge states of the various categories of learner for which the system caters. Each view is likely to consist of a sequence of learning units [1..N]. Each unit, in turn, has concepts [1..M] that are expressed in terms of component topics and levels at which these topics may be taught.

The types of representational structure involved in our implementation of knowledge based CAL are illustrated schematically in Figure 10.2. This shows how some particular universe of discourse may be organized into an appropriate set of domains (denoted by squares), concepts (denoted by circles), and topics (denoted by triangles). Inter-relationships between these various epistemological units are represented by directed arcs that connect together adjacent related items. A contiguous sequence of directed arcs that form a common relationship is referred to as a thread. Threads link together concepts and topics within any given learning unit. A thread is often used to represent a learning pathway for a particular student. Different threads may thus be used to represent different learning pathways and, to some extent, different views of a learning domain.

The various levels at which topics and concepts may be taught are represented by the system's repertoire of plans and scripts that cater for different categories of user. These relationships are indicated below in terms of generic Prolog knowledge structures:

```
concept(...........,<script>).

topic(.............,<script>).

usertype(<category>,<script>).

user (<identity>, <category>).
```

A user's category may change dynamically thereby forcing a change in script level. The system is therefore able to adapt and thus exhibit some sensitivity to the individual needs of particular user types. Currently, plans and scripts are manually produced. However, in principle it should be possible to facilitate the dynamic generation of each of these types of item through the use of heuristics that are developed as a result of machine learning activity (Self, 1986).

Structures of the type shown in Figure 10.2 form the underlying basis for our approach to knowledge-based CAL. Obviously, our implementation is heavily dependent upon the development and application of appropriate knowledge engineering techniques. Within this current project there are two areas where these techniques are being employed. First, for the development of an authoring facility that enables structures of the type shown in Figure 10.2 to be created. Second, to represent the organization

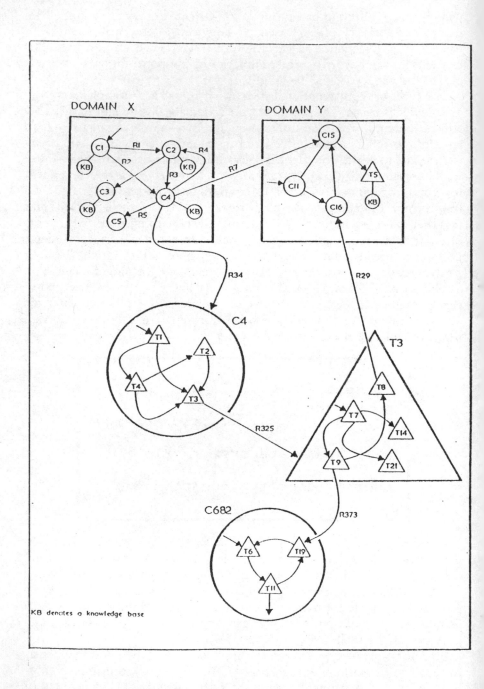

Figure 10.2 *A knowledge-based structure*

of the knowledge embedded within the instructional resources that are used to support teaching and learning operations. Each of these aspects of our work are discussed in turn in the remaining sections of this chapter.

10.3 Authoring for knowledge-based CAL

Several authors have commented on the severe limitations of the currently available methods of generating courseware material (Barker, 1987a; Bork, 1987; Whiting, 1987). In the light of these comments we have been investigating ways in which artificial intelligence methodologies might be used to improve both the authoring process and the student's interface to the learning materials that are embedded within sophisticated knowledge-based structures similar to that illustrated in Figure 10.2. In this section we therefore present an overview of the work we have been undertaking towards the realization of a linguistic interface that is capable of allowing courseware authors to create and manipulate these types of structure.

When designing an authoring facility for use with an interactive CAL system two levels of design need to be considered. First, there is the conceptual level in which the functionality of the author's interface is specified. Then comes the level of design that is needed to support the implementation phase. This latter phase is concerned with using the available interface technology and fabrication tools in order to realize the functions specified in the initial design stage. Each of the above aspects of our work are described in the remaining parts of this section.

10.3.1 Conceptual design

The conceptual command set which we propose should form the basis for a courseware author's interface to our system is presented in Figure 10.3. At present the commands fall into three basic categories that fulfil the higher level functional requirements of structure creation, navigation, and display, respectively. Each of these command subsets is briefly described below.

The creation commands enable domains, concepts and topics to be created and inter-linked in various ways. The command subset listed on the left-hand side of Figure 10.3 therefore provides the courseware author with a set of tools with which to generate knowledge based structures of the type previously illustrated in Figure 10.2. As we discuss later (under the title of media representation), a further set of commands is now needed in order to create knowledge bases (KBs) for different concepts and topics and also enable instructional material to be introduced into the system. We are currently working on the design of an appropriate subset of commands to achieve this.

Navigation commands enable users of the system to move around their knowledge-based structures and explore the representational frameworks that they have created using the creation commands that were described above. Currently, the navigation command set contains only seven

Creation Commands	Navigation Commands	System Browsers
Make-Domain[X] Make-Concept[C1] in Domain[X] Link[X—Y] in Domain [P] called [R1] Link [X] in Domain [Z] to [Y] in Domain [G] called [R7] Make-thread [T1] from [R1,R2,R3] called [J] Make-KB for concept [Q] Make-Topic [T23] within Concept [C2] Make-Topic [X32] within Topic [T23] Delete [T34]	Select Domain [Y] Enter Move-to [T23] Follow-Thread [T2] Next [Concept/Topic] Prior [Concept/Topic] Exit	Show All Move [Up/Down/Left/Right/In/Out] Show Concept(s) [Q,...] in Domain [Z] Show Topic(s) [R,...] in Concept [J] Show Link(s) [P,Q,...] in Domain [T] Show Thread(s) [S,TV,...] Show Concept(s) .... Colour [W] Make Topic(s) .... Colour [J] Make Link(s) .... Colour [M] Make Thread(s) ..... Colour [S]

Figure 10.3 *Conceptual command set for knowledged-based CAL*

primitive operations. The Move-to command allows any node within the currently active domain to be made the user's present node of interest. A domain (within its parent universe of discourse) is made active by means of the Select command. In contrast, the Enter command makes the logically initial node (marked with an arrow in Figure 10.2) the commencing point for system exploration. The Next and Prior commands allow node-at-a-time traversal of the framework. Similarly, the Follow-Thread facility allows an organized series of nodes to be accessed in a pre-defined order. The Exit command de-activates the currently active domain making a prior domain (if one exists) the active one.

In order to provide a facility that enables courseware authors to examine (in a global fashion) the logical structure of the frameworks that they create, a system browser facility is available. This presents views of the knowledge-based structures in ways that are easily assimilated by their users. The browser is controlled by a logical command set that is channelled onto the physically available control primitives of the target hardware. The browser maps the actual knowledge-based structure onto a 'graphics window' that is controlled by the subset of primitive commands listed on the right-hand side of Figure 10.3. These commands allow the complete structure to be displayed or sections of it to be isolated and viewed in greater detail. Provided colour graphics hardware is available the command set enables the author to display concepts, topics, links and threads in colours that are most meaningful to his/her particular authoring activity. One important feature that we have not yet considered and which must be investigated is the control of the view that particular author's have of the system. Controlled viewing is likely to be implemented by means of a Block command that prevents certain authors looking at certain types of object or segments of a shared knowledge-based structure.

10.3.2 Interface implementation

In order to implement the linguistic interface described in the previous section we have been using a version of Prolog that runs on a powerful minicomputer system (Salford, 1984). Our reasons for choosing Prolog for the initial implementation of the interface were (1) its highly interactive nature, (2) its rapid software prototyping capability, (3) the ease with which it allows the creation of data bases, (4) the potential extensibility of data base relations and clauses, and (5) the facilities it offers for the manipulation of list structures. This latter reason is particularly important since lists are extensively employed to represent most of the aspects of the knowledge structures of the kind shown in Figure 10.2.

Essentially, the interface system consists of four major components: a data base, a data dictionary, a command interpreter, and a snapshot facility. Within the data base each epistemological entity class used within our system is represented by an equivalent Prolog relation. As new instances of any of the allowed entity classes are generated new clauses are asserted into the data base thereby extending the number of entries within its parent relation. These relations are listed below in order to illustrate the

```
domain(<name>,<contents-list>,<linkage-lists>).

concept(<name>,<contents-list>,<linkage-lists>)

topic(<name>,<contents-list>,<linkage-lists>).

link(<name>,<to-object>,<from-object>).

thread(<name>,<contents-list>).

datadic(<name>,<entity-class>,<owner-list>).
```

nature of their arguments.

For each of the relations listed above the first argument is used to provide a naming facility; subsequent arguments are then usually list structures that specify ownership and inter-connection details. The data dictionary (which is also implemented as a Prolog relation) is used in a global way to keep track of each object's name, its entity type and its ownership details.

The command interpreter provides the author's operational interface to the authoring system. Its purpose is to analyse the text strings typed by the user, check that these represent valid commands and, if so, implement them. Each command offered by the interface is implemented as a series of Prolog goals. Obviously, textual command driven systems have severe limitations and so one important future development that we will need to undertake is an investigation of how pictorial dialogue methods might be usefully employed to facilitate authoring. Some initial design for such a facility (based upon the use of a mouse, icons, windows and pull-down menus) has already been undertaken (Barker, 1988; Barker and Proud, 1987). The type of pictorial interface facility that the author uses has been illustrated previously in Figure 1.8. Some considerable progress has been made towards the realization of this pictorial authoring system. However, significantly more development effort needs to b conducted before this type of authoring interface can be made operationally available to courseware developers.

The snapshot facility is responsible for generating pictorial representations of the current status of a knowledge-based structure. Unfortunately, this facility could not be easily implemented within the current version of Prolog that we are using – primarily due to the absence of any graphics primitives. Consequently, this function had to be provided by a post-processing facility programmed in Fortran. Although inconvenient, the mechanism by which this graphics processor operates is fairly straight-forward. When this authoring option is selected (perhaps via the Show All command listed in Figure 10.3) the command interpreter simply places a copy of the current status of the system data base into a text file. This is then used by the graphics processor to create pictorial views of the knowledge-based structure. It is hoped that future implementations of our system will be undertaken using a microcomputer version of Prolog that embeds appropriate graphics primitives (Borland, 1986) – thereby eliminating the need to adopt the approach we are currently using.

10.4 Media representation

Through the knowledge-based structures that have been described in the previous section we are able to provide a courseware author with an instructional design environment that enables the basic framework of a learning domain to be mapped out. The knowledge structures that are generated interactively at the designer's workbench (Barker, 1988) allow relationships between learning elements to be specified. However, the detailed pedagogic nature of those learning elements is not necessarily specified at the time the structures are produced. As we suggested at the end of section 10.2, this aspect of courseware production is dealt with in a subsequent phase of the instructional design process – media selection.

As we have described in detail elsewhere (Barker and Yeates, 1985; Barker, 1987a; 1987c; 1988), wherever possible we advocate the use of a multi-media approach to the implementation of learning and training processes. When selecting appropriate media it is important to consider how the available alternatives can be used to best advantage. Where several candidate media present themselves for consideration, a variety of other factors may also need to be taken into account before a final choice is made. For example, cost-effectiveness, communication bandwidth, ease of use, interactivity, and ease of sharing may all play a part in determining the optimum media mix to be used in any given situation. Of course, media selection will also be strongly influenced by the nature of the pedagogic processes to be implemented and the characteristics of the learning/ training activities to be supported.

Obviously, the most useful media will probably be those that are able to support knowledge and skill transfer using textual display, graphic/pictorial forms, and sound. Naturally, an authoring facility must provide mechanisms whereby each of these modes of knowledge transfer can be efficiently utilized by the courseware author and, the results of his/her labour then appropriately embedded within the host media that have been selected to support the instructional processes that are to be undertaken. Unfortunately, there are few (if any) really adequate tools available to support this aspect of the courseware production process. In view of this we have been giving considerable thought to the design of an instructional designer's workbench and the nature of the software tools that such a workbench should make available (Barker, 1988).

One important tool that we feel should be available is one that provides a facility to enable authors to create and maintain a 'concept dictionary'.

This concept dictionary must allow its users to keep track of the concepts (and/or topics) that they introduce and the media upon which these concepts are represented. It must also provide facilities for the instantiation of concepts – allowing for the fact that these instantiations may be retrieved from any of the media supported by the workbench. Because of its potential importance as a workbench component we have been modelling and exploring the properties of a prototype concept dictionary generator using Prolog as the implementation language.

The generic knowledge structure used to build a simple concept dictionary and a segment of a Prolog representation of such a dictionary are each illustrated in Figure 10.4A. Given that a concept dictionary can be created it becomes possible to use this dictionary to answer questions of the form:

Where can I find
  – a piece of text,
  – a picture,
  – a picture sequence,
  – a sound effect,
  – a narration,
  – a reference,
  – a piece of equipment,
  – an algorithm,
  – a learning strategy,
      etc
relating to concept X?

Answering such questions depends critically upon our ability to develop search algorithms that will access the Prolog data base and retrieve the details that are required. We are currently involved in specifying and implementing these algorithms.

An important type of imperative command that the workbench must support is one which requests the display of particular types of material at the workbench itself. For example, an author might make a request of the following form:

Show me the video disc representation(s) of concept X.

In order to support requests of this type two major problems have to be overcome. First, a number of generic structures are needed for handling media representations of instructional material. Second, facilities must be developed to enable the control of external storage media from within Prolog. The types of structures that we are currently exploring from the point of view of media representation are listed in Figure 10.4B. Because of the powerful facilities that it offers we have been particularly interested in the use of video disc as a storage medium for multi-media instructional resources. This medium is also attractive from the point of view of the ease with which images (and image sequences) can be retrieved. Consequently,

A: Building a Concept Dictionary

Generic Structure

```
concept ([<qualifier-list>],<medium>,<identity>,<location>,
                              <address>,[<presentational-details>]).
```

Prolog Representation

```
love([man,woman,nude_scene],videodisc,'PGB01','TP',16000,18000,[]).
love([woman,animal,dog,cat],videodisc,'PGB17','TP',1800,1950,[]).
love([children,adolescent_love],videotape,'OCT87A','PB',1372,1756,[]).
love([study_of,measures_of,intensity_of],book,'BK036A','GW',63,72,[]).
```

B: Generic Structures for Handling Media

Generic Structure

```
medium-type(<identity>,<start>,<finish>,[<whatever-else>],[<attribute-list>]).

    <attribute-list> ::= <attribute>|<attribute><attribute-list>
```

The attribute set [a_i] for any instructional unit is essentially a set of indexing terms that describe the content of the instructional unit.

```
For example:    vdisc(discid,start-frame,frame-count,[attribute-list])
                vtape(tapeid,start,playto,[attribute-list])
                cdrom( ... )
                film( ... )
                ohp( ... )
                slide( ... )
                book( ... )
```

Figure 10.4 *Knowledge structures for media control*

we have been actively involved in developing Prolog software to enable the control of a number of video discs that are attached to the author's workbench. Again, using Prolog, we are developing appropriate algorithms (in terms of goals such as findall(X,Y) and findany(X,Y) where X is a concept and Y is a medium) that are able to search structures of the type shown in Figure 10.4 and extract the information needed to retrieve pictorial knowledge from the video discs and display it to their user. Although we are some way from final implementations of these facilities the results that we have achieved to date are extremely encouraging.

10.5 Conclusion

Computer assisted learning methods are having a significant impact upon knowledge transfer for instructional purposes both in academic institutions and in commercial organizations. Too often, however, the very laudable aims of CAL are thwarted by inadequate and inappropriate courseware. Consequently, this chapter has emphasized the need for instructional software that is effective, efficient and adaptable to the needs of individual learners. One of our fundamental tenets is that CAL can meet these needs provided appropriate knowledge engineering methodologies are developed and are rigorously applied to the courseware development process. Unfortunately, implementing knowledge-based CAL is a complex process due to (1) the many different types of user likely to interact with the instructional system, (2) the wide range of dialogue levels needed to support effective communication, and (3) the difficulties associated with providing multiple views of shared knowledge domains. In this chapter we have described the approach that we have been adopting in order to generate a framework within which to investigate some of these problems. As soon as it becomes easily possible to create and maintain the types of knowledge-based structure that we have described in this chapter an attempt can be made to utilize them to support the generation of adaptive and flexible courseware for CAL applications.

10.6 References

Barker, P.G., (1986). Knowledge based CAL, 137-143 in *Proceedings of the 5th Canadian Symposium on Instructional Technology*, Ottawa, Canada, May 5-7, 1986.

Barker, P.G., (1987a). *Author Languages for CAL*, Macmillan Press, Basingstoke.

Barker, P.G., (1987b). A practical introduction to authoring for computer assisted instruction. Part 8: Multi-media CAL, *British Journal of Educational Technology*, 18(1), 25-40.

Barker, P.G., (1987c). Multi-media CAL, in *Tutoring and Monitoring Facilities for*

European Open Learning, (edited by Whiting, J. and Bell, D.), Elsevier/North-Holland, Amsterdam.

Barker, P.G., (1988). Towards an instructional designer's intelligent assistant, 127-134 in *Aspects of Educational Technology, Volume XXI: Designing New Systems and Technologies for Learning*, edited by Mathias, H., Rushby, N. and Budgett, R., Kogan Page, London.

Barker, P.G. and Proud, A., (1987). A practical introduction to authoring for computer assisted instruction. Part 10: Knowledge-based CAL, *British Journal of Educational Technology*, 18(2), 140-160.

Barker, P.G. and Yeates, H., (1985). *Introducing Computer Assisted Learning*, Prentice-Hall, Hemel Hempstead.

Borland International Inc., (1986). *Turbo Prolog Owner's Handbook*, Borland International, Scotts Valley, CA.

Bork, A., (1987). *Learning with Personal Computers*, Harper and Row, New York.

Christiansen,D., (1987). Artificial expertise, *IEEE Spectrum*, 24(1), 25.

CSIT, (1987). *Proceedings of the 5th Canadian Symposium on Instructional Technology*, Ottawa, 5-7 May, 1987.

FEU, (1987). *Courseware Directory*, FEU Courseware Unit, London.

Gillies, D.J., (1986). CAL in Canada: Innovations and their sources in teaching and learning, *Computers and Education*, 10(1), 221-228.

Leiblum, M.D., Derks, K. and Hermans, D., (1986). A decade of CAL at a Dutch university, *Computers and Education*, 10(1), 229-244.

Romiszowski, A.J., (1981). A new look at instructional design. Part I. Learning: Restructuring One's Concepts, *British Journal of Educational Technology*, 12(1), 19-48.

Romiszowski, A.J., (1982). A new look at instructional design. Part II. Instruction: Integrating One's Approach, *British Journal of Educational Technology*, 13(1), 15-55.

Russell, T., (1985). *Computers in the Primary School*, Macdonald and Evans, Plymouth.

Salford, (1984). *The University of Salford LISP/Prolog Reference Manual*, Second Edition, University of Salford.

Self, J.A., (1986). The application of machine learning to student modelling, *Instructional Science*, 14, 327-338.

Terada, F., Hirose, K. and Handa, T., (1985). Towards a self-paced learning support system, 39-44 in *Proceedings of the IFIP 5th World Conference on Computers in Education*, Norfolk, Virginia, USA, July 29 - August 2, 1985, edited by K. Duncan and D. Harris, North-Holland, Amsterdam.

Watson, D., (1987). *Developing CAL: Computers in the Curriculum*, Harper and Row, London.

Whiting, J., (1987). Conceptual design of advanced authoring and tutoring systems, paper submitted to *Creating Adult Learning - International Conference on Educational Design*, Middelburg, The Netherlands.

Whiting, J. and Bell, D., (eds), (1987). *Tutoring and Monitoring Facilities for European Open Learning*, Elsevier/North-Holland, Amsterdam.

Chapter 11
Designing and Developing Video Discs

George P.L. Teh
Institute of Education, Singapore

11.1 Introduction

The interactive video disc is one of the newer technological developments
that is associated with the microcomputer, and has been described by Levin
(1983), Teh (1984; 1986), Barker (1985; 1986), Kearsley and Frost (1985),
Uhling and Feldman (1985), Hannafin (1986) and Withrow (1986). From an
educational point of view, the most significant feature of the video disc,
apart from its enormous information storage capacity, is its ability to
provide multi-media learning sequences which may be stored on a single
disc: text, visual data, speech, computer programs, and still and moving film
sequences. A suitably programmed computer can in effect be placed in
control of a slide projector, film projector and tape recorder to provide a
multi-media lesson.

While interactivity has been available since the development of the
microcomputer, the addition of a high quality visual display in the
interactive video disc has facilitated the potential interaction to become
more realistic than the previously available computer graphics and printed
text displayed on a screen. Not only can instructional materials be
presented to students in a realistic and flexible format, but, results of
choices made during an instructional encounter can also be fed back to the
learner in a realistic manner. The interactive video disc has therefore not
only enabled enhanced interactivity in terms of quality visual display (both
motion and static) that can be planned into instructional sequences, but has
also enhanced the interactive control available at the student's console. It
has also allowed the student to impose an interactivity upon instructional
materials in a manner not previously possible.

Interactive video (IV) is therefore a unique combination of video disc and
microcomputer which has the potential to augment the existing attributes
of each medium separately. Until the relatively recent development of
interactive video disc technology, the combination of the visual richness of
film and television with the spontaneous qualities of interactive computing
has been unattainable. As put by Grabowski and Aggen (1984), the

interactive video disc systems are 'image rich' because they allow '... the learner to access any number or combination of motion segments and/or still frame imagery'. Given that the structure of instructional materials has been traditionally determined at the design and development stage of the materials, this revelation has enormous ramifications for instructional designers and courseware developers who intend using this technology.

11.2 Hardware and courseware design of the IV system

The overall development of the teaching system used in this project required the design and fabrication of a suitable IV workstation. It also required the production of appropriate courseware for use with this workstation. Therefore, in the remainder of this section, the various stages involved in developing the hardware and courseware materials are each briefly outlined.

11.2.1 Developmental phases of the materials

For developmental purposes, the project was divided into four integral phases. The relationship between these is illustrated in Figure 11.1.

Phase 1 was devoted to examining a suitable theoretical base for the production of the computer-video disc software to teach the concept of weather forecasting. This was to ensure that the design of the CAL courseware was related to a suitable psychological theory as a base.

This phase of the developmental project was to derive design dimensions based upon a review of the existing literature – especially that applying to:

(1) learning problems in geography,
(2) the shifting emphasis to cognitive psychology as inputs to instructional design, and
(3) the translation of these dimensions for video disc materials.

Phase 2 involved the recording of visual materials on 16mm film as part of a larger video disc materials project. This phase had four distinct but interrelated stages:

(1) selection and preparation of synoptic charts and diagrams;
(2) selection of satellite images to match the synoptic charts and diagrams;
(3) selection and preparation of diagrams and illustrations using graphic design techniques; and
(4) assisting the cinematographer/animator in preparing the synoptic charts, diagrams and satellite images for recording under the animation stand.

Phase 3 involved the preparation of the CAL courseware. This phase had two distinct stages:

(1) deliberations about selection of an appropriate programming language/authoring system to generate the initial coding for the CAL program; and

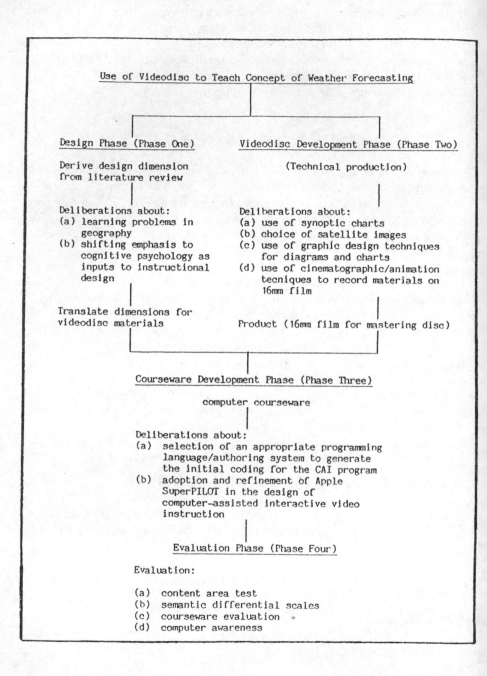

Use of Videodisc to Teach Concept of Weather Forecasting

Design Phase (Phase One)

Derive design dimension
from literature review

Deliberations about:
(a) learning problems in
    geography
(b) shifting emphasis to
    cognitive psychology as
    inputs to instructional
    design

Translate dimensions for
videodisc materials

Videodisc Development Phase (Phase Two)

(Technical production)

Deliberations about:
(a) use of synoptic charts
(b) choice of satellite images
(c) use of graphic design techniques
    for diagrams and charts
(d) use of cinematographic/animation
    tecniques to record materials on
    16mm film

Product (16mm film for mastering disc)

Courseware Development Phase (Phase Three)

computer courseware

Deliberations about:
(a) selection of an appropriate programming
     language/authoring system to generate
     the initial coding for the CAI program
(b) adoption and refinement of Apple
     SuperPILOT in the design of
     computer-assisted interactive video
     instruction

Evaluation Phase (Phase Four)

Evaluation:

(a) content area test
(b) semantic differential scales
(c) courseware evaluation
(d) computer awareness

Figure 11.1 *Phases of the developmental project*

(2) adoption and refinement of Apple SuperPILOT in the design of computer-assisted interactive video instruction.

Phase 4 involved an evaluation of the computer-assisted interactive video materials.

11.2.2 The video disc system
The video disc system employed in this developmental project included:

(1) a Disco Vision Associates (DVA) 7820-3 laser video disc system. A microprocessor for control of the video disc player operation is built into the DVA 7820-3. This feature enables the implementation of the play, search, slow forward or reverse, frame by frame review, frame display and audio commands. This internal microcomputer also allows for programming, but it is not possible to access the microprocessor instruction set directly. There are different ways in which the internal microprocessor can be programmed but in this developmental project, programming was achieved via an external host computer.
(2) an external control computer; the external host computer used in this project was an Apple-II+ microcomputer with twin drives and an external video disc interface. Through this system all the features mentioned above were achieved, including direct access to any frame within seconds. As configured for this developmental project, the following features were put under the control of the Apple-II+ microcomputer: slow forward, frame by frame review, frame recall and stop, speed control as well as freezing a frame for a closer study.
(3) an Allen Communication VM1 Card. This acted as an interface between the DVA 7820-3 video disc player and the Apple-II+ microcomputer.

The audio and visual information are recorded onto the disc through the medium of 16mm film. Each side of a disc has 54,000 frames. Each frame has a unique identification number (or address) that enables it to be independently and directly retrieved from the disc. A single TV frame is generated by each rotation of the disc; this allows approximately 30 minutes of continuous motion on each side of the disc. Both the Apple-II+ and video disc player operated on a NTSC colour standard, which enabled the video disc frames and microcomputer display to appear on a single screen but not simultaneously. The audio tracks do not play when a still frame or slow forward/reverse is being used. Music was generated using the Apple-II SuperPILOT software.

11.2.3 Production of the disc
The instructional materials used for this project were part of a larger video disc materials project. This part of the project involved recording the following information on 16mm film in readiness for mastering the disc:

(1) daily synoptic charts from the Western Australian office of the Bureau of Meteorology, and
(2) satellite imagery of two types:
    (a) daily images of parts of Western Australia from the American National Oceanic and Atmospheric Administration Satellite (NOAA7); and

179

(b) selected Australian images from the Japanese Geostationary Meteorology Satellite (GMS).

The recording of information on 16mm film for the mastering of the disc involved the following activities:

(1) use of graphic design techniques to prepare the selected visuals for filming; and
(2) use of cinematographic and animation techniques to film the NOAA7 and GMS slides and photos under the animation stand.

11.2.4 Control of the video disc

Of the range of possible interfacing and CAL authoring languages for controlling video discs in educational contexts reported by Jeffrey and Winship (1984), Barker and Singh (1985), Lee (1984), Zollman (1984) and Allen (1985), Apple SuperPILOT was chosen for the current project. The reasons for this include:

(1) it allows instructors with little knowledge of programming to write CAL lessons;
(2) the easy to use graphics and sound editors are useful in the preparation of charts, graphic, diagrams and music;
(3) it has improved screen presentation techniques; and
(4) the video disc can be readily accessed through programs written in this language.

11.2.5 Structure of the program

Before entering the instructional sequences proper, users are first required to complete a pre-test on the concepts of weather forecasting. Based on their entry learning abilities, learners may be directed to the basic modules (Modules 2-6) or advanced modules (Modules 7-14) of the program. The overall structure of the program is shown in Figure 11.2.

The introductory module is essentially a series of instructions to help students use the program.

The pre-test contains five items; one dealing with each of prediction of wind speed and direction, cloud patterns, relative humidity and general synoptic chart interpretation. Within each item students are first presented with text information and a visual and are then prompted to make a response. No chances or corrective feedback are given at this stage. The visuals are generated from either the video disc player or the graphics capabilities of SuperPILOT. Depending upon the number of errors made during the pre-test, students are directed to the basic modules when their score is two or less, or to the advanced modules of the program when their score is more than two.

The basic modules instruct students in elementary weather map interpretation, again using visual illustrations generated from either the video disc or the computer. The advanced modules assume an understanding of the skills in interpreting a synoptic chart, the use of satellite imagery, and the correlation between these two sources of information, and requires users to apply those skills in the learning of weather forecasting.

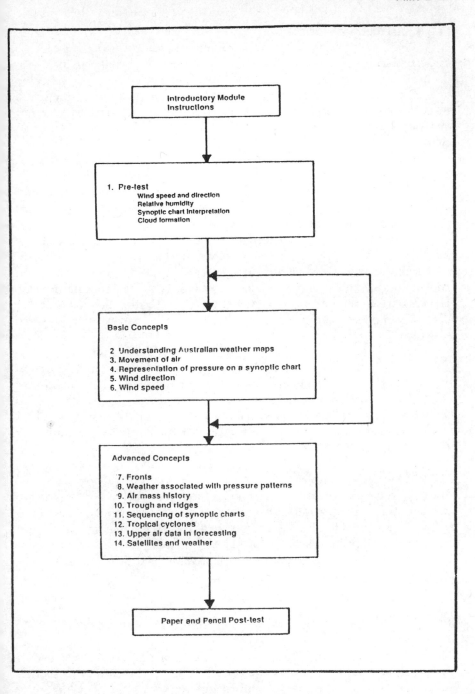

Figure 11.2 *Structure of an instructional IV programme*

11.2.6 Instructional format

While the presentation of the instructional sequences in these materials varies between segments, typically students are introduced to an idea with the use of a combination of text and visuals. This format is usually repeated several times in each segment – until the idea has been developed sufficiently for the student to answer a question concerning the current material. An example segment from Module 12 of the program is shown in Figure 11.3.

Instructional cues were presented in a variety of forms – sometimes on the video screen driven by the video disc player, but more frequently on the video screen driven by the Apple-II+ microcomputer. Occasionally, annotated charts and diagrams were used in conjunction with visuals generated by the video disc, but very often, computer text was used.

The visual information presented to students comes from either the video disc or the computer. The video disc materials were of course all pre-recorded; they contained pictures of sequential synoptic charts, matching satellite images and schematic diagrams of fronts, air masses and the like. The synoptic charts and satellite images were used both individually and in slow play mode to depict the changing weather patterns over Western Australia.

Frequently, slow motion images were used, but without sound. The series of synoptic charts produces an animated sequence when shown in the slow play mode. Still images from the disc with supporting computer graphics were also employed. Frame by frame review was especially used to show the nature and character of tropical cyclones and the use of satellites in weather forecasting. The sound facility of the computer was used to generate music at the beginning of each module.

11.2.7 The CAL program

The CAL program consisted of a series of modules which were designed to instruct students in various aspects of weather forecasting. These materials were designed to take full advantage of the interactive nature of both the video disc and microcomputer. These modules are shown in Figure 11.2. An example of a listing of the CAL program is provided in Appendix A.

11.3 Evaluation of the computer-assisted IV materials

The evaluation of the effectiveness of an instructional tool is as important as the actual development of the tool itself. Therefore, within this section a description is given of the techniques and methods used to evaluate the effectiveness of the learning resources produced during the project.

11.3.1 Subjects

The materials were initially trialled with a group of 14 undergraduate teachers-in-training, all of whom were enrolled in a social science unit. Ten

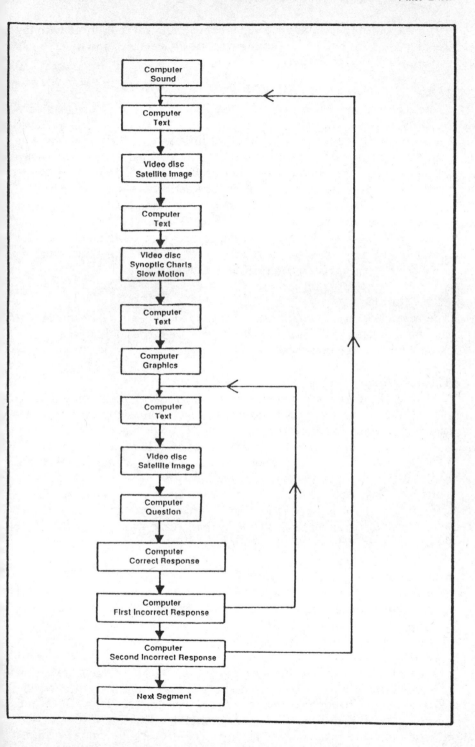

Figure 11.3 *An example segment (Module 12)*

of the students reported themselves as being totally inexperienced with the use of a computer while the remaining four (three males and one female) sometimes used a computer.

11.3.2 Procedures

Students were requested to complete a written pre- and post-test; each consisted of a weather forecasting test and a semantic differential scale concerning attitudes towards technologically-based learning systems. The post-test also contained another semantic differential scale dealing with attitudes about the video disc system used in this trial. Finally, subjects were asked to evaluate the weather forecasting program developed in connection with this project. The pre-tests were administered to subjects as a group during their normal class time. Each subject was then requested to work through the weather forecasting program individually, and to complete the post-tests. Each student spent about one hour working through the program and completing the necessary tests.

11.3.3 Results

The results of this evaluation are considered under four headings: the content area test, the semantic differential scales, the courseware evaluation and the correlations between various measures.

11.3.4 Content area test

Table 11.1 shows that although there was a significant improvement in the overall results, in terms of performance on each item, significant improvement was only observed on Question 1 (explanation of the term 'nowcasting'), Question 6 (identification of weather phenomenon) and Question 16 (the use of upper air data in explaining the apparent contradiction in a low pressure system). Interestingly, these three questions were also the most difficult. The fact that students were able to improve significantly in their post-test showed that the materials were adequate and sufficiently instructive as to increase students' performance significantly on these difficult questions.

11.3.5 Semantic differential scales

Subjects were asked to rate their feelings on three semantic differential scales: technologically-based learning systems (before and after working through the computer-assisted interactive video disc materials) and the particular video disc learning system used in the project.

With one exception, subjects did not reassess their prior opinions about technologically-based learning systems (Figure 11.4). The one exception concerned the colourfulness of technological systems. Subjects positively reassessed their feelings in respect of this matter. The profile of group means on this dimension is shown in Figure 11.4. Of interest is the fact that although subjects considered technologically-based learning systems would tend to be humourless, active, complex and colourless, only the view about colourfulness was significantly reassessed – positively.

Table 11.1 *Results of pre- and post-test on weather forecasting*

	n	Pre-test		Post-test		Difference	
		X	SD	X	SD	t	P
Overall	14	13.29	2.34	16.29	1.59	9.05	0.001
Q1	14	0.21	0.43	0.71	0.47	3.61	0.003
Q2	14	0.93	0.27	0.93	0.27	0.00	1.000
Q3	14	0.93	0..27	1.00	0.00	1.00	0.336
Q4	14	0.50	0.51	0.57	0.51	0.56	0.583
Q5	14	0.93	0.27	0.93	0.27	0.00	1.000
Q6	14	0.57	0.51	0.93	0.27	2.69	0.019
Q7	14	0.93	0.27	1.00	0.00	1.00	0.336
Q8	14	0.86	0.36	1.00	0.00	1.47	0.165
Q9	14	0.79	0.43	0.93	0.27	1.00	0.336
Q10	14	0.50	0.52	0.71	0.47	1.38	0.189
Q11	14	0.86	0.36	0.86	0.36	0.00	1.000
Q12	14	1.00	0.00	1.00	0.00	0.00	1.000
Q13	14	0.86	0.36	1.00	0.00	1.47	0.165
Q14	14	0.86	0.36	1.00	0.00	1.47	0.165
Q15	14	1.00	0.00	1.00	0.00	0.00	1.000
Q16	14	0.07	0.27	0.93	0.27	8.83	0.001
Q17	14	1.00	0.00	1.00	0.00	0.00	1.000
Q18	14	0.50	0.52	0.79	0.43	1.75	0.104

Subjects were also asked to rate their feelings about this particular video disc learning system upon completion of the interactive video disc lesson. The profile of group means indicates that feelings were largely positive (Figure 11.4). There were three significant areas of reassessment of opinion when compared to subjects' initial feelings about technologically-based learning systems – the video disc was considered less complex, more colourful and less active.

11.3.6 Courseware evaluation
Upon completion of the program subjects were required to complete a courseware evaluation form. As indicated by the group mean profiles shown in Table 11.2, the program was generally well received.

11.3.7 Correlations between measures
Correlations between measures used in the evaluation are presented in Table 11.3. No significant differences were found between the computer awareness of subjects and their pre- and post-tests scores in the content area. Neither was there any significant correlation between subjects' keyboard expertise and their pre- and post-test scores. These results suggested that the level of the subjects' computing experience or keyboard expertise did not affect their pre- and post-tests in the content area and

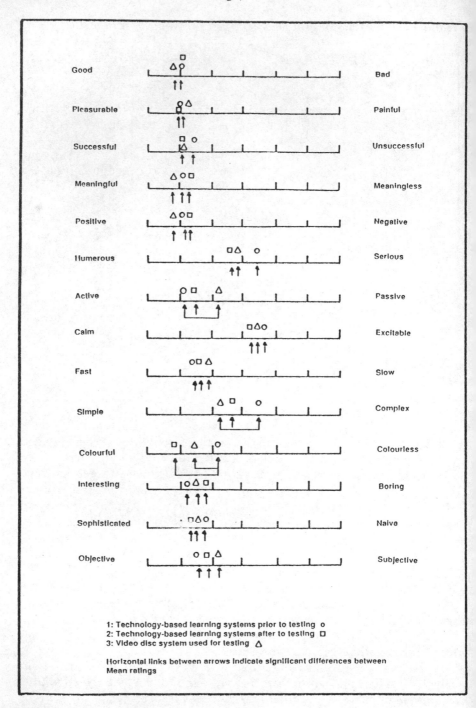

Figure 11.4 *Self-rating opinions by subjects*

Table 11.2 *Courseware evaluation – profile of group means*

	x̄	sd	SA (1)	A (2)	NS (3)	D (4)	SD (5)
Content Characteristics							
Understood text	1.64	0.84	:---x-:----:----:----:				
Good sequence of concepts	1.77	0.70	:---x-:----:----:----:				
Instructions simple and easy	1.93	1.00	:---x:----:----:----:				
Completeness of instructions	1.86	0.86	:--x-:----:----:----:				
Understood pictures and graphics	2.29	1.20	:----:x---:----:----:				
Instructional Characteristics							
Good definition of purpose	1.71	0.61	:--x-:----:----:----:				
Program achieved its purpose	2.14	0.54	:----:x---:----:----:				
Content presentation clear and logical	2.21	0.90	:----:x---:----:----:				
Appropriate graphics/sound/colour	1.64	0.63	:--x-:----:----:----:				
Motivational	1.86	0.54	:---x:----:----:----:				
Effective feedback	2.07	1.00	:----:x---:----:----:				
Lrnr contr rate/sequence of presentation	2.00	1.11	:----x----:----:----:				
Cognizance of previous experience	2.07	0.92	:----x----:----:----:				
Continuously interactive	1.93	0.83	:---x:----:----:----:				
Effective branching	2.07	0.83	:----:x---:----:----:				
Reinforced positive responses	1.64	0.75	:--x-:----:----:----:				
Technical Characteristics							
Effective information displays	2.07	0.92	:----:x---:----:----:				
Ease of use	2.07	0.62	:----:x---:----:----:				
Good use of computer capabilities	2.21	0.98	:----:x---:----:----:				
Reliability	2.21	0.80	:----:x--:----:----:				

Table 11.3 *Pearson correlation coefficients and probabilities between measures used in the evaluation*

	Pre-test Content Area	Post-test Content Area
Computer Awareness	.04 (.445)	-.15 (.305)
Keyboard Expertise	.33 (.127)	.25 (.189)

were contrary to previous research that computer experience might influence performance on computer tasks (Moran, 1981; Card *et al*, 1980). The results could be attributed to this particular interactive video disc CAL program which did not require much compulsory knowledge.

11.4 Conclusions

This project has demonstrated that it is possible to develop computer-assisted interactive video courseware that is appropriate to particular teaching/learning situations. The materials developed in connection with this project have shown that a wide range of the features available on such systems can be applied to develop effective learning resources.

Developing interactive video disc systems requires a lot of activity which must be conceptualized, organized and managed. For a single researcher or professional to design and produce the video disc materials (for example, materials for mastering the disc and the CAL program) is undesirable – if not impossible. Teams of individuals, for example, educational technologists, subject matter specialists, computer programmers, evaluation specialists, etc., must interact throughout the design and development process. These teams, working together, will probably produce more effective, cohesive and polished interactive courseware.

Although Fletcher (1979) maintains that it is difficult to develop effective interactive courseware and that there is a critical need for more technical instructional developers in this area, this project demonstrates that it is possible to develop effective interactive courseware provided the appropriate interfacing and CAL authoring language or programming language is judiciously selected.

The special attributes of interactive video for instructional purposes became apparent when the synoptic charts and matching satellite images were played in the slow mode. The animated motion generated enabled subjects to conceptualize the weather phenomena and weather patterns in a better perspective. Clark (1983) even agrees that the animated motion can serve as sufficient conditions to facilitate the learning of students.

Subjects' significant improvement in knowledge of weather forecasting after having worked through the instructional materials, their generally positive attitudes towards the video disc system and the courseware, suggest that the interactive video disc is capable of meeting an array of levels, styles and paces of subjects.

One important result which emerged from the evaluation of the computer-assisted interactive video disc materials was the apparent change of attitude of subjects towards the video disc system. Apparently, subjects found the video disc learning system less complex than they originally anticipated. This is an important aspect of instructional design for interactive video; even though the technology is complex, with appropriate courseware such complexity need not be apparent to the user. Instead, the learner should be able to concentrate on the learning task and be unaware of the complexities of the medium in use.

11.5 References

Allen, D., (1985). Linking computers to video disc players, *Videography*, January, 26-28, 30-32, 34.

Barker, P.G., (1985). Programming a video disc, *Microprocessing and Microprogramming*, 15(5), 263-276.

Barker, P.G., (1986). Video discs in education, *Education and Computing*, 2, 193-206.

Barker, P.G. and Singh, R., (1985). A practical introduction to authoring for computer assisted instruction. Part 5: PHILVAS, *British Journal of Educational Technology*, 16(3), 218-236.

Card, S.K., Moran, T.P. and Newell, A., (1980). Computer text-editing: An information-processing analysis of a routine cognitive skill, *Cognitive Psychology*, 12, 32-74.

Clark, R.E., (1983). Reconsidering research on learning from media, *Review of Educational Research*, 53(4), 445-459.

Fletcher, J.D., (1979). *Videodisc Overview*, ERIC Document Reproduction Service No. ED 175 447.

Grabowski, B., and Aggen, W., (1984). Computers or interactive learning, *Instructional Innovator*, 29(2), 27-30.

Hannafin, M., (1986). Research and development in instructional interactive video, *Journal of Computer-Based Instruction*, 13(4), 101-102.

Jeffrey, G., and Winship, J.A., (1984). Microcomputer controlled video disc in education, *Proceedings of the International Microcomputer Conference*, Perth.

Kearsley, G.P., and Frost, J., (1985). Design factors for successful video disc based instruction, *Education Technology*, 25(3), 7-13.

Lee, B., (1984). Interactive authoring languages, *AV Video*, October 1984, 22, 24-25.

Levin, W., (1983). Interactive video: the state-of-the-art teaching machine, *Computing Teacher*, September, 11-17.

Moran, T.P., (1981). An applied psychology of the user, *Computing Surveys*, 13(1), 1-11.

Teh, G., (1984). The use of the interactive video disc in teaching geographic concepts, paper presented to the Annual Conference of the Australian Association for Research in Education, Perth, November, 21-25.

Teh, G., (1986). Designing and developing interactive videodisc materials for instruction, 136-153 in *Selected Proceedings of EDUCOMP '86: Impact of Microcomputers on Education – Issues and Techniques*, Ngee Ann Polytechnic, Singapore.

Uhling, G. and Feldman, P., (1985). Interactive Video, *Education (California)*, 106(1), 3-8.

Withrow, F., (1986). The Videodisc: An Educational Challenge, *Journal of Educational Technology Systems*, 14(2), 91-99.

Zollman, D. (1984). Video Disc – Computer Interfaces, *Educational Technology*, 24(1), 25-27.

11.7 Appendix A: Listing of PILOT Module W12

```
v:apple
ts:v
ts:12;es
c:x=0
c:y=5
c:s=15
ts:s2
c:y1=6
c:x1=3
ts:f2;es
ts:gx1,y1
t:TROPICAL CYCLONES
sx:VIDEO2:EDELWEISS
ts:f3
ts:s1;t2
v:apple
*ep1
TS:V;ES
v:apple
ts:gx,y
T:Tropical Cyclones are very intense
:low-pressure circulations (with a
:clockwise circulation in the Southern
:Hemisphere) formed in the tropical
:seas off the north north-east and
:north-west coasts of Australia.
u:return
v:find(17787);video
w:s
v:find(17788);video
w:s
v:find(18101);video
w:s
TS;V;ES
v:apple
ts:gx,y
T:What you just saw are satellite
:images of Tropical Cyclones.  They
:develop in warm, humid open seas and
:travel slowly southwards towards the
:coastline.
u:return
TS:V;ES
v:apple
ts:gx,y
T:The next diagram shows typical tracks
:taken by tropical cyclones.  Notice
:that these cyclones affect only the
:coastal areas of W.A. and Queensland.
```

```
u:return
g:es0
gx:VIDEO2:TROCYC
w:10
g:es0
v:apple
ts:gx,y
T:These cyclones can extend up to 600
:Km in diameter.  Although they usually
:move slowly as systems, they generate
:tremendous wind force within their
:circulation .... as much as 250 Km/h
:.... and sometimes cause considerable
:damage.
u:return
TS:V;ES
v:apple
ts:gx,y
T:The next three charts are cross-
:sections of these cyclones.  Note them
:carefully.
u:return
v:find(18102);video
w:s
v:find(18103);video
w:s
v:find(18104);video
w:s
TS:V;ES
v:apple
ts:gx,y
T:Yet without them our northern
:pastoral areas could loose an
:important source of beneficial rains.
u:return
TS:V;ES
v:apple
ts:gx,y
T:Look at the satellite images of
:Cyclone Chloe. You should also notice
:the spiral circulation (in a clockwise
:direction) of the clouds.
u:return
v:find(17788);video
w:s
v:find(18101);video
w:s
TS:V;ES
v:apple
ts:gx,y
```

```
T:Study closely the next few charts.
:Note how tropical cyclones (like
:T.C.Bobby) are shown on weather
:charts.
u:return
v:slowfwd(17739,17746);video;wait
W:2
TS:V;ES
v:apple
ts:gx,y
T:Let's have another look at some
:satellite images and weather charts
:depicting these violent tropical
:storms.
u:return
v:slowfwd(17748,17753);video;wait
W:2
v:find(18101);video
w:s
v:find(17787);video
W:2
v:find(17788);video
W:2
TS:V;ES
v:apple
ts:gx,y
T:Look at the next satellite image.
:Note the coastal area affected by the
:cyclone and then answer the question.
u:return
v:find(18101);video
w:s
TS:V;ES
ts:gx,y
v:apple
T:1. Which part of the coastal area of
:W.A. is Tropical Cyclone 'Chloe'
:affecting?
c:a=1
c:n=2
*getal
pr:U
ts:v0,39,13,23;es
v:apple
ts:v;g0,13
th:>
a:
ts:v0,39,17,23
m:NW!NORTH*!PORT*!PIL*
ty:You got it right! Congrats!
uy:return
```

```
vy:find(18101);video
wy:s
jy:end
t(a=n):The north-west of W.A. ...... in
:fact in the Pilbara region.
u(a=n):return
v(a=n):find(18101);video
w(a=n):s
j(a=n):epl
t(a=1):Have another look at the
:satellite imagery then try again.
t(a>1 & a<n):Try again
u:return
v(a=1):find(18101);video
w(a=1):s
C:A=A+1
j:getal
*end
TS:V;ES
v:apple
ts:v
t:
t:
t:You've just come to the end of
:advanced module 6.
t:
t:
t:There're 2 more to come.
w:2
PR:W
v:VIDEO2:W13
V:REJECT
e:
*return
ts:g6,23
th:PRESS <RETURN> TO MOVE ON
as:
e:
```

Chapter 12
Video Discs for Interactive Learning

Judith Mashiter
University of Newcastle upon Tyne

12.1 Introduction

Video disc is still a relatively new medium. Attempts which have been made to apply video disc technology to educational purposes have been necessarily and predictably tentative. The two components in the intended application individually have been the subject of much research and analysis. Many comprehensive descriptions of video disc technology and studies of video disc based lesson design have been written (Parsloe,1983; Bosco, 1984; Jonassen, 1985; Kearsley and Frost, 1985; Braden, 1986). Extensive research in the fields of education theory and cognitive psychology has offered insights into how learning takes place and how it may best be stimulated.

The following discussion centres around the identification of different categories of learning. It is only when the objectives of a learning activity have been clarified that consideration can be given to the appropriateness and effectiveness of a technological innovation intended to enable or enhance that learning.

A selected range of interactive video disc developments are considered with respect to the opportunities for learning which they provide.

12.1.1 Categories of learning activity
Many recent curriculum developments in both secondary and primary education have acknowledged that the measure of a 'good' education is not indicated solely by the pupils' ability to recall facts. Understanding the implications of their knowledge, and the ability to apply the concepts in unfamiliar contexts is equally, if not more, valuable to the pupils. In most curriculum areas, explicit emphasis is now being given to such skills as the synthesis of data, the formulation and testing of hypotheses and the manipulation and representation of information. Thus learning entails more than the acquisition of concepts.

Learning activities might fall into one of the following three categories:

(1) concept acquisition, (2) procedural skill development, and (3) problem solving.

The 'concept acquisition' category needs no further explanation; it has been the prime concern of traditional teaching and of the examination of pupil learning. 'Procedural skills' are here considered to be those involving reason and thought. It is through generalized procedural skills that sense is made of existing conceptual knowledge, and by which new knowledge can be assimilated, or even 'discovered'. A specific example of a procedural skill, taken from science, is the identification of the dependent and independent variables in an experiment. Learning based upon problem solving is not a category directly equitable with the preceding two. Problem solving fits into the above paradigm only after some procedural skills have been demonstrated and some conceptual understanding has been developed. Without some degree of accomplishment in both these components, the learner is likely to experience difficulty in solving problems. Thus, problem solving is the application of procedural skills to concepts, in order to gain new information. It is quite readily accepted that the concept must previously have been understood. The element which is frequently neglected is the learner's ability to transfer or apply that concept. It is often assumed that this ability is either intuitive, or that it develops automatically through experience. A useful synonym for problem solving which might better indicate the necessary combination of conceptual understanding and procedural skills is the term 'research'. A clear distinction is drawn between the basic skills, or processes, involved in problem solving, (such as handling equipment or recording measurements) and the more cerebral procedural skills which determine their use.

Most teachers recognize the need for learning objectives to be clearly identified. Increasingly, the learning objectives, and the criteria against which progress is to be assessed, are being made explicit to the pupil.

There is, however, a drawback in explicitly concentrating on activities of just one of the above categories at any one time. It might be better if the pupil does not perceive that 'the lesson today is about how to draw a bar chart'; but instead that the context of the activity is arranged such that the opportunity for drawing a bar chart arises 'naturally' or 'spontaneously'. In this way a pupil is more likely to perceive the exercise as relevant and motivating and therefore become actively engaged with it. The teacher of the lesson, however, being mindful of the desired type of learning, must carefully construct the context and manage the activity in order that both conceptual hurdles and other procedural difficulties are minimized. For the graphicacy example, this would involve providing the opportunity to draw graphs which deal with concepts and utilize skills in which the pupil has previously demonstrated understanding and competence.

As with a reduction of procedural complexity in order to concentrate upon concepts, so with the desired emphasis on procedural skill development, the conceptual difficulty should be carefully controlled. A learner cannot be expected to successfully deal with unfamiliar concepts and develop skills simultaneously.

12.1.2 The raw materials for learning

Regardless of the category of the learning activity and regardless of the context of that activity, the learner is usually required to handle some form of data in some way. By the computer scientist's definition, data are without meaning. It is only when data are manipulated in some way that information results. This distinction between data and information is not difficult to understand with respect to an electronic machine. The computer's storage device cannot do anything with its collection of data; a humanly programmed set of instructions is needed if useful information is to be extracted. In applying this same definition to the human memory, we are more prone to blur the distinction between data and information. It is often assumed, albeit tacitly, that providing somebody with a quantity of data is equivalent to giving them information.

Data, then, are neutral. They have no intrinsic value. The number of ways in which a collection of data can be interpreted approaches infinity. It depends not only upon the person handling the data, but also upon their objectives (the category of their learning activity), their prior understanding and many temporal and trivial factors.

12.2 CAL and video disc

As has been discussed elsewhere in this book, CAL represents a powerful tool for the implementation of interactive learning processes. Combined with video disc even more powerful learning tools can be developed. In the remainder of this chapter some of these possibilities are explored.

12.2.1 CAL approaches to the use of data

With respect to CAL programs, there appear to be two alternative approaches to the use of data: (1) the storehouse with sophisticated tools, and (2) the closely focused concept-driven approach.

These approaches might respectively be considered divergent and convergent in their use of data. The storehouse principle partially acknowledges individual differences and requirements of learners by providing a wide range of data and the tools to operate upon them. However, often those tools either have evolved from such a strongly conceptual perspective that they, in fact, give a false impression of freedom while essentially directing the learner; or they are so non-specific that the learner cannot decide what to do with them. In contrast, the overtly concept-driven use of data must be very carefully constructed and managed in order to avoid providing a rigid and restricted sequence which approaches instruction rather than learning.

The decision to adopt either of these alternative styles of use has implications for the data to be incorporated into the system and vice versa. Constraints are imposed by the chosen hardware medium. Although the storage medium might be considered just that (a storehouse), features such as data retrieval time and display resolution can impact upon the potential use of data. More subtle constraints are imposed by the software and its design. Whereas a datum can be as simple as a number or a word, the inclusion of more complex types, for example, line graphs or even pictures as data items increases the ambiguity with which the data can be interpreted. In addition to the very type of the data themselves and the problems associated with their labelling (especially of pictorial items), there are other factors which influence their potential usefulness. The instructional design of a CAL program and the programmer's translation of that into software impose further restrictions on how the data can be accessed. A 'data point' is then characterized by its indivisibility and its possible approach and retreat routes; for example, it might be a sequence of animated graphics, always shown together and only shown after one particular, predetermined series of interactions.

A new medium – a new opportunity for learning?
Video disc provides a new medium on which data can be stored. That better, or even different, learning will result, is a *non sequitur*. However, video disc does allow a qualitatively different type of data to be stored, and subsequently retrieved, than other media. For this reason alone, new kinds of learning might be facilitated. Data, however they are arranged or accessed, are the raw materials of the construction of learning. They must be of a quantity and quality commensurate with the desired final construction.

12.2.2 Integration of CAL with classroom practice
Frequently, the introduction, generally of CAL programs, and specifically of interactive video programs, is treated in a way which denies a variety and diversity of learning activities. Considered more cynically, non-educational objectives appear often to have driven developments in educational technology, and thus, by implication, its use in the classroom. As Weller (1988) observes:

> Educational designs and techniques are frequently only reactions to the developing technology. The technology has emerged, and instructional developers have endeavoured merely to apply the technology for instructional purposes ... The term interactivity is being used, and misused, widely nowadays as a justification for the selling, buying and use of microcomputer-based instructional tools.

Teachers readily revert to asking questions such as 'What does it teach my pupils?', or 'Which part of the syllabus does it do?'. It is quite understandable that busy teachers want to know how a CAL program will integrate with their scheme of work and overall objectives. The answers to their questions are often not readily available, nor are the learning objectives of some programs transparent. Finzer (1981) uses an analogy to highlight the dearth of varied computer uses in schools. He suggests that traditionally, teachers have access to a cupboard containing chalk, pens, books, calculators, flash cards etc., but that there is no such cupboard for computer-based lessons. The implication is not necessarily that there is a dearth of good computer lessons, but that they are not organized, or indexed or even reviewed in ways that match up with teachers' information needs. Video disc applications will likely attract similar criticism.

12.2.3 Video disc applied to different learning objectives
The applications of video disc technology to learning can now be discussed with respect to the above categorization of learning activities and the consideration, in general terms, of the use of data by CAL programs.

Concept acquisition
The learning of concepts requires a particular use of the audiovisual storage medium. In essence, the instructional design relies on the trapping of misconceptions and the provision of appropriate feedback, remediation or redirection. Thus, a small fraction of the video disc provides a direct route to the acquisition of the desired, or 'correct', concept, and the vast majority of the disc is occupied with the largest possible number of predicted alternative, or 'wrong', offshoots of that route. The data is exhaustive, but only within the confines of the concept under study and within the chosen context. The selection, design or construction of material to be placed in such a database is founded upon the predicted interactions of the learner. Of course, the context is carefully and imaginatively constructed in such a way that the learner so empathizes with the given scenario that they are unaware of the sometimes complex branching which operates. Indeed, if the learner is to concentrate his/her effort (either implicitly or explicitly) on the acquisition of conceptual knowledge, then the procedural skills required of him/her should be appropriate to his/her level of procedural competence. This conceptually driven form of interactive design certainly results in the learner being highly motivated and drawn into the constructed simulation. The immediate response, especially when of the visual variety, is appreciated and effective in reinforcing aspects of learning such as perceived control, responsibility and the reward of success.

Procedural skills development
If the intended outcome of the learning experience is an increased ability in some procedural skill, then the learning activity should closely address that very issue. The interactive video system should allow the learner to interact with the data, and not merely with the hardware and software (i.e. this should not be confused with 'button pushing'). The procedures which might operate upon data include, but are not restricted to, the search, sort and index functions of traditional computer databases. There remain many unexploited aspects of using the data contained in a database, other than as a means to conceptual ends. A collection of various types of data, together with a versatile interface offers an ideal resource for the development of these procedural skills.

Problem solving

By reference to the earlier description of the problem solving category of learning activity, it will be apparent that the application of video disc to this objective requires a combination of those facilities for concept acquisition and those for exercising procedural skills. This requirement of a problem solving facility is met by many existing interactive video systems. It might not appear as such, due to the inappropriate concurrent use of partially developed skills and unfamiliar concepts. A particular learning activity is not fostered solely by the correct hardware and software; the emphasis given to the learner's use of data is crucial.

12.2.4 Distractions of interaction mechanics

The physical interaction which facilitates a non-trivial order of data processing must be as nearly transparent as possible. If this is the case, the intellectual process, whether conceptual or procedural is interrupted and possibly destroyed by the mechanics of interaction. The pupil's efforts and energies should be directed to the conceptual or the procedural development (interaction with the data) and not distracted by decisions concerning interaction with the system. The failure to achieve this can be likened to what happens when a touch typist or concert pianist consciously tries to think about which fingers are going where on the keyboard – the whole process falls apart. Learners should be spared the obstruction of having to deal with operational details of the system, save for it being an extension to their thinking power. Clark (1986) writes that

> 'A good interactive video program must deal directly with the user's concerns and requirements in ways that do not eat up scarce thinking capacity for tasks unconnected with the job in hand.'

Dugdale (1983) says that programs:

> should encourage students in productive thought and activity, rather than show off the capabilities of the hardware or the author; they should draw on the inherently interesting characteristics of the topic, rather than hiding it under graphics, animation and music unrelated to the learning task; and they should make students participate, rather than letting them watch and listen.

12.3 Video discs for interactive learning – some examples

A direct comparison of the various existing interactive video applications would neither be useful nor valid. The only conceivable justification for a comparison would be the medium they share. Yet even then, the applications are so various that such an exercise would be pointless in the context of this chapter dealing with learning. The only kind of 'information' which such specious comparisons can produce has little value in considering the educational effectiveness. An example of just such a comparison was made by Quinn (1987) after describing the range of curriculum related activities either included upon, or stimulated by, a disc designed to be used over a 12 week term. He commented that 'To put this in context though, [it] is only a fifth of the size of a Domesday disc'. The comparison is of unequals and is meaningless. Instead of this, then, the following descriptions serve as illustrations of different approaches to the use of interactive video. Their connection to the given categories of learning are discussed.

Domesday
Perhaps the most widely publicized, if not purchased, interactive video system in the UK is the BBC/Philips/Acorn 'Domesday' portrait of Britain in the 1980s. The intention was to collect together a resource of photographs, newsreel, statistical data sets, vicarious experiences (surrogate walks), maps, and text and then to provide the system's user with exploratory tools which permit access to those data items. The tools provide an impressive feeling of power. For example, by consecutive presses of a button, the picture on screen zooms from a satellite image, through aerial photographs and Ordnance Survey maps, to a photograph of, say, a village street, and in some cases, detailed plans and photographs of the interior of buildings. The structural design of the two discs and the control software is quite beautiful. The mechanics of orientation and movement around the disc are not immediately obvious or natural, but are comprehensible after initial instruction or recourse to the on-line help. In schools and colleges, Domesday systems have been welcomed, particularly by geographers, as an unequalled resource, 'bringing the outside world into the classroom'. The breadth and depth of data can give rise to endless topic-based studies, support for quantitative analysis at advanced levels, environmental case studies and numerous other spin-offs.

In terms of the possible learning outcomes described earlier, the Domesday discs are indeed a sufficiently rich database to provide opportunities for conceptual, procedural and problem solving based learning. However, the opportunities do not automatically induce the learner to use them. Whilst the quality of material and the implementation of the software interface can be highly motivating, they also carry the power to bewilder. Many Domesday adventurers have drowned in data! The tools are there and they can act upon a rich database. But what do you create with it? The cliché 'a solution looking for a problem' has been applied here. Conversely, there is a danger that such a magnificent technological accomplishment will be regarded, with awe, as 'a good thing'. The contribution it can make to learning might, at best, be considered of secondary import, and at worst, not investigated fully. Quinn (1987) remarks that 'The education potential is still being discovered, but the sheer volume of information itself is valuable ...' while O'Grady (1988) believes that 'In some ways Domesday is too attractive a resource; the temptation is to spend hours drifting through it'.

There are two practical problems experienced by many teachers who have attempted to use Domesday in their classrooms. Firstly, they are daunted by the enormity of the database. A considerable, and often unavailable, investment of time is required in planning the use of the resources in order that learners can exploit the system and extract anything but trivial information. Thorne (1988) writes:

> During the three weeks it was in the school, [the teachers] found that the initial excitement gave way to the horror of working out how to incorporate such a powerful tool into their everyday teaching.

The second problem is that of integrating the opportunities offered by the interactive video system with the broader objectives and methods of the classroom. Busy practitioners do not necessarily wish to be spoon-fed; but they do appreciate suggestions, guidance and examples of good classroom practice. Despite Quinn (1987) claiming that 'The educational value is pretty powerful. Put any good teacher in a classroom with Domesday in any area and there's so much in it for them', the provision of the latest technology, a mammoth data resource and a completely 'free-hand' does not guarantee the most educationally effective use of interactive video.

In acknowledgement of this feeling of bewildering disorientation which at first occurred with the Domesday discs, curriculum guides have been prepared by teacher trainers and researchers. They provide worksheet style notes which teachers can readily adopt or adapt. They hopefully operate also as stimuli to further development of local or topical interests. Paradoxically, the vast database which is brought into the classroom can also be perceived as a threat due to the hidden material it holds. Teachers know neither which data their pupils will discover nor what questions they might ask of them. This runs counter to the traditional situation in which the teacher is the holder of knowledge and distributes it at what he understands to be appropriate times in appropriate packages. The availability of easy-to-use authoring packages, through which teachers can develop customized applications might serve the dual purpose of allowing the production of immediately relevant and usable 'lessons' and also of increasing teachers' confidence in handling the system.

To date, the impression taken away by most Domesday users in schools has been disillusionment (a feeling that the database is interesting but does not tell me what I want to know), or frustration (I know the information must be in there somewhere but I can't find it!).

Ecodisc

Also from the BBC stable comes 'Ecodisc'. Although using the same 'Advanced Interactive Video' hardware as Domesday, Ecodisc is a very different product. It is designed to allow the user to simulate the running of a nature reserve. A range of variables are under the user's control and feedback is provided subsequent upon decisions made. One criticism which has been made of the simulation is that the feedback stops short of being visual. For example, if the user chooses to lay footpaths and car parks throughout the reserve, he/she receives messages of protest from conservationists etc.; he/she does not see the reserve with a web of concrete footpaths. This is an illustration of the difficult design decisions needed in developing interactive video. There has to be a line drawn somewhere between what can realistically be shown, and what is better than normal, or nothing. Any novel technology brings with it a hope for a cure-all. This is usually too optimistic. Certainly with interactive video, there are limitations to what it can do.

Despite the facility for the user to set parameters, the Ecodisc is largely a concept acquisition agent. The means through which the concepts of conservation are developed are varied and innovative. However, the access to data and the functions performed on that data are pre-defined and there are rules governing their sequencing. The labelling of the disc as a research tool would perhaps be inaccurate. It does not permit any original problems to be investigated, but only those pre-determined by the designer. The technique adopted for the simulation encourages the total immersion of the learner in the context of the nature reserve. Evidence of the efficacy of this approach is shown in various press reviews of the package. Reporters rise above commenting upon the hardware or the interfacing problems; they describe what they saw and did. For example, Cherfas (1987) writes:

> I got fully caught up in the reality of the reserve, spending far too long radiotracking mink and badger, hoping against hope to trap an otter, measuring pike, counting trees, the whole thing.

MIST

The potential for 'bringing the outside world into the classroom' has been placed at the centre of this interactive video project. Modular Investigations in Science and Technology (MIST) has been developed by Thorn EMI. It aims to provide a source of easily accessible stimuli for both teachers and pupils. The self-contained video sequences, 'modules', are short (no more than a couple of minutes) and have 'simpler' and 'more sophisticated' sound tracks. This approach has been well received by teachers who can readily use the medium flexibly as intended. It blends well with multi-media learning such as has more frequently occurred in primary than in secondary schools. Interaction is most commonly controlled by the teacher although, after practice, young pupils can manage the mechanics of modular access. A keypad is the basic communication channel for the rapid access into an indexed 'chapter' structure. The content presented is not reactive to the viewers' needs or desires beyond showing the correctly keyed snippet. The hardware on which MIST is implemented is Nebraska level 1 ('rapid, random access') (Parsloe, 1983), or, as the editor of the project materials describes it, the Model T Ford, not the Rolls Royce of educational technology (Mably, 1987). This absence of an external computer is a major psychological advantage when introducing the system to technophobic teachers. The deliberate stimulus or trigger nature of the MIST system implies that the dominant use of the materials is in furthering conceptual understanding. As such, the brevity and inherent conciseness of the module might be a very effective feature. Built upon a view of science education as 'how to find out answers' rather than 'knowing scientific facts' is what MIST claims to be. The video modules certainly stimulate investigative work away from the workstation. It is questionable whether the resources support procedural skill development or simply provide ideas for investigation; investigative work is encouraged as a means to a conceptual end, as opposed to the learning objective being the explicit development of procedural skills. Particularly significant characteristics of the materials are the inclusion of children performing experiments and the useful exterior shots of 'the real world'. It is perhaps just such an indexed resource of short video clips that Finzer (1981) envisaged paralleling a classroom cupboard.

The core concepts series

As would be expected, interactive video developments in the USA have been diverse. At one extreme, very teacher-centred discs have been produced and are very popular in classrooms. The pedagogical model used is that of direct instruction to the whole class and of mastery learning. The 'selling point' of the 'Core Concepts' series of video discs (System Impact Inc.) for teaching basic skills of mathematics appears to be their high quality instructional exposition. Teachers, who control the disc via a handset, can attend to individual pupils' difficulties and needs. They are freed from the chalkboard, by using a glossier version of instruction than they could consistently perform and can therefore spend more time and effort on remedial work. The pace of instruction from the disc is rapid and pupils are required to communally chant responses to on-screen questions. Both motivation and achievement are reported to increase with use of this technology (Straker, 1988; Henderson *et al*, 1983). What has not yet been researched is the retention of those basic skills several months after instruction. Again, the word 'skills' is used to describe the objectives of the learning which the disc enables. This use of the word differs from both the procedural and the data handling skills discussed earlier. The skills rehearsed on these Core Concepts discs are basic enabling skills of mathematics. They are rules to be learned and applied consistently. In this respect, the 'skills' better match the 'concepts' part of their series title. The discs treat the skills as something to be acquired. They do not require intellectual processing. Rote learning of when to apply which rule is the unfashionable adjective for this type of learning. Hence, the interactive video disc is being used to provide instruction which directs the learner towards a fixed, and recognizable end-point.

Palenque

At Bank Street College in New York, a very different theory of learning is being implemented through interactive video disc. Palenque is a Mayan temple site. The disc user is invited to explore it by 'walking' around the site or by visiting the site museum. At his fingertips are many 'tools'. Some, such as cameras and maps, are familiar to tourists; others are more especial. For example, the user can request that the scene be subjected to a 'time warp' – the ruined temple scene dissolves to one of its former state. A comprehensive help facility is provided through an on-screen 'friend' and archaeological experts on call. Game-like activities are numerous, but generally optional. The Palenque disc cannot easily be located into one of the defined categories of learning. It would more suitably be described as an information system; its users learn about the site. Nevertheless, the research which is being conducted into children's use of the disc might reveal features of interaction and of video disc design which are pertinent to more specifically educational materials.

Motion: a visual database
Here in the UK, a team at Cambridgeshire College of Arts and Technology have explored yet another potential application of video disc technology. In creating a resource for students and teachers of physics, the design exploits the frame-by-frame movement facility not available to the same high quality on any other visual medium. A collection of motion images has been gathered together to form 'Motion: a visual database'. No frills have been added. For example, no audio tracks have been laid down and software is functional, not fancy. The package provides an analysis instrument otherwise unavailable. It allows the path of a tennis volley, say, to be traced with a cursor, and it then uses the data to plot a graph from a suitable selection of forms. This most certainly allows for interaction with the video, rather than interaction with a computer program. It is nearer to computer-enhanced video than other examples of interactive video which could more aptly be described as video-enhanced CAL. Paradoxically, the simplicity, nay crudeness, of this system might prove to be its strength. The designers have explicitly prepared a pictorial resource; an event-by-event index of frame numbers is supplied with the disc. They have programmed some probes which can be used to investigate that data. They have then handed over to the user. There are no fixed 'lessons' to be followed, games to be played or skills to be acquired. Prior to using the disc, the pupil (or teacher) must plan what it is they are to investigate and how this might be achieved with the help of the technology. Interaction is initiated by the learner (or teacher), and they are forced to apply their procedural skills to the analysis. As with the Domesday discs, the value which can be extracted from this visual database depends largely upon the teacher's preparation of appropriate, relevant and motivating support materials or task assignment. Moreover, the intended audience is quite a specialist one. The disc can assist with concept acquisition, or procedural skills development, or it can be used as a research base for solving problems.

IVIS
A major interactive video initiative for schools in the UK was recently funded by the Department of Trade and Industry. Over a two year period, the Interactive Video In Schools (IVIS) project team developed eight discs covering a range of curriculum areas. The diversity of the interactive products and design methods was intentional. The range covers concept-driven and resource discs. Simulations allow pupils respectively to visit a

French town, where they 'talk' to residents and do some shopping; and to organize the staging of a school disco, in which they consider and control various factors including the location, admission charge, caretaker fees, hiring of the band etc. In this way, the designers have created 'an environment in which mathematical concepts, skills and techniques may be learnt in a practical way and related to real-life situations' (Plummer, 1987). A Life Skills disc contains scenarios presenting common teenage problems. These can be used as stimuli for related activities and discussion. Two of the IVIS discs directly address teachers. One of these provides opportunities for practitioners to compare recordings of classroom events with various educational theories; the other deals with subject-specific training for environmental studies. The 'Design disc' provides resources through which pupils can learn to appreciate good and bad design practice, and implement this in the design of a product. An exploration of the use of material drawn entirely from archives was undertaken in the production of a geography-based disc. In classrooms, pupils have used the 'open' software facilities to structure and present the material to suit a particular activity in progress. A pupil-as-researcher style of disc was located in the curriculum area of primary science; in addition to leading pupils through the concepts of energy, a dominant feature of 'Life and Energy' is its integration with related 'off-station' activities (Plummer, 1987).

With such a diversity of experience, the IVIS research and development can provide an extensive base upon which to assess the potential of interactive video in education. An attempt to disseminate these findings is the creation of a (human) network through which teachers share ideas of classroom experience of using the discs. An independent evaluation of the project is due to be published soon.

12.4 The interactive learning project

In contrast to the above-mentioned difficulty in comparing interactive video systems, there are design and realization problems common to all teams working in this field. As good educationalists would recommend, we ought to learn from each other's mistakes and also not 're-invent wheels'. It is for this reason that it might be useful to discuss at greater length the project with which I have been associated for over two years.

The Nuclear Electricity Information Group commissioned the School of Education at Newcastle upon Tyne University to produce three learning packages 'Risk, Statistics and Probability', 'Radiation and Properties of Matter' and 'Energy', for secondary schools. The Interactive Learning Project (ILP) was thus established with a staff of five full-time and seven part-time experienced teachers and lecturers and with a lifespan of three years. The sponsors of the project wanted, in addition to the production of learning materials, to discover just how children learn when using new technologies. There are therefore two foci to the project – research and production.

12.4.1 Research

While being strongly in favour of developing learning materials for the benefit of pupils, ILP has not naively neglected a consideration of the teacher's role and issues of classroom management. There are pedagogical as well as financial reasons for the study of the management aspect of classroom resources. Even should more than one interactive video 'workstation' be available, there are certain applications of the technology which operate better with, or even rely upon, a group of users, rather than an individual. Intuition might suggest that any interaction which is to occur between human and computer must be made on a one-to-one basis – there is only one keyboard, only one person can touch the screen at one time, there is only one mouse etc. This physical consideration is, as discussed earlier, merely one part of the interaction possible, and indeed, is essential for active learning. Pupils first have to decide what to communicate. Then there is the decision about who should communicate with the machine. But most importantly, there should be pupil-to-pupil interaction at a level above the prosaic key pressing. Of course, the quality of this interaction is not easy to measure, and will never be identical on two occasions or with two different groups. However, it should have a high priority on an evaluation checklist. The ILP has undertaken formative evaluation of its work. The findings of this research will be reported in due course.

12.4.2. Production

The project was fortunate in being able to have a 'dry run' in making a 'Development Disc'. The exercise yielded many benefits. The discipline of following ideas through elements of instructional design, piloting, flow-charting for disc and trialling in schools was something that could not have been experienced in any spectatorial way. Additionally, only through first hand experience could the possibilities, and limitations, of the visual medium be fully explored. Overseeing the production and post-production of film or video, and specifying requirements to a computer programmer also provided lessons in the effective and precise communication of ideas. The ideas of the team have grown considerably in sophistication during the project. Although the ILP team members rapidly enhanced their considerable expertise, a network of consultants was established. Their expertise, variously in classroom teaching, subject content and technological aspects was, and is, frequently called upon. Of paramount importance, though, was the opportunity which pressing the development disc provided for school-based trials of interactive techniques and contextual settings for the intended learning outcomes. In addition to observing the classroom use of the disc, a great many valuable insights have emerged from studies of video tapes of group work centred on an interactive video workstation. An analysis of these observations appears elsewhere (Atkins and Blissett, 1989).

Some seemingly trivial, yet extremely important observations were made during trials of the ILP development disc. As would be anticipated in any developmental work, there were ideas which have since been refined and expanded. For example, the use of video to simulate what would happen if radiation was 'turned off' has been developed into the reverse of this, in which the user must add energy to a 'black nothingness'. There are other ideas which have been modified or even abandoned. For example, an attempt to provide off-station tasks, and other 'take-away' material through the addition of a printer was found to be theoretically sound, but impractical on account of the noise disruption and time delay. This has led to more restrained use of the printer and an alternative system whereby cards are kept in a supporting resource box and are referenced from the disc.

12.5 What is the future for interactive video in learning?

The only certain answer to this question is that it is too early to say. Some critics have commented that the talking phase should be over, that there have been enough 'discovering the potential' projects and attention should now be directed to actually using the technology (Chambers, 1987).

Almost without exception, interactive video developers have declared their aim to be the improvement of learning, and not merely the furtherance of the technological aspects of educational technology. It is encouraging to observe that the once standard sales-pitch about the physical attributes of interactive video which prefixed any paper, conference speech or demonstration is being contracted and relegated to a hand-out for those not familiar with the technology. There does seem to be a positive shift from discussing learning about technology to learning with or through technology.

Some experiences of the introduction of computers into the classroom provide guidance and advance warning of potential pitfalls in the introduction of interactive video. At once the most obvious and the most difficult problem is the hardware/software circle – the dilemma facing manufacturers and developers in being the first to take a risk. Until an adequate, if not wide ranging, library of discs is available, investment in the expensive technology is unlikely. Until manufacturers are assured of a substantial market, they will not scale their production in such a way that results in a reduction of retail costs.

A further historical, and perhaps inevitable, 'problem' is the rate of progress itself. New developments happen so rapidly that education (which has been said to use the decade as it unit of time) cannot keep pace. This applies not only to the equipment obsolescence dilemma, but also to the application to learning. Before one idea has been thoroughly explored, another is vying to replace it.

No two of the interactive video projects outlined above have duplicated each other's endeavours. The ideas are all in what could be described as the germination stage. They might well grow and blossom in different directions. To fully exploit the power of the medium, we should now be consolidating and possibly integrating our findings, whilst not necessarily aiming to use one route to reach the same goal. The most harmful thing to do now would be to dismiss one particular style of interactive video as tried and of no worth.

12.6 Conclusion

In this chapter three categories of learning (conceptual, procedural and problem solving) have been described. As illustration of the variety of interactive video systems and programs, several recent developments have been outlined. The relationship between each implementation and the given learning paradigm has been discussed.

Video disc can store qualitatively different data to traditional databases. It allows for novel interaction with that data, and enhances existing data handling functions. The union of these two facilities offers new opportunities for learning. They carry implications for what is learned as well as how it is learned.

Further research effort needs to be applied to the realization of a truly versatile learning medium. Sophistication of interfacing tools is not sufficient. An expansive collection of data is insufficient. Of equal importance to the learner is the ease with which they can use their mind to select different kinds of learning as appropriate. Only then are the tools and data relevant and useful. A glimpse of such a learning environment is provided by Apple Computer's HyperCard system conceptual connections unique to an individual user or application. The addition of video disc to such a system is showing signs of offering some exciting and effective learning, in which the learner plays the key and central role.

As with any educational innovation, the use of video disc must be carefully aligned with educational theory and good practice. The resulting effect on learning must then be fed back into the curriculum to effect and hopefully improve future learning. Indeed, Clark and Salomon (1986) found that a change in achievement of ability following an innovation was not necessarily dependent upon the new medium introduced, and commented '... it was not the medium *per se* that caused the change but rather the curricular reform that its introduction enabled'.

We should set ourselves educationally determined goals and not become hooked on the intricacies or maybe idiosyncrasies of particular media.

12.7 Acknowledgement

The author greatly appreciates the help of Dr. Richard Gott (of Durham University) in the revision of earlier drafts of this chapter.

12.8 References

Atkins, M.J., and Blissett, G., (1989). Learning activities and interactive video disc: an exploratory study, *British Journal of Educational Technology*, in press.

Bosco, J.J., (1984). Interactive video: educational tool or toy?, *Educational Technology*, April, 13-19.

Braden, R.A., (1986). Visuals for interactive video: images for a new technology (with some guidelines), *Educational Technology*, 18-23.

Chambers, J., (1987). Interactive video: a genuine or imagined potential, *British Journal of Educational Technology* 18(1), 21-24.

Cherfas, J., (1987). So you think you can run a nature reserve?, *New Scientist*, 2nd July, 59-60.

Clark, D.R., (1988). Hard lessons for interactive video, *Educational Computing*, March, 41-45.

Clark, R.E. and Salomon, G., (1986). Media in teaching, in Wittrock, M.C.(ed.), *Handbook of Research on Teaching*, 3rd edition. New York; Macmillan.

Dugdale, quoted by Hawkridge in Hawkridge, D., (1983). *New Information Technology in Education*, Croom Helm, London.

Finzer, W., (1981). The gap between the image in the mind and the image on the screen, Math Network Curriculum Project, San Francisco State University (mimeo), USA.

Henderson, R.W. *et al*, (1983). *Theory-based Interactive Mathematical Istruction: Development and Validation of Computer-video Modules*, Santa Cruz, University of California; ERIC No. ED 237 327.

Jonassen, D.H., (1985). Interactive lesson design: a taxonomy, *Educational Technology*, 7-17.

Kearsley, G.P. and Frost, J., (1985). Design factors for successful video disc based instruction, *Educational Technology*, 7-13.

Mably,C., (1987). Interactive video as a school resource: Rolls-Royce or Model T Ford? in Laurillard, D., *Interactive Media: Working Methods and Practical Applications*, Ellis Horwood, Chichester.

O'Grady, C., (1988). Magical mystery tour, *Times Educational Supplement*, 17th June.

Parsloe, E., (1983). *Interactive Video*, Sigma Press, Wilmslow.

Plummer, B. (1987) The IVIS League, *Times Educational Supplement*, 23rd June.

Quinn, T., (1987). Is there life after Domesday?, *Educational Computing*, 19-23.

Straker, N., (1988). Interactive video: a cost-effective model for mathematics and science classrooms, *British Journal of Educational Technology*, 19(3), 202-210.

Thorne, M., (1988). National grid, *Times Educational Supplement*, 4th March.

Weller, H.G., (1988). Interactivity in microcomputer based instruction: its essential components and how it can be enhanced, *Educational Technology*, 23-27.

Chapter 13
Authoring for Multi-Media CAL

Philip Barker
Teesside Polytechnic

13.1 Introduction

The activities involved in preparing courseware materials for use in computer-based interactive learning envionments have often been collectively referred to by the term 'authoring'. This term has come to be associated with the preparation of courseware for both historial reasons and because of the similarities that it bears to the procedures involved in writing conventional text books. However, it is important to realize that the latter analogy cannot be taken too far. Because (1) of its highly interactive nature, and (2) of its multi-media composition, the procedures involved in the authoring of courseware are usually far more complex and difficult to undertake than are the corresponding processes associated with the authoring of text books. For this reason a wide range of courseware development tools are often needed in order to facilitate the production of instructional software. The nature of these tools and some examples of them will be discussed later in this chapter.

In previous chapters of this book we have established that multi-media CAL involves the co-ordinated use of several different logical and/or physical communication channels in order to effect a particular pedagogic objective. These channels may be used simultaneously (in parallel with one another) or in succession (that is, sequentially). The primary modes of communication used in a multi-media CAL dialogue depend upon the use of text, sound, pictures and various gestural and tactile operations. The latter are used in order to develop highly participative learning activities.

An important consideration to bear in mind when designing and producing courseware is the concept of 'learner control'. As its name would suggest, the learner control paradigm places the control of learning activity in the hands of the learner. That is, where there are choices available, the student chooses when to learn, where to learn, what to learn, how to learn, how fast he/she will progress, and the media he/she will employ in order to accomplish particular learning objectives. The significance of learner control in the context of developing multi-media CAL courseware is illustrated schematically in Figure 13.1.

This diagram shows some of the dimensions of learner control within a

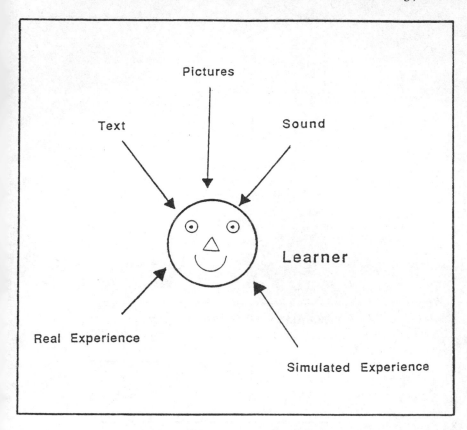

Figure 13.1 *Some dimensions of learner control*

multi-media learning situation. It suggests that there should be a variety of ways by which a student might choose to learn. Of the different methods available, some students will show a preference for real, live experiences while others will prefer the use of simulations. Similarly, some students will prefer to have material presented to them in textual fashion while others are likely to show a preference for pictures and/or sonic presentations. From the point of view of designing and authoring multi-media CAL courseware, learner control should therefore be regarded as being a student's personal preference and control mapping onto the various dimensions of the learning experiences depicted in Figure 13.1.

There are two other very important considerations that have to be taken into account when providing tools for courseware production. These relate to factors that influence the productivity and creativity of the courseware author. The factors that need to be considered are (a) ease of use, and (b) capability. These two properties of authoring tools will be discussed in more detail in the later parts of this chapter. Indeed, we would like to show (a) how ease-of-use can be accomplished through the use of appropriately defined tools and user interfaces (Barker, 1989), and (b) how it may be

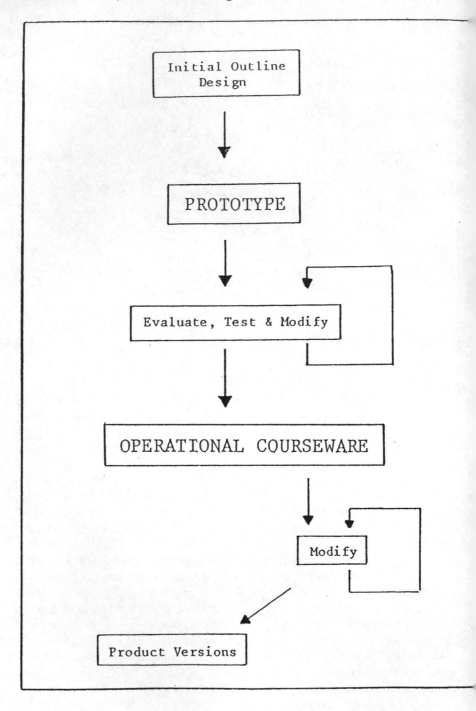

Figure 13.2 *The steps involved in a courseware engineering project*

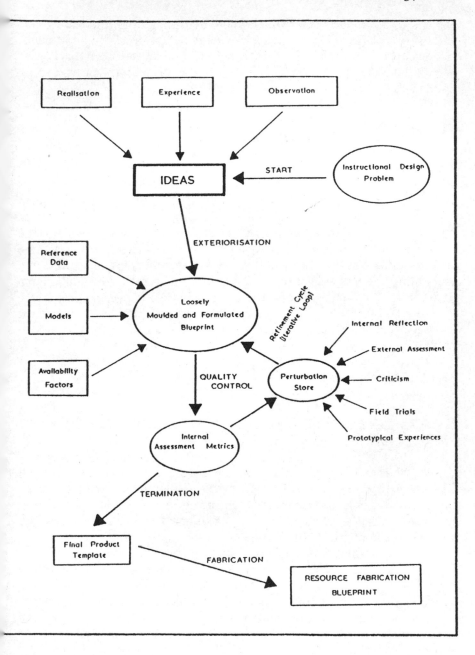

Figure 13.3 *Basic principles of courseware design*

possible to attempt to measure the potential utility and capability of an authoring tool in an objective way. However, before proceeding towards a discussion of these topics it is necessary to introduce a new term that is now being used to describe many of the activities involved in the development of instructional software: 'courseware engineering'.

13.2 Courseware engineering

The production of courseware is essentially an engineering activity. That is, units of instructional software are designed, brought together, tested and finally released as operational products. For this reason the term 'courseware engineering' has recently been suggested as one that would be appropriate to describe the many different activities involved in the preparation of instructional software (Barker, 1989). These activities range from analysis and specification through design, prototyping, authoring, and testing to the release of the final courseware product. The relationship between the basic steps involved in a courseware engineering project are illustrated schematically in Figure 13.2. Two of the most important courseware development processes, design and fabrication, are discussed in more detail below.

13.2.1 Designing courseware

A very simple and approximate model that brings out some of the relationships between the initial design stages that take place during a courseware engineering project is presented schematically in Figure 13.3 (Barker, 1988). The diagram embodies three important points. First, it lists some of the factors that influence the design of courseware. Second, it depicts the role of instructional prototyping (Squires and Millward, 1988; MacKenzie, 1987). Third, it introduces the role of a resource fabrication blueprint; this is usually expressed in terms of a suitable 'specification language' (Turski and Maibaum, 1987). A blueprint is a plan or scheme that specifies the content of the courseware and how it should be produced. However, it says nothing about the tools that should be used to produce it. Usually, this aspect of the courseware engineering process is left to the discretion of those involved in its actual fabrication. The various tools used to produce courseware are discussed in more detail in section 13.3.

From the point of view of courseware design, instructional prototyping is an extremely valuable technique since it enables initial design ideas to be tested out in skeleton form and at relatively low cost. The technique involves producing a computer-based 'mini-course' (the instructional prototype) covering the critical pedagogic and structural aspects of the CAL project as the first stage of the development process and then using this prototype as a design template. One major advantage of this approach to courseware development is that it allows the clients of the instructional software to see and experience the type of facility that will ultimately be produced - well in advance of the final production date for the courseware.

This is extremely useful since revisions (if they are needed) can be made to the courseware well in advance of its operational release. Further details on the instructional prototyping methodology and a critical discussion of its value as a courseware development strategy have been presented by MacKenzie (1987).

13.2.2 Courseware fabrication

Once the design blueprints have been drawn up the fabrication of courseware can commence. This normally entails two basic steps. First, there will be a need to create the knowledge structures that are needed to support the particular teaching/learning activities. Second, there will be a requirement to actually produce the operational programs that utilize the previously created knowledge structures and which are responsible for delivering instruction to the student(s). The knowledge engineering that is needed to produce the knowledge bases within any particular domain has previously been discussed in some detail in Chapter 10. Therefore, in the remainder of this chapter we concentrate primarily on the tools needed to develop operational courseware modules for the delivery of instruction.

13.3 Courseware development tools

The relationship of the authoring process to the process of instructional delivery is depicted schematically in Figure 13.4 (Barker and Yeates, 1985). Essentially, this figure illustrates how one person (the author) generates courseware for use by another (the student). In order to produce this courseware the author may use any combination of three basic types of tool: conventional programming languages, author languages, and authoring systems. The detailed nature of each of these types of tool are discussed in more detail elsewhere (Barker, 1987). Therefore, in this chapter we present only an overview of each class of tool along with a description of some simple examples that are needed for use in the latter sections of this chapter.

13.3.1 Programming languages

Although BASIC has been one of the most commonly used programming languages for CAL projects a number of other high-level development tools have also been employed. Despite its popularity, Bork (1987) condemns the use of BASIC and strongly advocates the use of more structured languages (such as Pascal or Ada) which can support the use of the Structured Analysis and Design Technique (SADT) for the creation of courseware (Kurtz and Bork, 1981). Similarly, in his work relating to the design of a portable authoring environment for interactive video, Anwar (1988) has shown a preference for the use of Modula-2. Each of these languages is extremely powerful. However, they are also very difficult to use by those who have not had any substantial programming experience.

The widespread availability of BASIC has undoubtedly been one of the

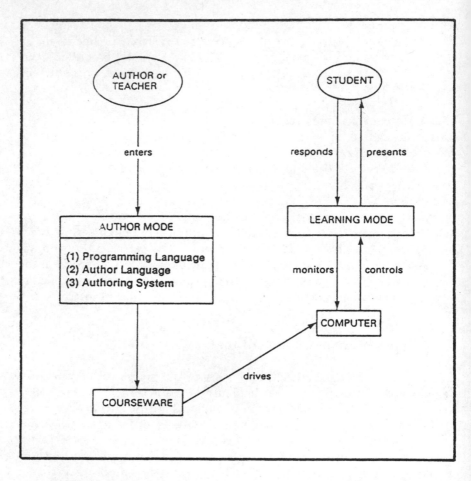

Figure 13.4 *Major types of courseware development tool*

major reasons for its extensive use as a courseware development tool. The appearance of a segment of courseware written in this language is listed in Figure 13.5A. This program segment is written in a dialect of BASIC that runs on an IBM PC (Hahn, 1988). When executed this code would produce the following multiple choice question on a CRT screen.

What is the capital of Arizona?

1. Tucson

2. Phoenix

3. Flagstaff

4. Prescott

>

When examining the BASIC program shown in Figure 13.5A it is

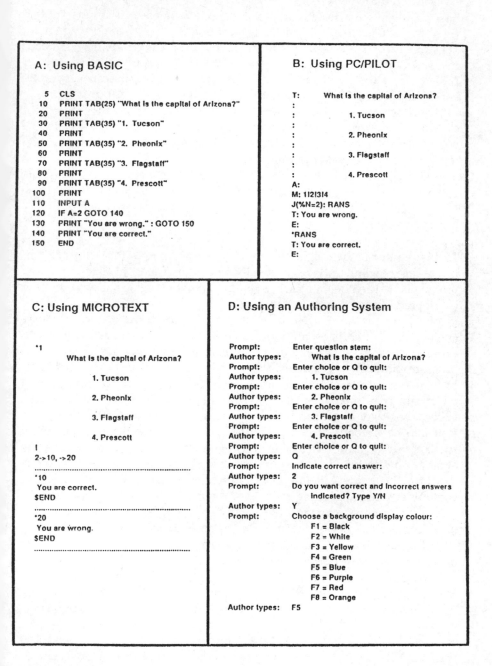

A: Using BASIC

```
  5   CLS
 10   PRINT TAB(25) "What is the capital of Arizona?"
 20   PRINT
 30   PRINT TAB(35) "1. Tucson"
 40   PRINT
 50   PRINT TAB(35) "2. Pheonix"
 60   PRINT
 70   PRINT TAB(35) "3. Flagstaff"
 80   PRINT
 90   PRINT TAB(35) "4. Prescott"
100   PRINT
110   INPUT A
120   IF A=2 GOTO 140
130   PRINT "You are wrong." : GOTO 150
140   PRINT "You are correct."
150   END
```

B: Using PC/PILOT

```
T:        What is the capital of Arizona?
:
:              1. Tucson
:
:              2. Pheonix
:
:              3. Flagstaff
:
:              4. Prescott
A:
M: 1|2|3|4
J(%N=2): RANS
T: You are wrong.
E:
*RANS
T: You are correct.
E:
```

C: Using MICROTEXT

```
*1
          What is the capital of Arizona?

               1. Tucson

               2. Pheonix

               3. Flagstaff

               4. Prescott
!
2->10, ->20
.........................................................
*10
 You are correct.
$END
.........................................................
*20
 You are wrong.
$END
.........................................................
```

D: Using an Authoring System

```
Prompt:          Enter question stem:
Author types:         What is the capital of Arizona?
Prompt:          Enter choice or Q to quit:
Author types:         1. Tucson
Prompt:          Enter choice or Q to quit:
Author types:         2. Pheonix
Prompt:          Enter choice or Q to quit:
Author types:         3. Flagstaff
Prompt:          Enter choice or Q to quit:
Author types:         4. Prescott
Prompt:          Enter choice or Q to quit:
Author types:    Q
Prompt:          Indicate correct answer:
Author types:    2
Prompt:          Do you want correct and incorrect answers
                     indicated? Type Y/N
Author types:    Y
Prompt:          Choose a background display colour:
                     F1 = Black
                     F2 = White
                     F3 = Yellow
                     F4 = Green
                     F5 = Blue
                     F6 = Purple
                     F7 = Red
                     F8 = Orange
Author types:    F5
```

Figure 13.5 *Examples of courseware development tools*

important to realize how much 'system code' is needed in order to obtain the required end result – that is, the presentation of the multiple choice question on a CRT screen and an analysis of the student's keyboard response. As we shall see later (in section 13.4) the amount of un-necessary coding effort that is needed to produce particular results can vary quite considerably from one courseware development tool to another.

Object orientated programming languages represent another important class of high-level programming facility that is gaining widespread popularity with respect to courseware development. A useful introduction to this approach to programming has been presented by Cox (1986). Two well-known examples of this class of programming language are Smalltalk and HyperTalk. HyperTalk is the programming tool upon which the Apple Macintosh HyperCard authoring system is based. HyperCard is briefly discussed in section 13.3.3.

13.3.2 Author languages

There are several different development strategies available for the production of CAL resources. Depending upon the particular strategy that is adopted, three different categories of computer user could become involved in the authoring of instructional software: (a) courseware engineers, (b) teachers and instructors, and (c) learners themselves. Professional courseware engineers will probably prefer to use conventional programming languages in order to develop their instructional programs. However, as we indicated in the previous section, for those who are not technically orientated (such as many of the people in categories (b) and (c) above) these languages can be difficult to learn and use. Consequently, as a means of overcoming these difficulties a class of courseware development tool known as author languages has evolved. An author language is an application orientated programming facility that has been specially developed for those interested in programming educational applications of the computer. When designing an author language simplicity of use is often one of the most important attributes to bear in mind. Because of the significant potential of the computer as an instructional resource a very large number of author languages currently exist. Barker (1987) provides outline descriptions of over 60 of these.

A number of different author languages have been mentioned in previous chapters of this book. For example, in Chapter 11, George Teh outlined some of his reasons for using the APPLE SuperPILOT language in his video disc project; APPLE PILOT and SuperPILOT have been described in some detail by Conlon (1984). A more recent version of this language (PC/PILOT) has also formed the basis of the work discussed by Reynolds and Meierdiercks in chapter 5. In contrast to these approaches, the work outlined by Judith Mashiter in the previous chapter has depended heavily on the use of MICROTEXT (Barker, 1984). These two author languages differ quite significantly both in their capability and with respect to the way in which they are used. Simple illustrations of the format of a PC/PILOT and of a MICROTEXT program are presented in Figures 13.5B and 13.5C, respectively. Each program implements the multiple choice question presented in the previous section. The significance of these programs will be discussed in more detail later in section 13.4.

13.3.3 Authoring systems

Author languages are generally much easier to use than conventional programming languages. Despite this, some people still find them difficult to use. In view of this, a third type of courseware development tool is available which makes the process of courseware production even easier than using an author language. Tools that fall into this third category are referred to as 'authoring systems'.

The way in which an authoring system operates is illustrated schematically in Figure 13.5D. By means of a suitably designed human-computer dialogue the author is guided through each stage of the development process and is prompted at appropriate points for material that is to be embedded in the final lesson. Figure 13.5D shows the type of dialogue that would take place if the author's intention was to produce the multiple choice question listed in section 13.3.1.

The authoring system illustrated in Figure 13.5D is not a very sophisticated one. Far more powerful systems exist. Three examples that have been mentioned in previous parts of this book are: HyperCard (Goodman, 1987); PROPI (ASYS Computer Systems, 1988); and Video-Works (Hayden, 1985). Each of these systems can be used to author multi-media CAL courseware.

HyperCard represents a new 'breed' of user-friendly, easy-to-use authoring system that is based upon a 'notecard' or 'notebook' metaphor. It enables users to create, store, edit and retrieve items of multi-media information that are organized into application orientated 'stacks'. The system provides a highly visual, icon-driven, direct manipulation end-user interface based upon mouse and keyboard interaction (Barker, 1989). A variety of levels of user capability is possible: browsing, typing, painting, authoring and scripting. The highest level of capability is scripting; it enables users to use the object orientated HyperTalk language (Shafer, 1988) in order to prepare scripts that monitor and control the behaviour of objects that constitute the user's interface to the system. Using Hyper-Card's 'button' facility it is possible to link cards and stacks together in quite complex ways – thereby enabling the easy creation of the types of knowledge structure that have previously been depicted in Figure 10.2.

Like HyperCard, PROPI is a mouse-driven authoring system that is based upon windows and pull-down menus. Using these facilities an author can create a pictorial 'lesson atlas'. This is a hierarchical collection of lesson maps – each map being a structured flowchart of the delivery strategy for a portion of the lesson. A lesson map consists of a series of nodes that are represented on the CRT screen by icons. Typical examples of node types include: input, output, decision, mark, question, group, and external. Each different type of map node can have an editor associated with it. Typical editors include: the text editor, the graphics editors, the animation editor, the music editors, the font editor, the picture wipe editors, and so on. The PROPI system generates PC/PILOT code. Although users do not need to program in PC/PILOT, it is possible (by means of external nodes) to incorporate code written in this author language (or any other language) into a PROPI lesson.

Animation often forms a very important part of a multi-media CAL lesson. Unfortunately, computer animation effects are usually very difficult to produce using conventional programming techniques. In order to overcome this problem, the VideoWorks authoring system provides an interactive environment that enables professional quality animation to be produced without the need for any programming experience whatsoever. It is a mouse-based system that uses the standard Macintosh pull-down menu interface in order to provide access to a range of tools for producing animation and accompanying sound effects. Some previous discussion of the VideoWorks system has been presented by Barker, Manji and Tsang in Chapter 7.

13.4 Towards an evaluation metric

Because there are so many authoring tools available it is important to try to formulate some mechanism that will enable their relative merits to be compared. Therefore, in this section two simple approaches are described. The first involves making a simple comparison of the ease-of-use of three different authoring tools. The second outlines a set of guidelines that are expressed in the form of an evaluation checklist that can be used to assess the relative merits of candidate authoring tools. These two approaches are briefly described below.

13.4.1 A simple comparison

Figure 13.5 contains various listings of segments of code that would (1) display a multiple choice question on a CRT screen, (2) allow a learner to select an answer by entering an option number, and (3) provide feedback to the student on the correctness (or otherwise) of his/her selected answer. Previously, in section 13.3.1, it was suggested that courseware develop-ment tools differ quite significantly with respect to the amount of coding needed to produce a given result. For the authoring tools shown in Figure 13.5, the numbers of system orientated keystrokes needed to achieve the required result, using each different system, are roughly as follows:

BASIC	186
PC/PILOT	46
MICROTEXT	26
Authoring System	4

It is easy to see from this simple illustration that there is a substantial reduction in the amount of un-necessary code as the above list is descended. Notice also that the screen layout for the MICROTEXT system depicted in Figure 13.5C (as produced by the courseware author) is very similar in appearance to what the user ultimately sees. MICROTEXT is an example of a 'What You See Is What You Get' (WYSIWYG) system. Increasingly, WYSIWYG interfaces are becoming a more and more important component of CRT screen editors and other courseware development tools. Interfaces of this type are discussed in more detail elsewhere (Barker, 1989).

13.4.2 A more detailed comparison

A variety of different methods could be used in order to evaluate the facilities available with any given courseware development tool (Leiblum, 1988; Barker, 1987). One useful method is to set up a collection of evaluation guidelines in the form of a checklist of questions that should be asked during any given evaluation exercise. Examples of the types of question that an evaluation checklist might contain are presented in Figure 13.6. In order to make the evaluation procedure more quantitative, each of the questions in this figure could be assigned a differential response scale and also allocated a numerical weighting so that quantitative comparisons could be made. Such a procedure would allow the relative merits of different authoring tools to be compared numerically.

Of course, it is important to realize that the list of questions included in Figure 13.6 is not comprehensive; it attempts only to cover some of the more important points that should be considered. Naturally, any attempt to evaluate the facilities offered by a complex and sophisticated courseware development tool is likely to be a difficult task. Often, even though an objective approach may be employed, final system selection is likely to be influenced by personal likes and dislikes, and by preferences to a particular manufacturer's product or equipment. Political and financial factors are also likely to have a significant influence on system selection.

13.5 Conclusion

Computers are now well-established as an instructional resource. However, developing computer-based instructional resources that are stimulating, pleasant to use and which accomplish high levels of knowledge and skill transfer is, in general, a very difficult task. Indeed, the production of multi-media courseware for CAL is an extremely challenging endeavour. This challenge arises because of the need (a) to incorporate high degrees of learner control, (b) to make available many different logical/physical channels of communication, and (c) to choose courseware development tools that are appropriate to the tasks involved.

Authoring for multi-media CAL involves quite complex and intricate courseware engineering activities. These need to be supported by a range of different types of software tool. Three broad classes of tool have been described in this chapter: programming languages, author languages, and authoring systems. Many of these tools are extremely powerful; they are

(1) Is the system easy to learn?
(2) Is the system easy to use?
(3) Does the system allow easy ammendment of courseware?
(4) Are different levels of authoring allowed?
(5) Can the author easily create screens of text?
(6) Can multiple text and background colours be used?
(7) Can the author define personalised character sets?
(8) Can multiple fonts and character sizes be used?
(9) Does the system provide facilities for audio support?
(10) Does the system provide facilities for graphic support?
                                        for slides?
                                        for video tape?
                                        for video disc?
                                        for CDROM?
(11) Does the system support computational graphics?
(12) Can text and graphics be freely inter-mixed?
(13) Can text and video be freely inter-mixed?
(14) Can computational graphics and video be mixed?
(15) Can video from different sources be mixed?
(16) Is colour easy to use?
(17) Does the system permit facile control/communication with
     other instructional aids and devices?
(18) Can other software systems be accessed during an
     instructional session?
(19) Is it possible to attach the courseware development and/or
     delivery workstations to a network via a communication link?
(20) Is the system microcomputer based?
(21) Is the system available on a range of microcomputer systems?
(22) Are mainframe/minicomputer development facilities available
     if they are needed?
(23) Can courseware be developed on a mainframe and delivered
     on a microcomputer system?
(24) Is the system well supported?
(25) Is the system well known?
(26) Is the system widely available?
(27) Are there consultants available should the need arise?
(28) Is the documentation easy to follow?
(29) Is the documentation well-written?
(30) Is there an on-line HELP system for authors?
(31) Can development and delivery modes be rapidly switched?
(32) Are there good facilities for debugging and testing courseware?
(33) Can the lesson strategy embed branching?
(34) Can the student recap?
(35) Is there an interrupt/restart facility?
(36) Does the system offer good computational facilities
     (for simulation and numerical work)?
(37) Does the system provide good answer checking facilities
     for tactile, numeric and textual responses?
(38) Can student responses be filed away for subsequent processing?
(39) Does the system provide support for input from a variety
     of devices such as:

keyboard?	mouse?
touch screen?	two mice?
touch pad?	tracker ball?
light pen?	joy sticks?
digitiser?	concept keyboard?

(40) Does the system provide facilities for the control of
     multiple displays?
(41) Can the activity on these screens be coordinated in various ways?
(42) Does the system enable the creation of student/trainee models?
(43) Can the system produce courseware for use in a group
     learning situation?
(44) Does the system permit the use of a database?
(45) Does the system allow the use of a knowledge base?

Figure 13.6 *Courseware development tools – evaluation checklist*

also very sophisticated. Because there are so many tools currently in existence, some method of comparison is needed in order to help authors select those tools that are most appropriate to particular applications. A checklist (in the form of 45 questions) has been suggested which could act as a basis for the development of a more substantial evaluation metric.

13.6 References

Anwar, A.K., (1988). A portable high-level programming environment for interactive video applications, CNAA M.Phil Thesis, West Glamorgan Institute of Higher Education, Swansea, Wales, UK.

ASYS Computer Systems, (1988). *PROPI User Manual*, ASYS Computer Systems, 104 Viewcrest, Bellingham, WA 98225, USA.

Barker, P.G., (1984). MICROTEXT: A new dialogue programming language for microcomputers, *Journal of Microcomputer Applications*, 7, 167-188.

Barker, P.G., (1987). *Author Languages for CAL*, Macmillan, Basingstoke, 1987.

Barker, P.G. (1988). Towards an instructional designer's intelligent assistant, 127-134 in *Aspects of Educational Technology, Volume XXI: Designing New Systems and Technologies for Learning*, edited by H. Mathias, N. Rushby and R. Budgett, Kogan Page, London.

Barker, P.G., (1989). *Basic Principles of Human-Computer Interface Design*, Hutchinson, London.

Barker, P.G. (1989). Courseware Engineering: Principles and Techniques, book in preparation.

Barker, P.G. and Yeates, H., (1985). *Introducing Computer Assisted Learning*, Prentice-Hall, London.

Bork, A., (1987). *Learning with Personal Computers*, Harper and Row, New York.

Conlon, T., (1984). *PILOT – The Language and How to Use It*, Prentice-Hall International, Englewood Cliffs, NJ.

Cox, B.J., (1986). *Object Orientated Programming – An Evolutionary Approach*, Addison-Wesley, Reading, MA.

Goodman, D., (1987). *The Complete HyperCard Handbook*, Bantam Books, New York.

Hahn, B.D., (1988). *PC BASIC for Beginners*, Edward Arnold, London.

Hayden Software, (1985). *VideoWorks User Manual*, Hayden Software Company Inc., 600 Suffolk Street, Lowell, MA 01854, USA.

Kurtz, B.L. and Bork, A., (1981). An SADT model for the production of computer based learning material, 375-384 in *Computers and Education, Proceedings of the 3rd IFIP World Conference on Computers in Education*, Lausanne, Switzerland, July 27-31, 1981, edited by R.Lewis and D. Tagg, North-Holland, Amsterdam.

Leiblum, M.D., (1988). A model for describing CAL authoring systems applied to TAIGA, *Computers and Education*, 12(1), 141-149.

MacKenzie, D., (1987). Instructional prototyping: a CBT development strategy, 157-163 in *Learning in Future Education, Proceedings of the International*

Conference on Computer Assisted Learning in Post-Secondary Education, edited by D. Norrie, Institute for Computer Assisted Learning, University of Calgary, Alberta, Canada, May 5th-7th, 1987.

Shafer, D., (1988). *HyperTalk Programming*, Hayden Books, Indianapolis, IN.

Squires, D. and Millward, R., (1988). The influence of new software environments on CAL development, *Computers and Education*, 12(1) 67-71.

Turski, W.M. and Maibaum, T.S.E., (1987). *The Specification of Computer Programs*, Addison Wesley, Reading, MA.

Conclusion

Philip Barker

In his book on electronic learning, Johnston (1987) distinguishes between three basic media: (a) audio, (b) video, and (c) electronic text and graphics. He reviews the importance of each of these media with respect to their individual effectiveness; he also comments on the potential of video disc (a 'hybrid' medium) because of its ability to mix sound, text and pictures. In the various chapters of our book we have used the term multi-media CAL to refer to this ability to integrate various teaching media and to utilize each one according to the type of instruction it is best able to promote. However, in mixing and integrating these media it is important to observe the central role of the computer both as an instructor and as a co-ordinator of instructional activity.

The next decade or so is likely to bring about a substantial increase in the use of technologies that support electronic learning. Some of the potential future directions of development that we are likely to see have been described in considerable detail by a number of authors (Barker, 1988; Barker and Manji, 1988; DELTA, 1987). However, although there is currently much interest in this approach to learning, it is important to realize that it is by no means new. Indeed, the use of radio, instructional television and computers has been quite widespread for many years. So, why is there likely to be so much interest in the future? Primarily, for three basic reasons. First, the falling cost of the computer and its related technologies means that there will be easier access to computer-based information and the electronic learning methods that it can be used to support. Second, as technology progresses there will be a growing need to maintain a highly competitive workforce through rapid re-training using new approaches based upon distributed information processing technologies. Third, there is likely to be a significant future requirement to provide controlled 'open' access to educational resources. Each of these three reasons is briefly expanded upon below.

Greater access to the resources for producing and delivering electronic learning is likely to have a number of 'knock-on' effects. Two of the most important of these are: (a) what, how, where and when people learn; and (b) the need for continuing 'life-long' education.

What people learn will obviously be influenced by the societies in which they live and the need for individuals and groups to survive within increasingly competitive environments. The way in which people learn will be strongly influenced by the learning technologies that are available, the centres of learning that are provided, and the nature of human cognitive forces. Where people learn will depend upon a number of factors – such as their age, their ability, the locality in which they live and the nature of their jobs. As we discuss below, centres of learning are likely to become increasingly open. The nature of learning locations is also likely to change; there will probably be a significant shift towards 'on the job' (Fricker, 1988) training and studying from home (Levrat, Tagg and Lovis, 1987). Because of time demands, particularly for adult learners, there must be a flexible approach to studying; it will need to be undertaken when and where it can be 'fitted in'. This flexibility of approach must also be reflected in out attitudes towards professional development and the design of accreditation and certification methods.

It is important to realize that we do not live in a static world; we live in a world that is rapidly changing. This change should have a significant impact upon curricula and the need for attitudinal change – both on the part of curriculum designers and students themselves. Curriculum designers must become flexible in their approach to course content; students should be taught to accept that education must be a life-long process necessitated by progress and technological advance.

Progress is an inevitable consequence of people's curiosity about the world, about themselves and about each other. Technological advance is therefore a natural outcome of human endeavour. However, progress means that the skills a nation has today will not necessarily be suitable for its survival tomorrow. There is therefore an important need to keep a watchful eye on technological progress and, if need be (as will surely be the case), retrain workforces with suitable skills to accommodate change and competition.

It would be altruistic to say that equality of educational opportunity is the only driving force underlying open access to educational resources. By open access we mean that learners are able to utilize a global stock of instructional resources quite independently of where these materials are located or where the students themselves reside. However, due to a variety of political, economic and commercial factors, access to resources will undoubtedly need to be controlled. Therefore, although totally unconstrained access is technologically feasible (Winders, 1988), in practice it will probably be necessary to allow access to resources based upon people's individual needs or their ability to pay for the resources that they use.

At the time when the idea of this book was first conceived we thought that its contents should adequately reflect the ongoing developments that were taking place in the area of multi-media CAL. Therefore, the various chapters in the book were each selected so that they would, in their individual ways, each contribute to the fulfilment of one or other of five basic functional requirements. These requirements were designed to illustrate the mechanisms involved in:

(a) designing and fabricating instructional resources;
(b) the global distribution of these resources;
(c) the local delivery of courseware materials;
(d) the effective use of instructional technology; and
(e) ensuring and measuring learning effectiveness.

As editor of this book I feel that our initial 'design aim' has been more than realized both in terms of the material that has been presented and in terms of the international flavour of its authorship.

Undoubtedly, from what has been written in the various chapters of this book, each author firmly believes that electronic learning (in the form of multi-media CAL) has a vital role to play in the future development of effective and efficient instruction. We have available today a wide range of technology to support the development of such learning systems. Our task for the future is therefore one of learning how best to use it to our advantage.

References

Barker, P.G., (1988). Interactive learning systems for the 90s, *Interactive Learning International*, 4(3), 6-16.

Barker, P.G. and Manji, K.A., (1988), New books for old, Programmed Learning and Educational Technology, 25(4), 310-13.

DELTA, (1987). *Development of European Learning through Technological Advance – Initial Studies*, Commission of the European Communities, DG-XIII, Brussels, Belgium.

Fricker, J., (1988), CBT in NatWest, *Computer Bulletin*, 4(3), 22.

Johnston, J., (1987). *Electronic Learning: From Audiotape to Videodisc*, Lawrence Erlbaum Associates, Hillsdale, NJ.

Levrat, B., Tagg, E.D. and Lovis, F.B., (1987). (Eds), *The Computer in the Home: Its Challenge to Education*, Proceedings of the IFIP TC 3/WG 3.2/WG 3.5 Working Conference, Interlaken, Switzerland, 7-11 April 1986, North-Holland, Amsterdam.

Winders, R., (1988). *Information Technology in the Delivery of Distance Education and Training*, Peter Francis Publishers, Cambs, UK.

Author Biographies

Philip Barker

Twelve authors have contributed to the preparation of this book. Some brief biographical details of each contributor are presented below so that readers can gauge the wide range of experience that each author brings into the various chapters to which they have contributed.

Philip Barker
Philip Barker is Reader in Applied Computing and Information Technology within the School of Information Engineering at Teesside Polytechnic. His research group is actively involved in research in three major areas of computer science: human-computer interaction, knowledge engineering and the design of interactive learning systems. He has published several books and many papers within each of these areas.

Robert DeSio
Mr DeSio is a graduate of Rensselear Polytechnic Institute and holds Bachelor's and Master's degrees in physics. He also attended the University of Minnesota and Harvard University, prior to joining the 20th Air Force in the Asia Pacific Theatre in World War II. He joined IBM in 1953 as a member of the Applied Science Division. He has held many management positions in IBM, both in the USA and in international operations. He has been Director of Advanced Market Development, Director of Scientific Computing and High Performance Systems, as well as Director of Systems Engineering. Prior to leaving IBM in December 1986 he was director of University Relations. Currently, Bob DeSio is Vice President for Development and Long Range Planning in the National Technological University in the USA.

Gareth Jones
Gareth Jones is Senior Lecturer in Staff Development in the Educational Development Unit at Teesside Polytechnic. Until 1988 he was Senior Lecturer in Educational Technology at the same institution and was Senior Course Tutor for an externally validated course in Educational Technology for teachers and trainers. He has been involved not only in teacher training but in media design and production for many years and is particularly

interested in the delivery of open and distance learning courses.

Karim Manji
Karim Manji is a Research Assistant working with the Interactive Systems Research Group at Teesside Polytechnic. His research deals with pictorial communication methods and their application to the design of human-computer interfaces. He is particularly interested in designing interfaces to new types of electronic book for the support of interactive learning.

Judith Mashiter
Judith is a graduate of Physics and Computing Science. After completing a post-graduate course in education, she taught Science and Computer Studies in an urban comprehensive school. She is currently working with the Interactive Learning Project at Newcastle University School of Education. This appointment allows her to pursue research interests in the application of new technologies, particularly interactive video, to learning in science.

Ken Meierdiercks
Ken Meierdiercks is a graduate of the University of Oregon. He also studied for his Ph.D in Instructional Design at this University. For several years Dr Meierdiercks acted as instructional designer in the Educational Technology Department at Singapore Polytechnic. He now runs his own CBT consultancy called 'Eagle Infotech Consultants' in Singapore.

Geoffrey Reynolds
Geoffrey Reynolds is a Lecturer in the Department of Electronics and Communications at Singapore Polytechnic. He is a graduate of the University of Queensland with a BE in Electronic Engineering. He has also studied at Mount Gravatt College of Advanced Education from which he graduated with a Diploma in Teaching.

Rodney Short
After leaving the sea Captian Rodney Short joined Singapore Polytechnic as Head of the Department of Nautical Studies – a post which he has held for many years. He has recently left the Polytechnic in order to set up a maritime consultancy based in the port of Singapore.

George Teh
George Teh is a Lecturer at the Institute of Education in Singapore. His particular interests lie in the area of interactive video in computer assisted learning and the use of Prolog in the teaching/learning process.

Tsang Lai-keung
Tsang Lai-keung is a member of staff at the Lee Wai Lee Technical Institute in Hong Kong. He is particularly interested in the application of CAL methods for vocational training applications. Tsang Lai-keung is Education

Chairman of the Hong Kong Computer Society. Some of the work described in the chapter to which he contributed was undertaken while he was on sabbatical leave in the United Kingdom working with the Interactive Systems Research Group at Teesside Polytechnic.

John Whiting

John Whiting is a lecturer in information systems and a member of the IKBS-User Modelling Research Group of the Instute of Informatics at the University of Ulster. His current research interests include the design of multi-media CAL and CBT authoring systems, the application of AI techniques to CAL and CBT production and use, and the development of distributed open and distance learning systems. He is currently working at the European Commission in Brussels for the DG XIII-F DELTA initiative. This involves a programme of research (and development) into the application of advanced computing and information technology to European open and distance learning.

Yeow-Chin Yong

Yeow-Chin Yong is Head of the Mathematics and Science Centre at Ngee Ann Polytechnic in Singapore. He received his BSc (Hons) in Physics and MSc (Plasma Physics) degrees from the University of Malaya, Malaysia. Yong's academic research interest lies in plasma physics computation. He is also interested in computer education, particularly in the area of computer aided learning and computer aided experimentation (CAE). He is the first co-ordinator in the polytechnic to develop and implement CAL in mathematics and science as well as CAE in physics. He leads a team of 30 academic staff in the development of CAL and CAE. Early in 1988, Yong set up a model CAL laboratory equipped with local area network facilities. This laboratory employs a classroom administration system and computer managed instruction in order to monitor the performance and progress of students.

Besides setting up this laboratory for CAL and CAE, Yong has also published many papers in these areas and presented talks at local seminars and overseas conferences. Yong is a fellow of the Malaysia Institute of Physics, a Chartered Physicist and a Member of the Institute of Physics (of the UK). He is also a Member of the Asia and African Association for Plasma Training.

Acknowledgements

Earlier versions of some of the chapters in this book have been previously published as contributions to learned journals, conference proceedings or collected works. The editor therefore wishes to express his thanks to all of those who have helped to disseminate his ideas by publishing the various subsets of his work that are now included, in updated form, in this present text book. Details of the work concerned are presented below.

An earlier version of Chapter 1 appeared two years ago in a book published by Elsevier/North Holland entitled, *Tutoring and Monitoring for European Open Learning* (edited by J. Whiting and D.A. Bell). The material presented in Chapter 3 formed the basis of a seminar that was given at an international workshop dealing with the problems of 'Creating Adult Learning Opportunities'. This workshop took place in September (1987) in Middelburg (The Netherlands) and was jointly organized by the Institute for Curriculum Development and the University of Amsterdam. A preliminary version of Chapter 3 is to appear in a book entitled *Creating Adult Learning Opportunities: Theoretical and Practical Communications on Educational Design for Adults* (edited by Fred Goffree and Harry Stroomberg). Finally, the material on 'Knowledge Engineering for CAL' (Chapter 10) is based on a modified and updated version of a paper that was presented at the IFIP European Conference on Computers in Education which was held in Lausanne, Switzerland, during the Summer of 1988. A previous version of this chapter therefore appears in the Conference Proceedings (pages 529-535) that were published by Elsevier/North Holland and edited by Frank Lovis and Donovan Tagg.

Philip Barker
School of Information Engineering
Teesside Polytechnic
January 1989

Subject Index

Author Index